THIRD MAN BOOKS

HOLLYWOOD DREAM

THE

THUNDERCLAP NEWMAN

STORY

Pete Townshend, a Band of 'Outsiders', and the Birth of British Indie Music

BY MARK IAN WILKERSON

THIRD MAN BOOKS

Copyright © 2024 by Mark Wilkerson

For more information:
Third Man Books, LLC
623 7th Ave S
Nashville, Tennessee 37203

A CIP record is on file with the Library of Congress.

Art direction by Jordan Williams and Amin Qutteineh
Layout by Amin Qutteineh

ISBN: 979-8-98990-891-2

CONTENTS

For Andy, Speedy and Jimmy

FOREWORD

Mark Wilkerson has brought into the present my early years at Ealing Art College in 1963. That was when Andy Newman – alias Thunderclap – enchanted me with his piano playing. And according to a legend I had almost forgotten, went on to advise me how to build my first home recording studio.

Andy, with the very young Jimmy McCulloch and John "Speedy" Keen, ended up in Thunderclap Newman, a band I created named after Andy, which – had I had my way – would have had a few more members. It was in 1968 I was attempting to gather a group of artists for a new record label I wanted to call "Talkus". They were, Andy Newman, Jimmy McCulloch, Tiny Tim, Arthur Brown, Steve Baron, Ron Geesin, Chris Morphet (known mainly as a photographer) and even some of the lunatics who ended up in a band called Bonzo Dog Doo Dah Band. One thing was missing for all those folk, and that was a hit song (although Arthur Brown had 'Fire' which was big hit in his back pocket, I didn't know that at first). I had a feeling I could write a hit for them, or that my friend at the time Speedy could come up with something. Speedy wrote the divine 'Something In The Air', and became the lead singer and studio drummer for the band, the only three I could keep my grip on that is.

Mark brings the many strands of this story together, one that unfolded even as I was bringing *Tommy* to The Who and beyond. My dedication, to help the waifs and strays and eccentrics of the music world together, continues to this day. I must admit that I learn more from working with other artists than I do working alone, and through them all have, like Rick Rubin, produced a philosophy of recording studio craft that sustains me every day. Creativity sparks creativity, and eccentricity in an artist is sublime – look at the list of chart-topping superstars of the past: they are all slightly nuts. They are all slightly brilliant too.

For me Thunderclap Newman was a great adventure and one I try to relive often. The recording studio at worst can be a grinding machine in some ways, but a happy place for me in particular, especially when I am in charge. For all three of them the success of their one big hit 'Something In The Air' saw each of them move on to new lives, and new adventures, some wonderful, some tragic. Who knew that great music could be created this way? Well I did even if the three members of the band were unsure at first.

I will turn to Wilkerson's book again and again to be reminded of my three dear friends who comprised the band Thunderclap Newman. It's carefully and devotedly researched with lots of input from all kinds of other friends of mine who shared their journey, and that itself builds a unique picture of the kind of Boiler Room world that musicians thrived in during the mid to late '60s. When the Beatles were hauling Mellotrons into the studio Andy Newman was hauling his massive Contrabass Saxophone along with his Kazoo.

This book says it all, that creativity and even hit-records sometimes, can be more about play than work. Musicians play, and when the hard work begins as it must, they sometimes fall by the wayside. The tragedy I spoke of earlier is simply that there was only one Thunderclap Newman album, the beautiful *Hollywood Dream*, recorded entirely in my home studio which was in a room meant to be a small bathroom. The saddest part of it all is that they don't exist today. This book brings them back to life.

- Pete Townshend

PROLOGUE

In early 1966, Chris Thomas was at a crossroads. He'd recently been playing bass guitar in a group called The Second Thoughts – really a *second* Second Thoughts, admittedly not as good as the original group which had formed in Ealing in 1963 and had performed alongside such luminaries as The Rolling Stones, Duane Eddy, and John Lee Hooker. This reconstituted edition of The Second Thoughts struck out on the continent with plans to perform in Sweden. It didn't work out, but they did play the fabled Star Club in Hamburg on the way back before the group disintegrated. Thomas then tried his hand at songwriting, part of a duo with his ex-Second Thoughts bandmate Pat Lyons called 'Hat and Tie', although they really wrote the songs separately. Thomas was a good songwriter – his song 'Finding It Rough' was picked up by the Everly Brothers – but the experience left him sorely disappointed, as he didn't get paid.

Going back to what he knew, Thomas formed a new band, called The Cat. He brought in a singer named Les Elliott, and the guitarist from the last iteration of The Second Thoughts, Pete Driscoll. Chris himself played bass. Their drummer, whose name escapes Thomas all these years later, quickly gained a reputation for being generally unreliable. "He would phone up at like 3 o'clock and say, "Oh, I can't do the gig tonight," and it's like – but we're playing in bloody Portsmouth!", Thomas recalls disdainfully. "So we had to scramble around and find somebody."

Drummer issues notwithstanding, Thomas began looking for opportunities to get The Cat into the recording studio. Through a mutual friend, he approached Pete Townshend, guitarist and principal songwriter for The Who, who'd broken through with three hit singles the previous year – 'I Can't Explain', 'Anyway, Anyhow, Anywhere', and 'My Generation', all penned by Townshend. Townshend had started a publishing imprint and had begun looking for talent to record on Robert Stigwood's new label, Reaction Records, which was in the process of releasing its first single, The Who's 'Substitute'. Thomas wrote Townshend a letter expressing his desire to work with him, and shortly thereafter the two parties met. "He offered a couple of different songs," Thomas remembers. "'Magic Bus' was one of them, which I didn't really see as a single – it was just like a Bo Diddley sort of thing. And then he wrote 'Run, Run, Run' and offered it to us, which we took."

It was with impeccable timing that John 'Speedy' Keen now entered the fray, fresh off a stint playing drums with The Eccentrics, a (mostly) English outfit who had performed in Italy for a few months over the winter until their prospects turned bleak and the group fell apart. Before that, Keen had played with that early, hot version of The Second Thoughts. Thomas, an Ealing boy like Keen, had seen them perform on several occasions. "They were a very good band, and they nearly made it; they nearly cut through," he said. "I remember Speedy was easily the best drummer around that I'd seen. Also he was a *very* funny guy. And the reason why he was called Speedy – apart from taking it – he had so much energy. He was sort of on a par with Keith Moon in terms of his drumming – slightly different, but that same kind of energy. And *loud* as a drummer."

Thomas duly asked Keen to join the band. "The big carrot of course was that Pete Townshend was going to produce us," Thomas said. "So Speedy didn't hesitate."

In short order, The Cat assembled at IBC Studios, 35 Portland Place, Marylebone, to record the new Townshend composition. The lineup for the recording of 'Run, Run, Run' was Les Elliot (vocals), Chris Thomas (bass),

Speedy Keen (drums), Pete Townshend (Guitar; Townshend hadn't been satisfied with Driscoll's guitar work), and a guest pianist: Graham Bond, of the noted jazz/R&B outfit and precursor to Cream, The Graham Bond Organization. The members of The Cat hadn't been aware of Bond's involvement until they arrived at the studio. "It was Pete's idea completely, like: 'This is Graham and he's going to be playing the piano,'" Thomas recalled. Townshend was at the helm as producer. The 'Run, Run, Run' session lasted only a few hours.

A few days later, Thomas received a message from Townshend advising the group to be at the studio the following morning – with a B-side. This presented an immediate problem, as The Cat didn't have any songs. "Although I was the writer in the band, I hadn't really written anything that I felt comfortable with," said Thomas. Keen offered that he had the basis of a song, a more promising option than any others available, so Elliott and Thomas quickly met the drummer in his bedroom at his parents' house in Hanwell where he played them what he had. "Speedy only knew one chord on the guitar, basically the 'F' shape, the bar chord," Thomas recalled. "So this whole song was written basically using just one chord, moving his hand up and down the neck of the guitar. So over a period of about an hour or two with Les, we actually fleshed this song out. I put different chords in it and Les added some lyrics." The song the trio came up with was named 'Club Of Lights'.

The following day, The Cat assembled at Spot Studios in South Molton Street, Mayfair, and recorded their new composition, with Townshend again producing. With A and B sides now complete, the group soon met with Robert Stigwood and discussed the plan to release their new single on Reaction Records. A release date was set: April 15th, 1966.

And then all went quiet. The Cat's version of 'Run, Run, Run' has never been released, nor has the B-side, 'Club Of Lights'. Speedy Keen suddenly, and quite mysteriously, left the group. Soon afterwards, another local group, The Birds, which featured future Rolling Stone Ronnie Wood, recorded a version of Townshend's song, but this too went unreleased until more than three decades later. The Who themselves would record and release their own version of the song later in 1966. "Everything seemed to stop, and I couldn't understand what was going on," Thomas recalled, still sounding perplexed all these years later. "And then I found out that Speedy had left the band to become Pete's driver! *Driving?* And it was like – what the fuck is going on? I was like – *what?* I couldn't believe it, I thought somebody was making it up. I hardly ever saw Speedy again."

Thomas was back to square one, with the fragments of a band and no single. "And so The Cat was out in the doldrums again," he said.

A few months later, Thomas received a surreal dose of clarity from an unlikely source: "So Speedy's vanished; I haven't spoken to him or seen him for months, and I'm walking down this road in Ealing – I remember exactly where it was: Spring Bridge Road in Ealing, and I'm walking over the railway bridge there, and a car stops. And this guy undid the window and said, "Excuse me, can you tell me the way to blah blah blah…" And he had a car radio, which was quite unusual in England in 1966." What was playing on that car radio blew Thomas's mind: 'Club Of Lights', by Oscar, released in June 1966.

"I said to the guy – "I *wrote* that song!", he recalled. "I'm listening to it and going "I wrote this!" – it was on the radio and I didn't even know it had been covered by anybody – I didn't know any of this! So I was kind of like, "What the fuck is this?" And of course at the same time, the guy who'd stopped to ask the way must have thought,

"Who is this fruit loop I've just bumped into?" and drove off, and I'm standing in the middle of the road there, going, "What happened?" It was totally bizarre. Speedy had actually – and I felt pretty angry about that, because he'd gone behind our backs – sold the bloody song as his composition and left us completely and utterly... nowhere." In fairness, Keen clearly considered it his song. "That was the first song of mine that got any publicity," he told *Sounds* in 1976. "He (Oscar) got a full-page ad in the *Melody Maker*... I thought – this is it! I only wrote it for a joke, when I was working with Pete."

But Thomas insists that the song was a group effort. "'Club Of Lights' was a hundred percent collaborative," he said. "A hundred percent. That's why I was so shocked – I just went: "What?" I thought, "Hang on a bit – that's not us doing it!" I just couldn't get my head around what was going on, and all the time this guy was trying to get directions somewhere."

Thomas, left standing there puzzled in the middle of the road, was left with one more reminder that life as a member of a musical group was not for him. "In actual fact, all of these things conspired to make me push myself into going into production at the end of 1967 for a hundred percent certain," he said. "That's when I thought, 'I must do this,' and that's why I wrote to George Martin and everything else happened. Because I was let down by the fact that when I wrote the Everly Brothers song I got no money; I didn't even get a copy of the record! I had to go and listen to it in the little record booth in the record shop and say, "Can I hear track four?" [laughs]. So I didn't get paid for that. I got stuffed basically when Speedy left and that all fell through. And then the next thing was the fact that I was persevering with a guitarist that I knew wasn't any good but I didn't have the heart to kick him out, and I just thought, it's no good relying on other people, I'm going to have to rely on myself, and I knew that eventually I wanted to be a record producer more than anything else anyway. I was much more interested in production than in playing or performing or writing."

Thomas's 1967 letter to Beatles producer George Martin led to his being hired to work as an assistant at Associated Independent Recording, the company co-founded by Martin. The following year he worked with The Beatles during sessions for their self-titled album, widely known as 'The White Album'. This was the start of a long and distinguished career, chiefly in production, working with such artists as Procul Harum, Roxy Music, Pink Floyd, The Sex Pistols, The Pretenders, INXS, Pulp, Elton John and, in a reminder of the smallness of the world that is the music business, a string of three Pete Townshend solo albums in the 1980s.

The short stint with The Cat changed Speedy Keen's life, too. From the moment they met, Keen and Townshend clicked. They became fast friends, driving to shows and listening to music together. Townshend began helping Keen organize and finish the dozens of scattered song fragments he'd scribbled down on various bits of paper. Before The Cat, Keen told *ZigZag* in 1975, his working life consisted of stints with groups where "I either ran out of money or got fired. Then I met Pete Townshend. The only thing that came out of those sessions in fact was my friendship with Pete which has been of more value than any friendship I've ever had. I remember going back to Pete's one day and he played me his early demos which for me was like the beginning of what I'm doing now really. I was so impressed by how they'd been put together and multi-recorded...it was a whole world that I hadn't looked at before. So he switched on the light for me that day."

The sessions with The Cat would also impact Townshend's trajectory. In a few years, he and Keen would join forces again, this time with Thunderclap Newman, a group that would attain a marker of success that he would never achieve with The Who. "Thunderclap Newman were my invention and my most enjoyable recording session, better than any Who session for me, and as far as I know my only genuine Number One in any role at all in the business," says Townshend today. "I still publish Speedy's Thunderclap songs by the way. I'm immensely proud of them and my part in their genesis."

PART ONE

CHAPTER 1

PETE

In 1963, Pete Townshend was an 18-year-old art student at Ealing Technical College, west London. Townshend was enrolled in a five-year course; he'd just completed two years of Foundation and was now beginning the first of three years focusing on his specialty: Graphic Design. "I went into graphic design rather begrudgingly because I had wanted to work on installation sculptures that involved small buildings and music," he recalled. "The sculpture school failed to get a diploma accreditation." However, the graphic design skills he learned were put to good use during The Who's formative years: "I used my talent for graphics in my early design work for the band," Townshend explained. "Target t-shirts, t-shirts and jackets with medals and chevrons, the Who logo with the arrow based on the male symbol etc."

Townshend's hours away from college at the time were devoted to music. He had been playing guitar for local group The Detours (which at this point included his future Who bandmates Roger Daltrey and John Entwistle) for about a year. The group played their own renditions of popular trad jazz songs on a busy circuit of local halls, peppering their set with a few Johnny Cash covers during their Sunday appearances at Douglas House, a U.S. servicemen's club near Hyde Park, a touch which the Americans appreciated and often rewarded by delivering a tray of Scotch to the band. Their equipment was transported to gigs in the van Pete's mother, Betty, used for her antiques shop.

Fellow student and future Bonzo Dog Doo-Dah Band member Roger Ruskin Spear attended Ealing Tech at the same time as Townshend. "I started off at Ealing in the mathematics department, not the art school," Spear said. This was at the urging of his father, the renowned portrait painter Ruskin Spear. "He put me off art school, really – he said "You don't want to go there... load of useless blokes go to that. You want to do something like mending peoples' televisions or something. Something useful." Accordingly, Spear enrolled in classes with an eye to doing something useful. "I did applied mathematics and physics, and I used to watch the art students going past the window to the café next door. And I just thought, 'Oh damn it, this is a bit better, really, than sitting in this classroom doing partial integration and differentiation', and all those sort of things."

Spear began frequenting the café, and soon became familiar with Townshend. "I used to try and teach all the art students multiple differentiation, drawing on the café wall," he said, "and I was aware of this bloke sort of coming in with a huge nose and a spotty bow tie and a yellow shirt and a blue jacket, and he'd be sort of grooving, and I thought 'Well there's a guy who's obviously enjoying being in art school!'"

Spear eventually moved to the art school, jettisoning mathematics in favor of the possibly less 'useful' but endlessly more creatively fulfilling subject of Fine Arts. "I think Pete was in our year, but he was very much opting for the graphics," he said, "so I never actually did any work with Pete in the studios, but we did sort of meet up in lectures, of these imported madmen that were brought in: Larry Rivers, and of course Gustav Metzger, the autodestructive artist, which gave Pete the idea to smash up his amps, and gave me the idea to blow up things onstage. So both the Bonzos and The Who got that from Gustav Metzger. So yes, it was happening – pretty exciting times, really."

"The art school had these midday lectures," recalled Townshend's college flatmate and longtime friend Richard Barnes, "and in many ways, thinking about Townshend's career and stuff, they were more influential than the rest of the art school. Nearly every one of those lectures had some kind of influence on him and his songwriting and so on. They were people like the American pop artist Larry Rivers, and there was another American, Robert Brownjohn, who was an art director in film – he did the credits for James Bond and stuff like that, very trendy – and there was David Mercer, a sort of left wing playwright. I always felt that David Mercer's thing was where Pete got his inspiration for that 'Substitute' *a plastic spoon in my mouth* thing. Anyway, there were others – Philip Jenkins, who was on the history of film and stuff. But Thunderclap was not part of that official thing as far as I know. Very odd, it was – a very strange sort of thing."

'Thunderclap' was the hastily applied nickname of another influential visitor to Ealing Tech around this time: An enigmatic pianist named Andy Newman, who gave a lunchtime performance at the school around mid-1963. Newman was a friend of Fine Art student Rick Seaman.[1] "Just for a bit of fun, I said, "Why don't you come to the lecture theatre and play?", Seaman recalled. To his mild surprise, Newman, whose presence at the school jarred with the typical jazz artists who performed there, accepted the invitation. "Roger and I used to play traditional jazz," recalled another member of the art school crowd, Clive Smith. "A bunch of guys that were a year or two ahead of us, who I also played with, were more into modern jazz. So they more or less organized this event every week and they brought in guys who would just gig around town, and there were some people who came in who were going to be playing at Ronnie Scott's that night. We attended all of them, so when Andy came in I can understand why everybody was a little nervous, 'cause he was not a famous musician." It was also Newman's first solo public performance.

---

1 "Dick was a *very* interesting guy," Barnes remembers. "He was really well-read and into philosophy and martial arts and stuff like that. He became a black belt at judo amongst other things." Barnes went on to promote performances by The Who and other groups at the Railway Hotel in Harrow and employed Seaman as a bouncer.

"Dick was so nervous that people would laugh," Smith recalled. "I mean, I don't know if you've ever seen Andy performing, but him sitting at the piano with a kazoo jammed between his mouth and the back of the piano, thumping out chords and singing on the kazoo is quite a novel image."

"I thought, 'Goodness me, this is not going to go very well'," said Seaman. "So I put one or two posters up which were complete bullshit really, and I dreamt up this 'Thunderclap' name to make him sound more interesting." Townshend saw the posters and was intrigued.

"We all thought Thunderclap Newman must be an obsolete jazz star, so we all collect in the lecture theatre," Townshend recalled in 1970. He and Barnes took their seats among the roughly 70 students who attended. "It was very, very bizarre," recalled Barnes of the performance by the bespectacled and rotund Newman. "For instance, Andy was a very eccentric-looking guy, and overweight, (Townshend's recollection was "the first image I got was his shape, which was a bit like a turnip") and he came and sat at the piano onstage with a kazoo kind of fixed so he could play it." Newman set a metronome going on top of the piano and began to play. "I don't know whether he had sheet music," said Barnes, "but I don't think he looked at the audience once – he came in and he sat down and played this strange stuff, almost like he was some drunk that had come in and couldn't play the piano, really banging away. But after a while you could see he did know what he was doing; he *could* play the piano. But he played in these strange, heavy, thumping minor keys that were slightly different."

Townshend later described Newman's music as "primitive but exotic, absolutely unique." Newman performed mostly what Barnes recalled as "his own weird compositions" that day, but Townshend was particularly struck by his take on a few popular contemporary tunes. "Barney and I were blown away by his "method" when applied to a few Beatles songs the audience had asked him to try," he said. Newman "played for an hour until he was stopped," recalled Barnes. "The students went wild at the end."

"Anyway," he added, "it was really interesting and I'm sure some people walked out but Pete thought he was a genius; he just thought it was incredible."

At the time of his performance at Ealing Tech, Andy Newman was far from an established musician: He was a 20-year-old telephone engineer with the General Post Office, the U.K.'s postal and telecommunications carrier. He'd been working for the GPO for four years. Soon afterwards, Seaman gave Townshend a copy of a recording called *Ice and Essence* featuring Andy Newman on piano and 'Richard Cardboard' (Rick Seaman) on percussion. "There were only two copies of this album which were cut from a tape recording of some of Thunderclap's numbers performed by himself and Dick in a church hall," Barnes recalled, "and it was an amazingly inventive album with all sorts of convoluted time changes. It had an eerie, delicate, echoey quality about it and Pete played it constantly." Seaman points out that 'Ice and Essence' was simply the name of one of the tracks, a track that "was done in Andy's parents' front room in his house."

Newman had "incredible inventiveness," Seaman recalled. "He would dream up tracks with names like 'King George VI Reservoir Blues' and things like this. Extraordinary stuff." Seaman's contribution to the collection of recordings was minimal. "I'm not musical at all," he said. "It was just literally on one track Andy suggested that I play some percussion and it was literally whatever was hanging about – an old biscuit tin or something like that I bashed out a bit of rhythm on."

Townshend still has his copy of *Ice and Essence* – a vinyl test pressing. In 1971 he told *ZigZag's* John Tobler that the recording was "absolutely amazing." In 2001, Townshend had the seven-track recording restored and digitized by his then brother-in-law Jon Astley (whose studio, incidentally, happens to be in Pete's former home in Twickenham where Thunderclap Newman first met and went on to record most of their work). He released the title track online, and later released a limited run of the entire recording on compact disc.

Newman's performance on the Ealing Tech campus and the *Ice and Essence* recording had a profound impact on Townshend. Barnes laid the groundwork:

> The thing is, this was 1963 and major changes were happening in this country. Suddenly it was like people worshiped young people after we'd been ignored before that, and it all sort of started to happen – this youth revolution – and of course we were part of that, and another thing was smoking marijuana, which in those days was very exciting – very obscure and interesting. So – bear in mind, there's me and Pete, we're at art school, every day is fucking exciting, every day is interesting, we're stoned, long-haired, we're doing art, we're meeting people, we've got a school below us which is all gorgeous women in the fashion school, it was wonderful! And then [laughs] Andy was so *unbelievably* straight. When we saw him, it was kind of a culture clash. I mean, we used to get attacked in the street for having long hair, it was unbelievable. But Andy was this GPO engineer, 9-to-5, really straight, collar and tie, and I think that was part of the appeal! I thought Andy was great, but Pete was *obsessed* with him. Utterly obsessed. I think he fell in love with him. We used to say it was like something out of a child's comic book; he was just like a character.

As they still hadn't met him, Newman remained an enigma to Townshend and Barnes, who shared a flat on Sunnyside Road across the road from the art school. "One day Pete and I saw Thunderclap Newman coming along the opposite side of the street," Barnes recalled in his 1982 book *Maximum R&B*. "We were both very stoned and totally in awe of this mysterious figure. He was shaped like a barrel, chinless, and he walked along with his hands behind his back and looked like some mysterious, eccentric professor out of a *Rupert* annual. We followed him, hiding behind cars, totally struck by fear, wonder and reverence for this odd genius."

"I'll always remember this 'cause it was so odd," Barnes recalls today with a chuckle. "Pete said, "Look!" I said, "What?" He said: "*Look!* It's Andy Newman, walking along the road!" And he was getting very excited. We didn't know him then; we hadn't met him – we'd just seen that concert. And so Pete said, "Let's follow him and see what he does!" So we followed him – it was *absurd!* Hiding behind parked cars, dashing from one car to the other in case he turned round. This was St. Mary's Road, the main road from the art school. We followed him for about half a mile, just looking at him! He used to walk along with his hands behind his back, it was really odd. Pete would say, "Look – he's stopped and looked in a window!" When I look back now, it's a very strange thing."

Not long after this episode where Townshend and Barnes stalked Newman as if he were some rare and exotic animal, he visited their flat. Townshend hung on his every word. "Newman held forth about the valuable contributions Bix Beiderbecke[2] made to jazz before he died,"

2 Beiderbecke was an innovative American jazz cornetist and pianist whose recorded legacy, despite spanning only seven years, remains hugely influential. He died as a result of chronic alcoholism in 1931, just 28 years old.

Barnes recalled, adding, "Pete went through a Bix Beider-becke period for the next three or four weeks." Newman loaned Townshend and Barnes some of his favorite records, namely 1920s and '30s American jazz. Barnes recalls one such track by the Hoagy Carmichael Band (featuring, among such other jazz luminaries as Benny Goodman, Tommy Dorsey and Gene Krupa, Newman's hero Bix Beiderbecke on cornet) called 'Barnacle Bill The Sailor'. "It was a party piece; a wonderful sort of novelty song," said Barnes, "and so Pete learned it and he used to sing it – learned it all: *Who's that knocking at my door / It's Barnacle Bill the sailor!* He learned the words and all the voices. He should have done it on one of his solo albums!"

CHAPTER 2

ANDY

"I just played piano, solo, for about an hour in front of the audience," Andy Newman explained in 2009 when asked for his recollections of the performance at Ealing Technical College that had left Townshend and Barnes transfixed. "It was just to fill some time in because they'd had some very important artist – I think it was (jazz trumpeter) Shake Keane and his band – but they'd had to drop out at the last minute and so I came in and took over. I just played, as I say, solo piano, and apparently Pete was in the audience."

He went on in this understated, matter-of-fact manner to describe the recordings he'd made with his friend Rick Seaman. "Rick and myself had been playing a bit of music together and doing a bit of recording onto an old Grundig tape recorder and Rick played the recordings to Pete, and for some reason he liked them." Predictably, Newman's appraisal of *Ice and Essence* was lukewarm: "To me, it wasn't that good, but everyone else seemed to think it was alright." Pete, of course, didn't just think *Ice and Essence* was "alright." Barnes' observation in his book *Maximum R&B* was that "Pete became slightly obsessed with him and regarded him as a sort of undiscovered genius... Pete played [*Ice & Essence*] constantly". This was news to Newman, who was positively flabbergasted when told of Barnes's memories regarding the impact both the performance and the recording had on Townshend.

"Did he really?" Newman asked slowly, clearly amazed. "I didn't know that," he said finally after a long pause. I then read Barnes' recollections in full to an uncharacteristically quiet Newman, who had apparently spent the preceding four-plus decades completely unaware of the degree of Townshend's admiration for him. After another long pause, he finally spoke up: "I *say*... I didn't realize that... [pause]. Well, well, well... you've taken my breath away there," he said, punctuating his comment with an incredulous laugh.

To speak with Andy Newman was to pry open an encyclopedia. The man knew a great deal about an enormous number of subjects, particularly in the fields of music and technology. Early 20th century American jazz was an area of particular expertise. When I informed him that Pete went through a Bix Beiderbecke period for about a month after hearing Newman's discourse on the merits of Beiderbecke's musical genius, Newman, after again offering an incredulous "Did he *really*?" dove straight into a monologue on Pete's love of a Beiderbecke record featuring Eddie Lang.

"I know one thing," he said, clearly pleased that his favorite subject had been broached, and rediscovering his natural verbosity:

> Pete got very fascinated by a record that Bix Beiderbecke was on with a band called the Jean Goldkette Orchestra where the guitarist, Eddie Lang, did a very interesting set of chords before the vocal refrain and apparently he spent quite a lot of time trying to learn the chords. Eddie Lang was superb – he was probably the first great jazz guitarist in history. He precursored Django Reinhardt and the other great guitarists like Kenny Burrell and Barney Kessel and Carl Kress and – oh God, I'm trying to think of all the great jazz guitarists. He could not only play the solos; he was an extremely good accompanist. In fact, he was so good that when Bing Crosby started his solo career, he signed a contract with Brunswick, and he had written in the contract that he would not record unless Eddie Lang was in the orchestra. Eddie Lang had to be on the session, otherwise Crosby would not sing. That's what he thought of him as an accompanist.

Eddie Lang, incidentally, was the guitarist on the Hoagy Carmichael Orchestra's aforementioned recording of 'Barnacle Bill The Sailor'.

Newman's encyclopedic knowledge was paired with an unbridled joy at sharing this knowledge with an interested party, leading to our handful of long conversations in the summer of 2009. In addition to regaling me with stories about his own life and career, he veered off into subjects as diverse as Muhammad Ali, cricket, Benny Goodman, and the pronunciation of 'baroque' (my use of the American pronunciation clearly jarred with him and he repeatedly – but politely – corrected me). When the conversation turned to Pete Townshend's father, a saxophonist with the R.A.F. Dance Orchestra, Newman again proved an enthusiastic wealth of information:

> Cliff Townshend was a beautiful player – he played my soprano sax at a party; he was really good. And he was a really sweet man. He was a saxophone/clarinet man with The Squadronaires, which was the R.A.F. dance band during and a little bit after the war. And in this country it was one of the three top bands of the services. There were two very good American bands, Glenn Miller and Sam Donahue, and there was The Squadronaires. Now I was talking to an American guy… now what was his name… he was a trombonist in Glenn Miller's band, he was saying that the favorite band amongst the American armed forces was Sam Donahue, who was the Navy band. They all preferred him to the rest. But he said if they couldn't get Sam Donahue, they would settle for The Squadronaires. But none of the Americans liked Glenn Miller's band, amazingly enough.

To which I responded with surprise, given that Glenn Miller is the one who's typically mentioned first. "That's right," Newman replied. "But most of the actual servicemen, if it came to a choice, they'd get Donahue, and if they couldn't get Donahue, they'd get the Squads, and they'd only have Glenn Miller if they couldn't get the other two. Which I was quite surprised about, because you'd think the American bands would have a much more authentic sound than a British band. But apparently they liked it! …There was another guy I met who actually played with Cliff Townshend in The Squadronaires, he was a bass player, and *he* said he thought Sam Donahue's was by far the best band, and he couldn't understand why Glenn Miller was getting all the publicity."

Conversing with Newman was a delight, but as Richard Barnes observed, he could at times veer off into the most arcane subjects. "Andy was a strange person and he was very obscure," said Barnes. "He had an encyclopedic knowledge of really unimportant, obscure things, it seemed to me. Like – he'd go on about some kind of Soviet scientists that had done experiments on dogs living near railway tracks, and you'd go, "*What?*" And he'd say, "Yes – Professor Krupkin, in his research, discovered that…" and you'd go, "What the fuck?" *No one's* interested, you know? And it was amazing – he could hold forth with anyone in the world on this obscure subject, and he was like that. And he could get quite argumentative about it. I should imagine he spent a very lonely life, 'cause he was an oddball, and that's probably how he got into the piano. I should think he was shunned at school and all of that."

* * *

Andrew Laurence Newman was born on November 21st, 1942 at Osterley Nursing Home, Isleworth, west London,

the same town where Pete Townshend was born two and a half years later. Newman was a big specimen right from the beginning. "I vividly remember seeing him for the first time, when the family came round and my mother was back from the nursing home," recalled Newman's brother Robin, six years older than Andy. "He was quite a big, heavy, strong baby." By age 26, Newman was a strapping lad: 6' 2", and 15st 9lbs.

Newman grew up in the west London borough of Hounslow, attending Alexandra Primary School. His father, Charles, was Parks Superintendent for the Middlesex Borough of Heston and Isleworth (later absorbed into the London Borough of Hounslow). Charles had met his wife, Alice, who worked with her sister at the Ministry of Pensions, while he was a student at Kew Gardens. Alice's family lived on Kew Green, next to the Greyhound pub, in a cottage they rented from the church. Charles lived in nearby Willow Cottages, just a few steps from the river. In January 1928, when the Thames flooded, the residents had to be rescued by horse and cart. Charles and Alice later had two children: Sons Charles (b. April 1936) and Andrew.[3]

Because of Charles's job, the Newman family resided in a house with a large garden on the edge of Lampton Park, the largest park in the borough, a house that has since been sadly demolished, but fittingly, the land from which has been absorbed into the park. "We were there many, many years and it was a delightful area," Robin remembered. It was the perfect environment for Andy to explore his interest in birds and wildlife, passed on to him in particular by his maternal grandfather, a plumber by trade who worked in a munitions factory during the war.

Young Andrew's interest in nature and a budding

---

3 The elder Newman clarified: "My official name is Charles; the family name was Robin – Andrew always called me that."

independent streak landed him in a spot of trouble when the family embarked on their first post-war holiday, to Holland-on-Sea on the Essex coast. "He disappeared," Robin recalled of his brother, only two years old at the time. "We were frantically looking, walking around this little estate of bungalows where my mother had got a fortnight's holiday she'd booked from an advert. I went round the back and I remember they hadn't noticed he'd disappeared and I said, "Where's Andrew?" He wasn't there – and I went round the back of the estate, looking everywhere, and they went round the other side, and we met at this pond." And voila – there was Andy, enjoying the view. "He'd just simply gone to see the ducks, and that was probably his first interest – he was very interested in wildlife."

Accordingly, Andy studied *Wood's Popular Natural History*, a widely read Victorian book and one of many in the family's collection. His mother was a voracious reader and was passionate about the arts. Robin remembers her reading Osbert Sitwell's four-volume memoirs, and her affinity for listening to the BBC's Light Programme and Home Service on the radio, the sopranos Elizabeth Schwarzkopf and Elisabeth Schumann among her favorites.

Richard Barnes paid a visit to the Newman family home in the mid '60s. "His dad was a park keeper," said Barnes, something Robin was quick to correct: "He was Superintendent of Parks, not a park keeper." Barnes went on: "Quite a nice job, and you'd get this lovely little cottage with it – a wonderful little house with the white picket fence at the front, and again, it's like something out of a nursery story, you know: "*Andy lives in the little house…*" Andy's like that eccentric professor in the *Rupert* annual – it's as if he was supposed to be part of it, and his parents and everything else, but there's been a screw-up somewhere along the line and he's ended up in real life. He's supposed to be two-dimensional in this book, but he's not."

The front room of the Newman home featured an old and delicate wood-framed Eavestaff upright piano with brass candlesticks, an instrument which used to belong to Andy's great grandmother. "My father used to like Victorian ballads, and he used to vamp on this very old piano," Robin recalled of Charles, one of ten children, the son of a tortoiseshell spectacle frame maker from Birmingham. "I suppose his father used to like them. 'Silver Threads Among The Gold'; very Victorian, you know."

Andy soon began to demonstrate his own interest in playing the piano, a development which did not bode well for the delicate heirloom in his front room. "He effectively destroyed it, because it wasn't loud enough," Robin recalled ruefully. "Which is a great pity. It was a family piano, and if it had been properly treated... My father used to play it without damaging it, so I think Andrew could have done so." By the time he was a teenager, Newman had physically outgrown his parents and brother, which may help explain matters.

Newman had begun playing at an early age, explaining to *Melody Maker's* Chris Welch in 1969 that he had been "banging the keys of the piano for some years, and it wasn't until the age of nine that I was able to master 'We Are The Robbers Of The Wood'."[4] He later explained that he'd learned to play by watching the hands of his father and those of one of his teachers when they played the piano.

At age 11, Andy began attending Bulstrode Secondary Modern school, right next door to Alexandra Primary. It was at Bulstrode that Andy met Rick Seaman, who became

---

4 Written by Frederic Norton, from the Oscar Asche musical *Chu Chin Chow* which was based on *Ali Baba and the 40 Thieves*. *Chu Chin Chow*, which had premiered in 1916 and ran for more than five years, was adapted for the screen in 1934 and enjoyed a resurgence on the stage in the early '40s. The play's popularity continued well into Newman's childhood, with a radio play and even a traveling *Chu Chin Chow on Ice* show emerging in the early '50s.

a lifelong friend. "My first memory of Andy is we were in the playground at the school," Seaman recalled, "and there was an alleyway where the kids went and the railway beyond it, and there was a copper who used to give the kids a hard time when they were coming to school. I was near the railing and I saw Andy telling this copper off, pointing at him, and I actually heard him say, "You are a public servant!" This was a kid of 11 or 12. I didn't know him, but he was a great big fellow. I thought, God, there's something unusual here, you know."

Seaman also recalled Newman playing the piano in the school assembly hall at lunchtime. "Andy would sometimes play at the piano and sing and stuff, and a few kids would hang around, and he had fun doing it," said Seaman. "I can remember him singing Pinetop Smith.[5] He used to sing, 'I'm Sober Now' – he used to love that song."[6]

By the time he was a teenager, Andy's interests were wide-ranging: 1920s and '30s dance bands and New Orleans jazz, ornithology, astronomy, and a variety of technical subjects. Richard Barnes recalled Newman having an enormous model lighthouse – presumably that he'd built himself – in his bedroom: "One of the things he had in his room was this model lighthouse which was about four foot tall! Fucking amazing! And painted on it was something like THE WHEATSTONE BEACON. Red and white striped and all. And I thought – that can't be a toy – it's too big! I mean, I wanted it – and I'll die without having one. So amazing and weird, you know – but wonderful."

Newman also set up a novel home surveillance system.

5 Smith was an influential 1920s boogie pianist whose 'Boogie Woogie' was arranged for big band and recorded by Tommy Dorsey and His Orchestra in 1938, becoming Dorsey's best-selling record.

6 The image of young Andy singing this song at school is made even more delightful by the lyrics, which include the lines *I been playin' the blues round here for you the whole night long and y'all ain't bought the first jug somehow / I don't mind playin' anytime that y'all can make me drunk, but Mr. Pinetop is sober now*

"Andy lived in this little house in the middle of a playground, and he wired it all up so that he could see or hear anybody approaching," Clive Smith recalled. "He was incredibly technically minded and just loved the technology. I think he made his own multi track tape recorder at one point."

"He was certainly interested in a large number of technical things," Robin remembered. "He had books about all sorts of things – I think he'd more or less educated himself, having gone to a Secondary Modern school where you get a basic education, but not very much more." By this time, Andy's older brother had taken a more academic route, attending Latymer Upper School in Hammersmith, followed by Cambridge University, where he obtained his teacher's diploma.

Andy, meanwhile, stayed on at Bulstrode Secondary Modern until 1959, where he found things increasingly difficult. "The secondary modern schools, normally they left at fifteen, but the headmaster, Mr. Dennis, was very keen on building up what he called a Sixth Form, which is what grammar schools had," Robin recalled. At one point during his Sixth Form year, Andy's progress was sufficiently poor that Mr. Dennis called a meeting with the young man's parents. Robin remembered his father's disappointment in Andy, who surprisingly found mathematics particularly difficult. Presumably this struggle is what led to what happened next: "Andrew eventually left and went straight into the post office," Robin recalled. "He was much more practical than I was; he was always interested in technical things, particularly electricity, and in fact in the end, I'm not quite sure whether it was his choice or my mother decided it would be a good idea, but he got into the post office – telephones." 16-year-old Newman undertook his training at Wheatstone House, the GPO Telephone Exchange building, named after the scientist and inventor

Charles Wheatstone, who presumably impressed Newman enough that he named his model lighthouse after him.

Newman's apprenticeship began a successful tenure with the GPO. "He took to it quite well," Robin recalled, adding "he was taller than me – bigger and stronger, but I don't think he liked climbing up the telephone poles, which they had to do as part of their training. They had an older chap supervising them. Andrew and he kept up a friendship into – well, until the chap died. He eventually moved to the Forest of Dean and Andrew visited him once or twice." Robin also recalled his younger brother bringing home his first pay packet and "ironing the notes with a linen iron to make them nice and smooth."

An early purchase Andy made once he started earning an income was a sturdier piano: A second-hand, iron-framed upright model on which he continued honing his craft. He was entirely self-taught, hammering away in the front room. "As far as I know, he never had any formal lessons," said Robin of his brother, who reported 'none' under MUSICAL EDUCATION in a 1969 *NME* questionnaire.[7] "He sort of picked up his own thing. The rhythm and, I suppose, the loudness – it does sound a bit odd. If it sounds original, it's because it *is* original."

In addition to developing an interest in a wide range of musical instruments, Newman began buying second-hand records, which is probably what sparked his interest in American jazz. Robin added that during his national service in Scotland in the mid-1950s, he was "posted on a trail near Fife and the nearest town was St. Andrews, and I bought quite a few of these 78 RPM records. Andrew got very interested in them and borrowed them so he could

---

7 "My family tried to dissuade me from music because they did not think it made money," Andy told *Record Mirror* in 1969. "Then my mother heard that a little boy next door was supposed to be a budding musical genius, so she arranged for me to have lessons, not to be outdone. However, I did not take them."

copy them." Robin specifically remembers some Jimmy Shand recordings among them – Shand was a Scottish accordionist who played traditional Scottish dance music. "So – apart from the jazz – he was very wide-ranging in his interests."

In 1969, Newman answered a series of biographical questions for a profile in the *NME* which provides some additional insight into his childhood years and his personality. He listed 'Richard George Seaman' as his best friend and his 'first professional appearance' as occurring at Hanwell British Legion Club, while his 'first important public appearance' was the aforementioned lunchtime performance at Ealing Technical College in 1963. Newman notes that his radio debut was "West of England radio, 1953 as a result of car accident," while under 'most thrilling experience,' he cited "1400 volts while working with GPO." His favorite color was yellow; favorite food lobster, and, fittingly, under favorite drink and clothes, the ever-practical Newman listed "water" and "functional". He listed a "kitten named Tania" and "a grass snake" under PETS and cited "little chicken farm" under PERSONAL AMBITION. His professional ambition, he wrote, was "to innovate music."

The more musically centered questions offer further insight. Under 'instruments played', Newman listed piano, soprano, tenor and bass saxophones, kazoo and flute. Although he rather surprisingly listed contemporaries Fleetwood Mac as his favorite group, the rest of his influences were markedly of another era: Bing Crosby and Peter Dawson were his favorite singers, Chopin and Elgar his favorite composers, and, under 'biggest influence on career', Newman listed the 1920s-era American ragtime/jazz pianist Jelly Roll Morton.

Morton's influence can certainly be heard in Newman's playing, which has proved hard to put a name to. Speedy

Keen was asked how to describe Newman's playing during a radio interview in 1975: "Boogie pianist is perfect," Speedy said. "He's a 1930's boogie pianist." In the early days, Newman's playing was compared to that of Morgan 'Thunderclap' Jones, a Welsh pianist and songwriter who released his popular 'Hurricane Boogie' in 1956 on Oriole Records. The song's opening featured a clap of thunder, hence the nickname. Jones wrote dozens of songs, including The Shadows' million-selling 'The Stranger' (1960), Craig Douglas' 1960 hit 'Heart of a Teenage Girl', and Mark Wynter's 'Dream Girl' (1961). Jones also wrote and played on Johnny Kidd & the Pirates' 'So What' (1961). Newman and Jones would eventually meet, as we shall see in a later chapter. While the pair shared a similar style, Newman's playing is heavier and more firmly ragtime-rooted than the more frenetic and showmanlike Jones.

"It's difficult to say who influenced my revolutionary style," Newman told *Melody Maker*'s Chris Welch in 1969 with rather uncharacteristic panache, possibly due to the fact that the interview was conducted in a pub. "I would say it was a cross between Bix Beiderbecke and Debussy," Newman said, citing in particular Beiderbecke's piano solo on the Debussyesque 'In A Mist,' in which one can certainly hear elements of Newman's technique. "Andy was a genius in his own orbit," says Pete Townshend when asked to describe Newman's playing. "He had a technique of chordal and percussive playing rooted in the piano style of the great jazz cornet player Bix Beiderbecke. Bix only played piano rarely but when he did he had a poignant, poetic style. Andy based his technique on that."

Newman's friend Clive Smith, also a pianist, noted: "He was not a trained piano player, he just figured it out himself, and he was doing these really interesting inversions that are really quite sophisticated, you know – when you're just playing piano and you want the bass end to say certain things, and to color the chord in a certain way, and he did it naturally, which was amazing."

At some point, Newman began performing in public, but cautioned me, "all I'd been doing was very, very amateur and, arguably, slightly semi-pro in a few cases where we actually did get paid for little public performances as well as sitting in with other little bands where I could be of help. I doubt if I earned more than a fiver." He later recalled performing with "a guy called John Brown and Mick Carver, and there was also a Hawaiian band I've forgotten the name of."

Andy left home around 1965 after some difficulties between the strong-willed 23-year-old and his father. "He got on perfectly well with my mother, possibly not so well with my father," Robin recalled. "I know they didn't get on. When he was younger, he was disobedient. Andrew basically did what he wanted to and didn't care about fitting in with other people. And, of course, dad wasn't a very big, strong man; he was fairly small, and Andrew was taller than he was, so that was probably another difficulty. My father was a quiet sort – he was very fond of reading, he wasn't a bully or anything like that at all. I suppose he had rather old-fashioned ideas about how children should behave."

While Robin observes that they "got on well enough," the two brothers drifted apart, seldom making contact with each other. Robin embarked on a teaching career which took him to Crosby, near Liverpool, for five years before he returned to the much closer to home Lewisham. "By this time, Andrew had long since left home," he recalled. "Andrew didn't keep in touch; at one point my mother didn't even know where he was," recalls Robin, who revealed that the family discovered Andy was living in "quite a respectable area of Ealing," when Newman's landlady happened to telephone his mother about some concern or other.

Newman's interests in a wide variety of musical

instruments and also more technical subjects led him to begin experimenting with recording at home, something he started back when he was still living with his parents. "I was playing other instruments, mainly wind instruments," he said, "and what I wanted to do was proper, full orchestrations, and being an amateur musician and having people around who really didn't know anything about music and didn't understand the whole sort of concept of how an orchestration goes, I thought, well, the only way to do it is to get two tape recorders, record your basic track on the first one, and then dub through a mixer to the second one, with a microphone in the mixer, and add the second instrument, and then bounce back the other way putting the third instrument on. And I managed to do a few recordings like that. The technical quality was appalling because by the time you get to four overdubs you've lost a hell of a lot of quality, and all the faults in the system build up, and I didn't have terribly good equipment to work with anyway."

Despite a distinct lack of musical ability, Rick Seaman ended up helping Newman with his recordings. "How I later got to connect with him I really don't know, it's a bit of a mystery to me because to be honest, we had absolutely nothing in common," said Seaman. "I did eventually get to know him a bit better and went round to his parents' house and made recordings with a piano and a kazoo – he made a kind of extension to the kazoo which was like a big funnel which he used to rest where you would normally rest the music on a piano, and he would play, and it was really quite extraordinary."

In the months after Andy's performance at Ealing Tech, the Newman-Townshend connection continued sporadically, with the pair occasionally discussing music and Newman intermittently providing Townshend with examples of his latest recordings, some of which had over twenty multi-tracked instruments. "These recordings were played to Pete, and he thought it was a very good idea to try and do it," said Newman.

"Pete was starting to write and what really turned him on was that Andy was over-recording his music on tape machines," Barnes recalled.

> It sounds really crude now with all the sophistication, but just the mere fact that with two reel to reel tape machines you could record on one and then overdub on the other one. Pete was absolutely fascinated that Andy was doing it. I think he probably met up with him a lot more than we did together, you know – probably met him as well on his own, 'cause I think he'd gone and looked at him recording and stuff like that. Andy was a post office engineer, you know – I suppose one of those guys we used to see at the side of the road and their boxes full of wires and they'd sit there and wire them together and fix up the phone lines. So he was very technical, but Pete was also technical – a lot of these musicians are very technical, and into electronics and stuff like that. And so they probably clicked on that level.

The degree to which Newman influenced Townshend, if at all, is difficult to gauge. When asked if Townshend sought his advice when it came to multitracking, the typically self-deprecating Newman said, "I think he more or less was able to work out how it's done. I might have answered a question or two." Conversely, Richard Barnes observed, "I don't know whether Pete would agree with me, but I think Andy was a major influence on him because of this over-recording and overdubbing and all that stuff."

"He didn't really influence me," said Townshend when asked about the impact of Newman's multitracking on his own techniques. "But he was multitracking before me I believe." And of course when dealing with someone whose every thought has been recorded over the past six decades, there's a conflicting statement: "Thunderclap was working in the electronic communications division of the British Post Office at the time and made multi-tracked home recordings using two tape machines," Townshend wrote in an online diary entry in 2001. "This was my first exposure to this method of multi-tracking, one I used myself from 1964 onwards for my own songwriting. Later, you may or may not know that I 'created' a pop group called Thunderclap Newman and the man himself was of course a member. My then friend Speedy (John) Keen was writing quantum songs like "Something In The Air" and I was excited to record them in my own home studio that Thunderclap himself had inspired. Several of the early tracks from their first album were recorded by jumping back and forth from tape machine to tape machine (a la early Phil Spector) rather than using multitracks." In his book *Before I Get Old*, Who biographer Dave Marsh provided one more piece of evidence supporting the idea that Thunderclap did indeed influence Townshend, stating that Pete acquired a reel to reel tape recorder after being exposed to Newman's work.

It was during the latter half of the '60s that Newman began receiving queries from Townshend regarding recorded work. "In 1966, I had a visitation from Mr. Townshend who asked me to record for his label 'Talkus'," Newman told *Record Mirror* in 1969, adding, "devaluation set in later in the year so just as well the label did not come about."

Newman received another request from Townshend during the second half of 1967. "I got a message from Pete saying that he wanted me to do some film music," Newman recalled, "and so we went to his flat in Eccleston Square, and he sort of told me roughly what he wanted.

At the time he was gluing a guitar back together which he'd broken. He gave me a Nagra reel to reel portable tape recorder which at that time I think was considered the best portable tape recorder money could buy; I think they've still got them in the film industry now. Anyway, so what happened was I went away on the basis of what he'd said he wanted, and I recorded some stuff and sent it back to him with the tape recorder."

Newman recalled that the music was intended for "a guy from the BBC West of England film studio, and apparently they were training producers who were students at Bristol University. I think they actually put the thing into practice when we did the promotional film for 'Something In The Air'... Of course, Pete wasn't there on that occasion, because most of the time he was away on tour in America. We used to get these very amusing stories coming back of the slight disagreements between he and other members of the band."

This instance of Townshend soliciting film music from Newman didn't come to fruition, but the guitarist kept him in mind and would call on him again the following year, with far more meaningful results.

CHAPTER 3

SPEEDY

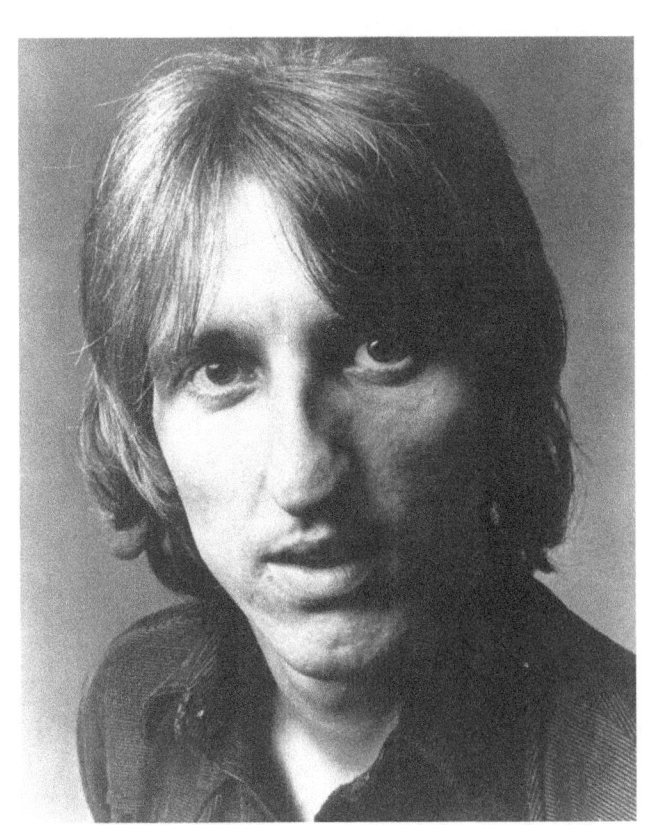

On June 29, 1966, Pete Townshend drove to Sheffield University, where The Who were scheduled to perform that evening. Townshend had driven straight from London Airport after a flight from New York where he'd met with the notoriously combative music executive Allen Klein as part of an effort to extricate himself and The Who from the unfavorable deal they had signed with producer Shel Talmy. Townshend arrived in Sheffield around 10pm to find that his bandmates had already given up on him and left. Exhausted, he turned around and headed back for London.

Townshend was driving the car he had purchased just a couple of months earlier: A 1963 Lincoln Continental Convertible, a big, black American car with a silky-smooth ride – a little too smooth for the fatigued guitarist, who fell asleep at the wheel. He woke up "upside-down in a ditch with petrol dripping in my face, and a police officer asking if I was OK," he recalled in his 2012 memoir *Who I Am*. "I gave the breakdown man my Rickenbacker 12-string as a reward for pulling me out of the ditch."[8]

"Now in those days the motorways didn't have crash barriers on them," Andy Newman told me years later in a possibly embellished and implausible but thoroughly entertaining retelling of what I assume is the same event:

Fortunately, where he went to sleep, the ground next to the motorway was flat; he went straight

8 Townshend had had another accident the previous month. "…I was driving down the M1 motorway in the early hours when I ran into an accident that had happened ten minutes earlier," he recalled in *Who I Am*. He braked too late and his car skidded. "At the very last moment of my skid, I smashed tail-first into a Jaguar that had rolled over, and still contained two trapped elderly people waiting for an ambulance. They already had multiple injuries so that bump caused them considerable pain. I felt terrible for them, and shame for the habit I'd fallen into of driving too fast when the road was empty. I was convicted of careless driving and heavily fined, although I didn't lose my licence."

through a fence and into a farmer's field. The problem was, the farmer was ploughing the field and it had messed up his day's work. Anyway, he gets out of his tractor and he starts screaming at Pete, you know: "You irresponsible young so and so," blah blah blah, "they should bring back national service, sort you hooligans out!", and all the rest of it [laughs]. Pete woke up and when he realized what had happened, he apparently put his hand in his pocket and pulled out £50 and gave it to the guy. Suddenly, *oooh*! The guy was all over him! "Oooh! I'm sorry sir! Don't you worry, we'll get you out of here. Are you all right sir?" £50, that was his price. But of course, obviously, it could have been a lot worse than that. He could've, you know, hit something really solid or whatever, so I think after that, he always had Speedy along to drive for him. Particularly on the way home.

* * *

John David Percy Keen was born in Ealing, west London, on March 29th, 1945, the son of Walter and Margaret Keen. Margaret worked at a soap factory in nearby Brentford while Walter was a laborer at a local builder's yard. "During the war, he used to drive tank transporters, massive great, that carried 100-ton tanks," Keen wrote of his father in the memoir he began in the early 1980s. It was never finished but provides some beautiful insight and reveals the same observational skills that helped make Keen such a good songwriter.[9] "Anyway, he had to nip home to see mum

9 I've taken the liberty of correcting Keen's punctuation and spelling errors in any excerpts. Hence, Keen's creative spelling – such as 'listerning' and 'oppersite' – has been cleaned up, and his lengthy sentences, often spanning ten lines or longer and punctuated with only commas, have had a few full stops thrown in.

who was living with granny at the time, driving his huge long lorry into the cul de sac," Keen continued. "He nips in for tea, and when it was time to go, he found he couldn't back the lorry out again without knocking down a wall on the bend where Ramsay Road met the main road. Well, after an hour of trying, he ended up just smashing the wall down – he was quite famous in Ramsay Road after that, and I think he got into trouble with the Army. Good though to have that kinda story of your father. My dad had a great sense of humour, he always laughed when he told that story." John Keen was a storyteller, and by many accounts could weave an enthralling yarn in person, but it's clear both through his song lyrics and the fragments of his memoirs that he could do this on the page as well.

The Keen family – Walter, Margaret, young John and his sister, Patricia, four years older, lived on the ground floor of 102 Murray Road, a Victorian terraced house in Ealing. Speedy shared a bedroom with his sister. "My sister had the bed near the window which always bugged me because she could see the stars and I couldn't and she would always go on about it," he wrote. "One of her favorites was, "Look, I just seen a shooting star!", the one thing I always wanted to see."

Keen's grandparents and an assortment of aunts and uncles lived nearby. His paternal grandmother, 'Granny Keen', held a special place in his heart. "She was a wonderful woman," he wrote.

> We used to sit by her iron stove… She told me the story of the Rags woman, who used to come round every week to collect the best suits from the men. The men would wear the suits on Saturday nights and to church on Sundays, it was important to them to look smart at least one day of the week, then on Monday the woman would come round to

collect the suits to take them to be pawned for the week's food and baccy money, then on Friday when the men had their wages she would go and get them out again for Saturday and Sunday night. That's how working-class people had to live to survive and still be thought of as part of the community. The Rags woman came round every week until one day she was found in an alley just down the road, she had drank a whole bottle of carbolic, it's a cleaning fluid, and died, it's a dreadful way to die and she must have been so unhappy. The story of the carbolic lady has always stuck in my mind.

In those days I would have to go to the shop for granny's five Woodbines, which were three pence old money, incredible that isn't it. We used to sit in front of the stove, and she would give me a puff of her cigarette which was heavy going for a six-year-old. I loved her and still think I loved her more than anyone else.

The Keens would take the shuttle from Acton Town to South Acton, known as the 'Ginny Train', to visit Speedy's maternal grandparents. "My mum used to say, "Come, we're going on Ginny to Granny Skinner's house"," Speedy wrote. Because Keen's grandfather was a park keeper, his grandparents lived at Ramsay House, situated at the edge of South Acton Park. "One of the things I loved when I visited Granny Skinner was I could play in the park, or play on the railway which ran down the side of the park," Keen wrote. "It was 1950, steam trains went clanging by on their way to Acton goods yard. I used to love standing on the bridge and lean over the side and look straight down the funnel as it went by; it wasn't a good idea really 'cause sometimes you would get a face full of soot and hot ash. ...Granny and Grandad Skinner's house was gas lit and I remember sitting in Grandad Skinner's lap and always falling asleep with the gentle drone of their voice as they talked and the gentle hiss of the gas lamp."

Keen's typewritten recollections[10] reflect a strong sense of family and community during his childhood. He recalled beautifully the street party on Murray Road celebrating the coronation of Queen Elizabeth II on June 2, 1953, when he was 8 years old. "All the streets were blocked off round our way, we had a big tea in the middle of the road, and in the evening the mums played the women at football," he wrote.

> I remember helping my dad put our radiogram through the front window of our house into the front garden so the grown-ups could dance in the evening, then he fixed up these lights across the road, then he had the cheek to plug them into the lamppost opposite our house... it was a fantastic evening for us kids, because we stayed up late and all the parents got so drunk that they all became so happy you could get away with anything, smoke a fag, drink beer, eat loads. It was lovely, the music blaring down the road, seeing all the neighbours having a good time, it was wonderful.

In addition to working full time at the soap factory, Keen's mother cleaned the canteen at Beldam Rubber Company in Brentford on Saturdays. "I always went with her," he wrote.

> ...In the canteen in the left hand corner was a piano, that's where it all started. While mum would polish

---

10 "I have to stop now because the typewriter is disturbing the neighbours," he typed at one point.

the floor in the canteen I would get lost in a world of my own on the piano, and though I didn't understand what I was doing I used to get so carried away that they used to come and complain. It was a really old out of tune piano, but …it was the first time I could get completely lost in something that didn't involve someone else. This gave me back something, this wonderful noise, this powerful sound, I could create thunder and lightning, at the top end rain snow drops, the sound used to bounce around the empty canteen, it was a wonderful time. I heard things in that piano that I hadn't heard before, it was terrible when my mum stopped working there.

Although he wrote in his memoirs that his mother was "uptight" and his father was "a miserable sod most of the time," Keen told Vivien Goldman of *Sounds*, "I always got along well with my family. My sister is fantastic," he said of Patricia, who had struggled with rheumatic fever since 9 years of age. The following decade was a seemingly endless series of hospital visits, culminating with a stay at the Canadian Red Cross Memorial Hospital in Taplow, which at the time was a center of research regarding rheumatism in children. "Every time we went to the hospital they'd say we don't know how long she's going to last," Keen said. "…She was under the threat of death for five years, but she's one of those people that just barrages you with happiness, she's got rosy cheeks… It was very hard for me when I was a kid because when she was in hospital I used to get 2/6d [the equivalent of 30 pence] a week pocket money, and when she was at home I used to get nine pence. Then they used to say to me, she's got a bad heart, don't you frighten her. So I used to spend the rest of my life going *DADADAeeDADA* darting out of cupboards and yelling, so that I'd get my 2/6d, y'know wot I mean?" Perhaps it was in response to one of these ambushes by Speedy that led to his sister one day pushing him off the ledge of an upstairs window, leaving him with a chronic back injury and a fear of heights, something that particularly bothered him when his father enlisted him to help with roofing work.

There were also tender recollections of his father, such as Keen's account of him caring for a pigeon with a broken wing. "We put it in the greenhouse, and he fixed a sort of splint on the broken part, and it stayed in the greenhouse for about five months while it healed," Keen wrote. "Then one day dad let it go, and I never forget it flew up in the air then did a big circle and landed on our roof by the chimney and you know from that day until we moved it was always on the roof, every day, it was amazing."

Keen attended Little Ealing Primary and Junior Schools, followed by Little Ealing Secondary Modern, all just a short walk from the family home on Murray Road. He joined the Boys' Brigade at age 9 but soon lost interest. "I liked the Boys' Brigade, they gave me a uniform, and I felt like I had joined the Navy," he wrote. "We used to play games and make knots and things like that but I don't think it was a very rich brigade at that time because we just met in a church hall with not very many facilities, we used to have to imagine it was a ship. I soon got bored with it and preferred to tell my mum I was going, but I used to hang around with other boys who told their mums they were going but didn't." He and his friends would play at Boston Manor Park, a short walk from the end of Murray Road. "It had big iron gates and a big pond, tennis courts, huge greenhouses, and a childrens playground," he recalled. "More important it had woods, the place all the cowboy fantasies were lived out. It used to be a thing to go to Saturday morning pictures, and watch Buck Rogers or Robin Hood, then relive the films in Boston Manor Park on the Sunday afternoons."

Keen's school experience was predictably negative for such an adventurous child. "I don't have many memories of school life except sitting looking out the windows on sunny afternoons, wishing I wasn't there," he wrote. "I was always getting the cane for being late, I used to go through all the back alleys to get to school… I loved those alleys, you could always guarantee walking to school on your own. During my last days of school I found it more and more difficult to leave the alleys and actually go to school at all… it was much easier to carry on playing than going through the gates of that grim place Little Ealing Secondary Modern." He recalled once being "caned so badly my father came to the school to complain and ended up throwing some books at the teacher."

Around age 11, Speedy began working at George West's builders yard with his father and his Uncle Monty on Saturday mornings. "I used to clean up the yard and paint ladders and things like that," he wrote.

> My father drove a little grey van at the time which was a converted baby Morris, you know the tiny little ones with the spoke wheels, it was lovely and we had many adventures in that van me and my dad, to this day I've never worked out why he was always so miserable in the mornings. It had a profound effect on me, it made me never want to get up early ever again. George West used to do a lot of factory maintenance as well as private work for fairly well to do people. Father rarely got the factory maintenance side of things, he had no push my dad, he would do a job for anybody, and no matter how big he'd only charge them half a dollar 2/6 old money. Many Saturday afternoons were spent fixing someone's roof in the rain and wind, and they'd say at the end of it, "How much

I owe you Wally?", and he'd say, "That's all right mate,"bung the ladders on the van and we'd be on the way home, soaked to the skin.

Keen's fragmented memoirs are rife with his love of cars, trains and motorcycles, such as his recollection of having to help start his father's Standard Big Nine motor car before family trips to the country on Sundays. "If it was cold it would be murder on the fingers, and the more it wouldn't start the more times dad had to turn it, with the engine kicking back all the time, and dad getting angrier and angrier," he wrote. "Sometimes it wouldn't start at all, and he would be in a bad mood all day. I used to hate that car until it started, then it would be the most wonderful thing in the world, often taking us far from Murray Road, into the country."

Keen began to develop a love of music in his early teens, picking up an affinity for '50s rock & roll from his cousin, Robin. At some point in the late '50s, Granny Skinner bought him his first drum kit. "I have a lot to thank her for," he wrote. "I remember forever being clouted round the ear for making a noise, but I loved those drums, I felt I had this native rhythm in me and only drums could bring it out. The first time I played drums in public was at a social club my parents went to, when the band let me play to show how good I was. I was pathetic, but it showed I was heading in the right direction. The next time I played live was in the local youth club when I thought the drummer was so terrible I got up and asked him if I could have a go."

When Jim Marshall's music shop opened in nearby Hanwell in 1960, Speedy quickly became a regular visitor. The shop catered in particular to drummers in the early days, Marshall himself being a former drummer and giving lessons to many students, including Mitch Mitchell, later to reach fame with the Jimi Hendrix Experience. "That shop changed my life," Speedy wrote. "His son changed the way amps were made forever, but what he had for me was drums." Keen's becoming known to Marshall opened up doors for the young drummer. "How I started playing music was, I went to Jim Marshall's shop, and he gave me work," he said later. "I went all over the continent thanks to him…. all kinds of bands, thousands of gigs."

In the aforementioned *NME* questionnaire, Keen lists his first professional appearance as 'Birmingham Redcaps 1960', likely the first example of work resulting from his relationship with Marshall's music shop. Keen would have been only 14 or 15 years old at the time. Alan Morley, Redcaps drummer for the duration of the band's short life, has no recollection of Speedy sitting in, but does allow that it may have happened on a date when he was otherwise indisposed, a not unthinkable scenario, particularly when considering they sometimes played as many as three shows in one day.

In parallel with the musical developments, a rebellious streak emerged during Speedy's adolescence. "At school I ran with the hooligans and tried to act tough," he said in 1973. "I tried to prove myself but I couldn't make it – I was the one who was done over, the one who got stuck head-first down the toilets[11], the one who was always caught." Bored and restless, Keen left school around age 15, worked a variety of jobs and dove into music and motorcycles. If Keen was riding legally, his interest in motorcycles would have blossomed after he turned 16 years old in March 1961. "I used to go to the Ace Café with Johnny Brooks, he was a good rider and I learned a lot from him," Speedy recalled in his memoirs.

---

11 "I remember being held in the bog head first while they flushed the toilet on your head," he wrote in his memoir, "but once you had been through this you could happily smoke in the bog as a club member."

I eventually got a bike of my own, it's the one I had the terrible crash on, I shouldn't have been allowed to ride it. It really was an absolute wreck – it was a Triumph Speed Twin and I tore around so much I got the name Speedy.[12] It was much better to have a motorbike then, they were loud noisy things and you didn't have to wear a crash helmet. The big thing was to meet up on Sundays and go down to the coast, sometimes as many as thirty or forty bikes would get together and head for the coast, the noise was terrific, and fantastic.

Keen spent a short time working at a motorcycle shop before leaving for a job as a petrol pump attendant at Haven Green, Ealing, but it too was short lived. "I remember the man who ran it really didn't like me," he wrote. "In the end I got the sack because Friday nights my friends would bring the motorbikes round to fuel them up, and one Friday night he caught me. It was my first sacking with many more to follow." A series of jobs followed: He worked as a center lathe operator at Ottways, who made binocular lenses, then went back to working with his father at George Wests's yard again, then as a delivery boy at a butcher's shop. "The job entailed cutting up meat and delivering it," he wrote. "I had my motorbike then, and because the carburetor was leaking I put a jam jar underneath held by elastic bands. It leaked so much I used to have to keep stopping to empty the jam jar into the tank so I was always late."

12 "It comes from a long time ago, really," Speedy explained to Dutch radio host Wim Noordhoek in 1975. "I used to have a motorbike called a Speed Twin, and to get anywhere as a drummer in the early days, you had to do what I'd term as a Keith Moon, do you know what I mean? ...You had to be fast and furious – and everybody used to call me Speedy from the motorbikes. And it just escalated from there to the drums."

Keen wrote that he "always seemed to be falling off" motorcycles. One final accident led to him swearing off riding forever. "There was a guy down the road who worked in another butcher's shop who had a fantastic Bonneville, a bike I dreamed of owning one day," he wrote. "Well one lunch time, I don't know why, he came on the back of my old wreck, and I'm sure he wished he had never, 'cause while I was showing off trying to overtake a lorry on a bend down Popes Lane we had a terrible crash, and he broke both ankles and took out 3 vans with us. I've never seen him since, or been on a motorbike since. I remember waking up in the hospital with this huge copper sitting next to the bed reading a Beano." With this mention of police involvement, one wonders if Keen's motorcycle license may have been revoked or suspended as a result of the crash.

Regardless, Keen's interest in motor vehicles soon turned to the four wheeled variety. His father bought the converted Morris work van he'd been driving and gave it to his son. Despite some mechanical deficiencies, "I managed to pass my test in it," Speedy wrote.

It was the hottest day of year 1961, the van had no hand brake and the speedo didn't work, I was so nervous about these things that I thought I would never pass, anyway the instructor was a clever man and realized I was a good driver… when I did the emergency stop he and the orange box he was sitting on went flying to the back of the van nearly sending him out the back doors. "Pull over there," he said, and I thought 'this is it', laughing he said "don't worry, you've passed," then he said "nip across the road and get us a bottle of Tizer and take us back."

As we drove back my father was sitting on the

side of the road with his head in his hands like he was crying. "Is that man with you?" the instructor said. "Yes," I said, "He's my father." "He doesn't seem to have much faith in you," he said. "Better go and tell him you've passed and stop him crying." It was one of the greatest days of my life, passing my test. It meant freedom at last – I could go everywhere I wanted to go, it was wonderful. I went everywhere in that van until it was smashed up.

Smashed up? "The old man smashed it to bits one morning because I wouldn't get out of bed," Keen explained.

In 1962, 17-year-old Keen began playing drums for Ealing group The Krewsaders, who played mostly Shadows covers at local dances and weddings. Speedy brought his friend, bassist John McVie, later of Fleetwood Mac fame, to the group as well. "I can't remember much about the gigs we played except we wore white cricket jumpers with a red badge and a big K on it," Keen recalled. The Krewsaders disbanded early the following year when McVie left to join John Mayall's Bluesbreakers. Keen seems to have gone adrift around this time, straying from the rock & roll life and associating more with a criminal element. "How I finally got myself accepted was when I put some geezer through a shopfront," he told Nik Cohn. "Actually it was an accident, he sort of stumbled but the impact was fantastic and after that I was the iron fist. The heavies used to come down to the dancehalls whenever I had a gig, and then I got put on probation, which was another plus."

Keen thus developed a tough-guy reputation, which stuck long into his musical career, despite his soft-spoken singing voice and hippie inclinations. "Speedy was a really nice guy," said filmmaker Richard Stanley, who befriended and worked with Keen during the Thunderclap Newman years, "but he also seemed to be the sort of guy who could look after himself, you know, in the night – he kind of seemed to be that way, quite tough and so forth." Pete Townshend later said his first impression of Keen was "quite scary actually; I'd heard he had been in prison for a couple of years." Which appears to have been true. "Pathetic," Keen told Cohn. "Absolutely ridiculous. I got involved with a couple of geezers who were working a fiddle with stolen savings books, where I had to go into different post offices and make withdrawals. Ten pounds a time was the maximum and my share was a third. I wore a cap and blazer and tried to act like a school kid, because I was still all fresh and innocent-looking. After three days a cop knocked at my front door and I jumped out the back, straight into the arms of half a dozen more."

There appears to be a gap in Keen's musical career from the early '63 breakup of the Krewsaders to his mid-1964 joining of another Ealing group, The Second Thoughts, a void which may have been due to his imprisonment. If the 18-year-old Keen was in prison during this period, he was likely in a Borstal (a U.K. Youth Detention Centre), which at the time housed offenders up to age 23. Details on this subject are difficult to ascertain due to the fact that U.K. prison and Borstal records are subject to a blanket 100 year closure rule. Keen doesn't mention prison or Borstal in his memoirs[13], but does mention "I had got into trouble for something I didn't do, I might add," and that he had been on probation. At the time, he had an ill-fated love affair with a girl named Linda; ill-fated because it emerged that her father was his probation officer.

By mid-1964, Keen was back to the generally more wholesome pursuit of drumming. His tenure with The Second Thoughts began as their residency at the legendary

---

13 The title of Keen's first solo album, 1973's *Previous Convictions*, offers a nod to his checkered past.

Ealing Club was winding down. By this time, the Keens had moved to 53a Townholm Crescent in Hanwell, about a mile and a half northwest of their former home on Murray Road. "It seemed as if we were really going downhill," Speedy recalled. "I mean, all I could see from my bedroom window was scrap yards, but I got an old piano and really started to try and write songs."

Keen was "a drummer with a manic force of energy bar none," recalled Second Thoughts singer Pat Lyons, who lived with Keen at his parents' house in Hanwell for a few months "until we were shown the door by his mum for taking too many liberties," he wrote in his memoir, *Psychedelic Days*. "It all came to a head when we got stoned and started playing two drum kits – a face-off at 4 in the morning after we had barricaded his bedroom door with two mattresses. It brought all the screaming neighbors out on the street, the Law and the Council were called in, and his parents were threatened with eviction."

From the Ealing Club residency, "we were able to graduate to the London R&B circuit proper," recalled Lyons. In the coming months, The Second Thoughts would perform regularly at the Studio '51 Club near Leicester Square, the 100 Club on Oxford Street (where they performed in support of groups such as The Graham Bond Organization and The Tridents, featuring guitarist Jeff Beck), and Klooks Kleek in West Hampstead, where on October 12, 1964, Keen and company supported blues legend John Lee Hooker. Wrapped around all of these dates were semi-regular appearances at Ealing Town Hall (Thursdays) and the Ealing YWCA (Saturdays). Lyons recalled that the group's repertoire included "…covers of songs like 'You Can't Judge a Book by Lookin' at the Cover,' 'Mona,' 'Roadrunner,' 'I'm a Man,' and a couple of Wilbur [sic] Harrison songs. That was the backbone of our show; in no time at all we became the most popular band in the area, playing Scout halls and town halls… We started to bring in decent money."

The Second Thoughts "were great and had a good chance of getting somewhere," Speedy wrote in his memoirs. "We even played the Marquee in Wardour Street, it's a night I'll never forget," he recalled. Unfortunately, it was for all the wrong reasons. The appearance, supporting the increasingly popular Moody Blues, took place sometime shortly after the November 1964 release of their single 'Go Now', which reached number one the following January.

> We were so nervous, it was a really big break for us. In those days the band would go on first and play a number to warm up the audience then our singer Pat Lyons would come running on the stage and we would start our set. Because we were playing such a big gig and because we wanted to look professional we borrowed a plug box, because you usually had trouble trying to plug everything in somewhere, there in the middle of the stage was our borrowed plug box, and as I have said we went on and played our opening number, when we finished on came Pat at incredible speed, tripped over the plug box which he didn't see because there had never been one before, blows all the amps immediately and as he's falling shouts thru the very loud PA system "What cunt put that there?!" So ended our big night at the famous Marquee club and the Second Thoughts soon after.

The Second Thoughts remained together long enough to pay a visit in the Spring of 1965 to R.G. Jones recording studio, near Wimbledon. It was Speedy's first recording session. The group recorded two songs – Wilbert Harrison's

'Let's Stick Together', and T.J. Arnall's 'Cocaine Blues'. These tracks apparently went unreleased. Keen wrote his first song in the back of the van enroute to the session. "I forget what it was called now, but I remember they were very impressed by it," he recalled.

This iteration of The Second Thoughts didn't last much longer, but Keen was soon off on another adventure. After watching The Second Thoughts perform at Beat City on Oxford Street in April, the French singer and Fontana Records artist Teddy Raye approached guitarist Tony Duhig, bassist Mickey Holmes and drummer Keen and asked them to serve as his backing group for a month in Madrid, Spain, augmented by a saxophonist. "A right one he turned out to be," Keen wrote of Raye, whom he said "thought he was Frank Sinatra."

> We flew there, it was the first time I had flown and I wondered where the parachute was, I was desperately searching under my seat, when I found this cord, by accident I must have pulled it, anyway it was all very embarrassing because this rubber dingy started to inflate and I nearly got put out of the plane.
>
> When we arrive in Madrid we were taken to this …cheap hotel, and the next day started to rehearse at the Club Consulado, the biggest night club in Madrid. It was French rock with a few Frank Sinatra numbers thrown in. It was all totally different to anything I'd played before, and it was hard work trying to please the Teddy, he wanted me to play this kind of cack handed drumming which I couldn't get used to at all.
>
> Anyway after a few weeks rehearsal with him we went down very well, I even got my picture in the paper, *Batterista Extraordinaire* it said, I

sent it home to mum and she's still got it. Well we worked our balls off for a month and then come pay day, and after a bowl of soup and an orange every day the whole band was looking forward to it. I remember him saying, "You pack the equipment away and I'll meet you back at the hotel," which we did, and about two hours later we got back to the hotel and there was a telegram waiting for us, it was "I used to be a big star in France a long time ago and this money will help me become a big star again, sorry stop," and there we were: No money, the hotel bill to pay, plus we had these stupid suits made and there was the tailor waiting to be paid.

Despite an arduous journey home, Keen and company had been successful enough in Madrid that upon their return to London in May, they quickly made plans to add a singer and return to Spain on their own. They brought in former Second Thoughts bandmate Jon Field on organ, and added singer Tom Newman, from local group The Tomcats. The new group called themselves Los Tomcats and promptly set up a gig at Ealing Town Hall to pay for their trip back to Spain. "For some bizarre reason Speedy had looked after the money," Newman said later, adding "but Speedy wasn't the kind of guy that you could actually trust looking after your money [laughs] and Speedy pissed it all against the wall… So as soon as Speedy revealed himself as being thoroughly untrustworthy, we sacked him."

Keen wasn't out of work for long. In early July, he got a call from a band looking for a drummer. The Eccentrics had just wrapped up a month-long residency at the legendary Piper Club in Rome, and their drummer, John Kerrison, had left the band due to homesickness. With the rest of the group wanting to stay, guitarist Peter Maggs and bassist Roy Robinson returned to the U.K. in search of a replacement. "Neither of us knew Speedy beforehand," recalls Maggs. "We simply went to Jim Marshall's shop in Hanwell and asked around." By the end of July, Keen was in Italy performing at the Piper Club with The Eccentrics, engaged in a residency that stretched through August, an enjoyable period for several reasons. The other band playing at the Piper during this period was Equipe 84 (Team 84), one of the biggest bands in the country – known as 'Italy's answer to the Beatles.' Speedy and co. befriended Romano Morandi, the group's bassist/vocalist at the time.

The Eccentrics lived up to their name during and in between performances. "We did used to lark about a bit," Maggs recalled. "Using feedback, I would use the guitar to simulate an antiaircraft machine-gun. On another occasion, Roy and I acquired cap-guns and during a dull interlude chased each other around the club pretending to be cowboys. One memorable time at the Piper, we found some straw somewhere, and proceeded to cover Speedy in it as he was playing, until he looked like a haystack with just his drumsticks visible still going up and down."

It was also at the Piper Club that Speedy met Lydia Kern, a Berlin native living in Rome. Kern was an actress, visual artist, singer and model who sang in clubs, appeared in a few films, and released some singles under her name, including a song entitled 'Down By The Riverside'. Her parents both having died when she was very young, Kern had lived in an orphanage in Germany from which she repeatedly escaped. She lived in France for a time before moving to Italy where she met Speedy. "He said she was the most gorgeous woman that he'd ever seen," Speedy's friend Emma-Jane Hughes recalled. "He just thought she was amazing because of the art and creative side, and he said she just looked glamorous the whole time. He said she never had to do anything – she'd get out of the car at petrol stations and someone would just run over and offer to fill the car for her." Despite the fact that she knew very little English, Speedy and Lydia quickly became close.

Keen was writing songs during this period, but they were fragmented and unfinished. He also began singing a little. "I do remember him trying to write songs in Italy using a guitar he blagged from The Rokes[14]," recalled Maggs. "He was a good drummer, and I think we fixed him up with a mike at the Piper Club at least for backing."

After the Piper Residency, future Rome area gig prospects for The Eccentrics quickly dried up, chiefly since the group's contract with The Piper Club precluded any appearances within 150km of the city, so as not to attract business away from the club. "When the money ran out we slept in the van one night and then the Rokes allowed us to sleep on the floor of their apartment on the Via Cassia," Maggs recalled. "Speedy had met Lydia, and for a while he and I stayed in her apartment. [Eccentrics singer Mick] Liddell had met an Italian girl and she took him off and fed him, while we were living on the Rokes' charity with a plate of egg and chips once per day – or pancakes at Lydia's. It was round about this time that we parted company with Liddell." Meanwhile, Keen and company heard that their friend Romano Morandi had left Equipe 84. "It seemed logical to join up with him," said Maggs. "He said he could get us work around his home town of Modena, so me, Speedy, Roy and Bruce moved up there in October/November 1965. I shared a room with Speedy in a seedy hooker's hotel for several months."

"I first saw The Eccentrics on stage at the Piper," recalled Morandi. "I was still with Equipe 84. To the Piper crowd they were like the Stones, surely because they were from the U.K. John Speedy was crazy as nuts! At some point

14 The Rokes were another British band playing in Italy at the time.

he tried to learn the Modena dialect.[15] He was extremely funny and as a drummer he was a hard hitter! He was just crazy."

The newly named Romano and The Eccentrics performed in theatres in northern Italy. "Genoa springs to mind," Maggs recalled. "We just played good old fashioned rock'n'roll, playing covers of popular bands. Our specialty was to make a lot of noise, and I used to do a Townshend take-off banging my guitar on the amplifier and using feedback. Frankly unoriginal and derivative, but the audiences appeared to enjoy it."The group lasted for only three or four months, playing their final show at Lake Garda on a Saturday night, January 15th, 1966. "It was winter in northern Italy and bloody cold with snow on the ground," said Maggs.

> We were living in a seriously poor hotel along with some working girls, and just about earning enough to pay for the hotel and meals at a local café. It was Roy who decided that he had had enough, and I am glad of it, because we were going absolutely nowhere. As the person with some knowledge of Italian, I was detailed to explain to Romano that we were calling it a day and returning to England. After the gig at Garda we drove for 26 hours in one go across Europe without a heater in the van.
>
> It was well into Sunday when we left, arriving at Ostend late on Monday for a 4 or 5 hour crossing. I was the only non-driver at the time, so Roy, Bruce and Speedy took turns driving while I navigated and tried to stop the windscreen from icing

---

15 Maggs remembers Keen learning 'the dialect': "Speedy did go into a manic phase from time to time. He got to know a few swear words in Italian dialect – as did we all – and used to repeat them continually to the amusement of our Italian friends."

up inside. I badly screwed up around Innsbruck, and we made a very long and unnecessary diversion, crossing the border high up but with magnificent scenery. The trees were covered in snow and looked magical.

Speedy and his bandmates returned to the U.K. on January 18th, 1966. Keen's girlfriend Lydia, now five months pregnant, initially remained in Italy. "I came back from Rome, leaving Lydia there, to break the news to my parents," he wrote in his memoirs. "It came as a bit of a shock, but when a few weeks later Lydia turned up at the door they had to accept it." The pair moved into Speedy's tiny bedroom in his parents' home, a cramped arrangement that was stressful at times. With the added complication of the language barrier, Lydia found the atmosphere quite cold and kept to herself. Her husband was frequently absent, away on drumming gigs.

It wasn't long after his return to the U.K. that Speedy Keen first worked with Pete Townshend, at the aforementioned sessions with The Cat, recording 'Run, Run, Run' and 'Club Of Lights' at IBC and Spot Studios, respectively. Although Keen later said the group "didn't exist a few months later," they apparently performed at least one live gig, with a local newspaper reporting a planned performance at Ealing's Blue Triangle Club on Thursday, March 24th, five days before Speedy's 21st birthday.

As a result of the sessions, Keen had found someone who could organize the chaos of his creative output, while Townshend found a friend, and the writer of several songs which remain of enormous importance to him to this day. The pair apparently clicked right away. "...we were very close and it was like an instant friendship," Speedy told *ZigZag* in 1975. "After a few weeks of knowing him I felt like I'd known him all my life."

"We found that we'd both been formed by a lot of the same experiences," Townshend said in 1973.

We'd had the same flashes and we progressed from there. He had incredible potential, I knew that straightaway, but it was all unrealized and disorganized. He'd keep having ideas but there wasn't any framework for them and they'd get thrown away. He was also amazingly insecure; he wouldn't expose himself in any way. Every time he made a move towards expressing something real he'd suddenly draw back, and he'd cut off dead. He was suspicious of everyone and everything, which you could understand, and that made him paralyzed. So probably the basic flash he got off me was reassurance, because no one could have been more insecure than me and yet I was using it somehow and managing to function. Gradually he understood that you can't spend your whole life hiding; if you don't risk getting burned, you just stagnate and die.

"Speedy had a hundred wonderful, really smart and catchy song titles ready to go, but few songs," says Townshend today. "I facilitated his demo process, and taught him how to just jump in and complete lyrics. I think I lent him a tape machine. His previous band in Ealing with Pat Lyons played gigs at a pub in Ealing Broadway, and had a decent following. But Speedy had never completed songs on his own. I explained to him that collaboration was just for finishing, polishing, finalizing… it was better to stay close to your first thought even if it seemed silly. His best idea was a project called *Summer City* that may well have set part of the scene for the holiday camp in *Tommy* (although the idea to actually force it in sideways came from Keith Moon). I actually have a demo of *Summer City* with me on drums, but it was Speedy's concept. I think it was about Utopia, the reverse of 1984."[16]

In April 1966, Keen began driving for Townshend, "not as an employee, but as a friend," Townshend recalled. Keen wrote fondly of this period in his memoirs. "The best time we had was when we first hung around together, he used to buy different cars and I would drive them; he would drive to a gig and I would drive home."

> Sometimes we used to go in the Lincoln, put on 'Green Onions'; he had a record player in the Lincoln with a twenty watt amp, so it was really loud. Then we'd drive the motorway, arrive at the gig, smash up a guitar or two then drive back. I remember the time we got the XK2 Jaguar and he had a new bigger engine put in it, a bit too power-ful for the car really, and the guy who did it said, "Whatever you do, don't go over 40 miles an hour," and we set off for Leeds or somewhere like that, we were crawling down the road by usual standards and we went on like this for some time, we couldn't stand it any longer, he said, "I'll put my foot down a little way and see what it can do." The next thing I remember it had spun round twice, and we were facing the wrong way, I think it was something to do with too much torque between the axle and the gear box, but they were great times for me and I will never forget them.

16 "Summer City is a dream of a city," read an article in the Swedish music press in June 1966. "The dreamer is the Who's guitarist, Pete Townshend. In the city there is a street where you smash shop windows, another street lined with clubs. Juice and Coca-Cola squirt out of the fountains. In Summer City, the houses are blue, green and crowded. It is a city where all adults are barred. The city is in Pete's imagination, but it may become reality as a musical."

Despite the occasional squabble – in his Who biography *Before I Get Old*, Dave Marsh recounts a story of Keen being ejected from a moving vehicle by Townshend in the middle of a roundabout one night – the pair grew closer. Keen told friends at the time that Townshend was his best friend. "Speedy was rather compliant I suppose," Townshend says today. "He fitted in with what I wanted to do musically when playing around in the studio or in life. We were both still young enough to be a bit silly. Beneath his soft exterior was quite a hard nut I think, but he came across as loving and kind. I needed that at the time. The other members of The Who were just awful to be around." Indeed, infighting constantly plagued The Who during this period. In late May, Keith Moon left the band after an onstage altercation that left him with a black eye and a leg injury that required stitches. Speedy filled in as The Who's drummer during at least one of the five gigs that occurred during this period before Moon resumed drumming duties.

The first tangible result of Townshend's work with Keen was 'Club Of Lights,' which had been recorded by Paul Nicholas, then recording under the name 'Oscar'. The song, Keen's first published writing credit, was released by Reaction Records on June 3rd, 1966, published by Pete Townshend's year-old imprint, Fabulous Music.[17] Keen later described the song as "fucking terrible!" It was catchy, bubblegum pop, receiving some airplay on the pirate radio stations and making a brief appearance on the Radio London charts before dropping out of sight.

Speedy and Lydia's daughter, Patricia, was born on May 5th, 1966 in Hammersmith. Their tiny accommodations became even more cramped. "Mum would apparently

---

17 Richard Barnes: "You know, he nicked the name Fabulous Music from me! I was going to start a company called Fabulous Promotions. It was taken from the magazine 'Fabulous'. I just thought what a great onomatopoeic word. I don't mind, I just thought – 'cheeky sod'."

often paint with me on her knee and dad would be constantly in and out of the home, often under the influence of drugs such as pot and LSD," Trish Keen recalled. Mum was working on an oil painting called 'City In The Sky', or 'Castles In The Sky' – it was a painting of castles floating on a cloud in the sky." Speedy observed Lydia's creation and filed it away, perhaps helping to inspire a future song. Townshend occasionally visited Keen's home in Hanwell – in fact, he wrote the song 'So Sad About Us', later recorded by The Merseys and then The Who, in the living room.

By the summer of 1966, Pete Townshend had moved into a large single-roomed flat at the top floor of 87 Wardour Street, Soho. "It was a beautiful, light room with half-moon windows," Townshend later wrote. "A carpenter knocked me up a bed and some shelves for my tape machines and disk-jockey rig, and the flat became my recording studio and personal nightclub, though I rarely slept there. …The studio was big enough so I could play the drums, and I learned how to play keyboards on a clunky Hohner Cymbelier electric piano I had bought from Jim Marshall." Keen became a frequent visitor. "We used to work together a lot on music," Townshend said. "I used to help with his demo recordings and he used to play drums on mine. He was my driver, and so we covered a lot of ground together when The Who toured the U.K., and he was a good safe and sober driver. He helped me lug gear around as well.[18] I think both of us smoked a bit of marijuana, and maybe drank a bit together too, but that was not the basis for our compact. We brainstormed a lot, mainly about song-concepts, and even album concepts like *Summer City*. It was fun. He insisted on pacing around

18 The sixth-floor space had no lift, and one can imagine Speedy carrying drums, amplifiers and other equipment up the stairs.

when he talked, head down, throwing out ideas. He also happened to be a good drummer, and I needed that too from someone in my circle because trying to get Keith Moon to play conventional drums was obviously a tough call."

"His demos destroyed me," Speedy told Nik Cohn in 1973. "I'd heard his stuff with the Who and I knew he was heavy but the demos were years ahead of anything. He was writing songs then that the Who are still recording today and I couldn't believe them. For the first time I saw how much was possible – how much creativity you could contain alone, how much you could achieve without dependence on anyone – and at last I started to suss myself. I began to put things into perspective, the experiences I'd survived, the changes I'd been put through, and I tried to use them, instead of letting them use me."

Speedy Keen and Lydia Kern were married at Ealing Registry Office on November 16, 1966. Patricia was six months old. After the marriage was official, "we all went to the pub over the road for a drink," Speedy recalled. But things were far from rosy for the newlyweds. Keen was frequently absent, working on demos or driving for Townshend. In addition, he was increasingly using drugs such as pot, acid and speed. Lydia strongly disapproved of her husband's drug use and the parties he'd attend with his friends.

Further examples of Keen's songwriting emerged. In July 1967, he shared a writing credit on 'Something's Coming Along,' the B-side of the single 'Tremblin' by the Swinging Blue Jeans. Another early Keen composition was 'Armenia City In The Sky,' which appears to have been written in 1966. "I remember the song, so maybe he played it to me around the same time that he played 'Club Of Lights'," Chris Thomas recalled.

"That was really very early stuff and the first real big

thing I ever did," Speedy said later, "but I was still very unsure of what I was doing." He and Townshend recorded a demo of the song together.[19] "It's about anything you want," Keen later explained. "If you're an Irishman it could be a pub with free beer, if you're hung-up it could be a place without hang-ups, if you're a fucking maniac it could be a place in the sky with a thousand chicks, and so on." Townshend thought enough of the song that it was recorded by The Who on October 20th, 1967 at IBC Studios. Speedy sang the high chorus with Roger Daltrey. The song became the opening track on the album *The Who Sell Out*. "This was the first time an outsider had contributed an original song to a Who album, and it never happened again," Townshend wrote in his memoir. He later commented, "we were short of material – we wouldn't have used it otherwise."

It wasn't until after the song had been recorded that Townshend discovered he'd misheard its name. "Speedy said to me, "You've got the wrong title there, mate," he said later. "So I said, "What do you mean…?" He said, "This Armenia, that's some place in the Balkans, isn't it?" So I said, "Yeah, 'Armenia City…'" and he said "No, *I'm An Ear Sitting In The Sky*." [laughs] That's supposed to be the title. 'I'm An Ear Sitting In The Sky' – it was a song that he wrote when he was on some bad acid!"

By late summer 1967, Lydia, who'd found work at a petrol station, found a flat of her own and moved out, taking 14-month-old Trish with her. Speedy, who later wrote that that the relationship ended "thanks to interfering people and my lack of sense," told Nik Cohn, "I was gutted. I was finished. I thought I'd never stop losing."

---

19 The fact that this demo was not included in the 2021 'Super Deluxe' edition of *The Who Sell Out*, which included 14 previously unreleased demos, doesn't necessarily mean it's missing. "The number of demos was limited," Townshend explains. "There are several left unreleased. I don't think I came across the demo when I was researching because I was looking for unique pieces."

After Lydia's departure, he dove further into music, moving into Townshend's often vacant Wardour Street flat. Keen became a paid employee of Track Records, earning £15 a week driving for Townshend and writing songs. "I owed so much to Track," he told *ZigZag* in 1970. "They'd kept me alive for two years before anything at all happened. I used to creep into the office on my hands and knees every week and say, "I've got this great song" and they'd give me some bread and I'd keep saying, "I'm just finishing it off Kit, it sounds fabulous," and they kept on for a couple of years."

After Keen had delivered 'Armenia / I'm An Ear', he set to work completing a song that began life titled 'Spotting Trains', later to become 'Accidents', "which I told them was about children's accidents but wasn't sick, and there was no-one else writing about children's accidents, so I lasted another 4 months on that one," he said. "So that's how I started... and by the time 'Something In The Air' came out, I owed them a lot of money."

CHAPTER 4

JIMMY

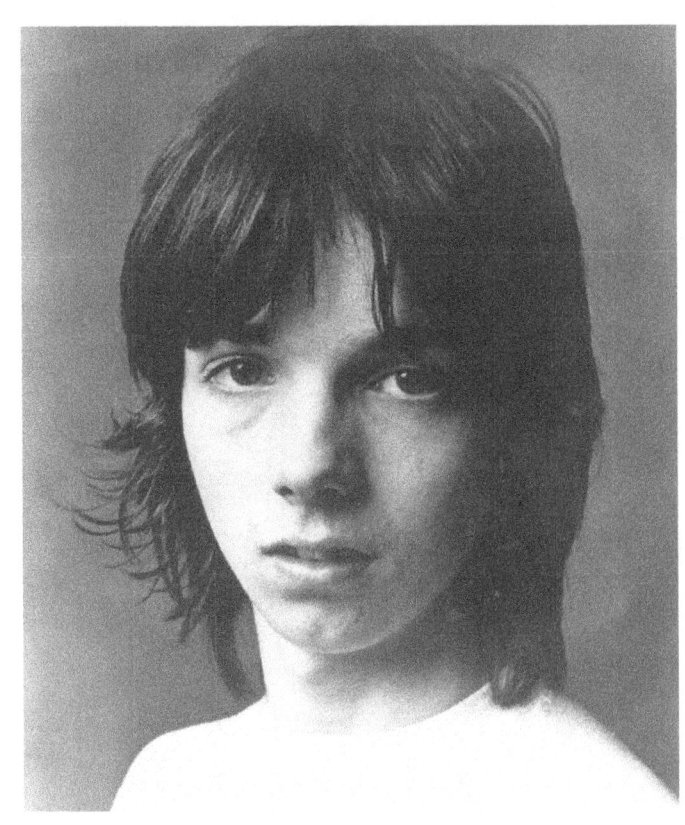

Promotional photo of Jimmy McCulloch, 1969.

Vernon Brewer's desk was just inside the door to the Track Records office at 58 Old Compton Street, Soho. It was the first piece of furniture one would encounter upon entering, which perhaps helps explain why drummer Steve Palmer remembers Keith Moon strolling through the door and turning this same desk upside down one day. This position (when the desk was right side up) provided Brewer with a prime vantage point from which he could see all comings and goings related to Track business. Brewer, Track Records promotions manager, remembers sitting at this desk one thankfully less eventful day in 1968 when "the door opened, and there's this woman with this young chap carrying a guitar; he was holding his mother's hand with one hand and a guitar in the other," he recalled. "It was Jimmy McCulloch and his mother – and they were looking for work."

Pete Townshend was already familiar with McCulloch, as the young man's group, The Jaygars, had supported The Who on May 8, 1965 at the New Palladium Ballroom in Greenock, Scotland. Jimmy was all of 11 years old at the time, dwarfed by the enormous hollow-body electric guitar he was playing. His brother Jack, who played the drums for The Jaygars, was 16. "He was a kid," Townshend recalled of the younger McCulloch. "The family were still calling him a 'wean' (a wee one). I met him first in Greenock, Scotland, a very tough part of the area outside Glasgow, a shipbuilding town already in decline. He was already playing electric guitar eloquently and cleanly, carefully, but with amazing panache. Beneath it all was a man who would become a fiery, hard-drinking, fall-down Scot!"

The next time Townshend saw McCulloch perform onstage was in the cavernous great hall of the 'Ally Pally' – Alexandra Palace, north London, on April 29, 1967. The event, named the '14-Hour Technicolor Dream', had been organized as a benefit for the counterculture newspaper

International Times, in need of funds to cover legal costs after a recent police raid. McCulloch was there with his group One In A Million, named as such after their supremely talented guitarist, now age 13.

Alexandra Palace's great hall was packed with an audience of as many as 10,000.[20] "There was a stage at each end and, for much of the time, two bands would be playing simultaneously," rock archivist Pete Frame told *Q* in 1995. "In between the two stages was an old-fashioned fairground helter-skelter with a light show playing all over it." Social Deviants singer Mick Farren added, "Nobody had ever played a gig this big. It was a rectangle the size of Paddington Station with similar acoustics. Because of the helter-skelter, we couldn't see the band playing at the other end of the hall, but we could hear it, like a slightly more melodic version of the 3.15 from Exeter pulling in at the platform."

Although several of the acts listed on the event's poster (by Mike McInnerney, who later designed The Who's *Tommy* album art) ultimately didn't appear, there was no shortage of talent on the night, with The Soft Machine, John's Children, The Move, Arthur Brown, and, appearing onstage in the very early morning hours, just as the sun began to stream through the great hall's glass roof, Pink Floyd. "Syd was just manic, and everything went through dozens of echo units, and you couldn't tell the beginning from the middle from the end," Townshend, who was there filming some of the acts, recalled. "I was stone cold sober, which may have been the worst way to see them."

Conversely, one act that did perform at the '14 Hour

20 Among the audience "were John Lennon, Pete Townshend and Kit Lambert," wrote Mark Blake in *Pretend You're In A War: The Who & the Sixties*. "The latter quickly discovered that peace and love would only get him so far. After Lambert was turned away for not having a ticket, he was given a black eye by one of the doormen when he refused to leave."

Technicolor Dream' but *wasn't* on the bill was The Cat, Chris Thomas's group, consisting of the same lineup as the previous year, but with a new drummer occupying the role vacated by Speedy Keen. Thomas remembers watching One In A Million. "They had this tiny, tiny little guy playing the guitar," he recalled. "I think he played a Rickenbacker, like the ones that Pete used to play. I certainly remember that the guitar was almost as big as he was." Pete Frame relayed to *Q* his memory of the group playing some "Love numbers, and Jimmy did this incredible solo. Townshend was watching them."

* * *

James McCulloch, Jr., was born on June 4th, 1953, at Overtoun Maternity Hospital in Dumbarton, Scotland, two days after the coronation of Queen Elizabeth II. Jimmy's father, James Sr., worked as a marine engine fitter; his wife, Lillian, was a hairdresser. There was one other child, Jack, born in October 1948. In Jimmy's early years, the McCullochs moved from Clydebank, a few miles northwest of Glasgow, to Cumbernauld, designated a 'New Town' in 1955 as part of the effort to ease overpopulation in the Glasgow area. Cumbernauld, thirteen miles northeast of the city, offered a more rural setting, with lower density housing and green space – a better situation for a growing family. The McCullochs' new terraced home at 7E Kyle Road was in Kildrum, the first area of the new town to be planned and built. Jimmy quickly grew to enjoy exploring the local countryside and playing football with his friends on the local brand-new red ash pitch.

Jimmy was steeped in music from the very beginning. "I was just brought up on music, and it's been born into me, and I've had the chance to be able to play," he told American DJ Roy Leonard. "My dad was a trumpet player – jazz, trad stuff – and I was brought up on Django [Reinhardt]. I love the guy. He's a genius... I was brought up with that at the age of three or four. I was going to my dad's concerts. He played the Clydebank Town Hall. I was tempted to have a go at playing Dad's trumpet but, being very thin, I didn't have the wind for it."

McCulloch's father played the trumpet in the Duntocher Silver Band, a local semi-pro jazz outfit. "My father, he was a musician, and my grandfather, and my great grandfather," Jimmy observed in a 1970 interview used to promote Thunderclap Newman's *Hollywood Dream* LP. "I had this sort of like gift when I started up, you know?," he continued. "I like music, I like to listen to music, and I like playing it. Doesn't really matter what it is." Accordingly, young Jimmy dabbled with the piano, drums and saxophone at an early age. When he enrolled at Kildrum Primary School, he joined the school choir.

It was when he saw '50s U.K. rock & roll star Tommy Steele on television at age four that Jimmy decided he wanted to play the guitar. "No one thought he was serious until he got one," Jack McCulloch told biographer Paul Salley. "It was amazing to see. When he brought his first guitar home, he was playing tunes within an hour, which was incredible." Jimmy, perhaps emulating his father, practiced his craft with rare discipline. James Sr. certainly helped drive his son's desire to improve. "I spoke to Jimmy about this; I said, "How come you were so good so young?"," recalled Jim Avery, who performed with McCulloch in Thunderclap Newman in 1969 and worked with him again in the early '70s. "He said it was because he was playing an acoustic guitar that he had as a little boy. He played it so well he wanted to get an electric, and his father said you cannot have an electric until – he gave him a book of chords written by Wes Montgomery – jazz chords, written by the man who invented those chords. And so Jimmy studied it and learned how to play like Wes Montgomery when he was a little boy, like 9 years old. So his dad said, "Great, I'll buy you a guitar." And he bought him a Gibson or whatever, and… a star is born."

Jimmy's father bought his son a Harmony H77 "which was about twice as big as me," he told *Sounds* in 1975. "It was a giant semi-acoustic and cost about £14." Now that he had sufficient volume to be heard amongst the other instruments, he started practicing with his father and brother. "Jim, Jackie and their dad used to wake us up on Sunday practicing: Jim on guitar, his brother on drums and their dad on trumpet," neighbor Billy Keene told Salley. The brothers continued to accompany their father when the Duntocher Silver Band performed, and played during the intermission – just Jimmy and Jack, alone. "When we started, it was just the two of us," Jack McCulloch told Salley.

> …we played instrumentals by The Shadows, The Ventures and Dick Dale-style numbers. The idea was that it would give us experience on stage. Before we had a band, my brother and I would do the same type of thing during the interval at a bingo hall as well… We had a gig doing that every Thursday night… it was all part of our education because when you're young, you don't fear getting up and playing in front of hundreds of people. So, when we first started putting bands together, we noticed a lot of people had a certain amount of stage fright, which we could understand, but we probably had about 50 gigs behind us before we formed a band. We had no fear about going up on stage.

Jimmy thus began to accrue vital onstage experience at an incredibly young age. "My playing experience is the main thing – all the things I've played," he told *Guitar* in 1975. "When I started it was the Shadows and the Ventures and Sandy Nelson. I was always interested in rhythms. From that I think I got a rhythmic way of playing guitar; not rhythm guitar, playing lead in rhythmic patterns. Melodic as well – I got an influence from Django Reinhardt, 'Sweet Sue', 'Ain't She Sweet?' and stuff like that." McCulloch was self-taught. "My father wanted to take me to a teacher, but I thought I'd develop better on my own," he told *Melody Maker* in 1971. "I got a chord book and practiced scales and took to the guitar very quickly."

With McCulloch's wealth of natural ability and extraordinarily disciplined practice habit, a standout guitarist quickly began to form. "When I first started playing guitar I used to listen to Cliff [Richard] and the Shadows and, once I could tune the guitar, I'd learn the solos note for note," he said in 1975.

"He practiced from the moment he got up in the morning until it was time for school," Jimmy's mother Lillian told Beatles scholar and author Ken McNab. "And then he would come in at lunchtime and start again. The Beatles were his heroes. He was too young to have seen them live, but he had the records and he listened to them all the time. He had a terrific ear, everything was by ear. He would hear a song on radio or television, then pick up a guitar and get it very quickly. He was an average pupil at school, but he found something in music that he could do very well." Jimmy actually did see his heroes perform live. On June 7th, 1963, fourteen-year-old Jack and ten-year-old Jimmy traveled to Glasgow to attend their first concert: The Beatles, performing at the Odeon.

Jimmy's cousin Steve Adams remembers visiting the McCulloch home on Kyle Road around 1962 when Jimmy was about 9 years old. "My main memory was that he was a normal child with an incredible talent even then," Adams recalled of his cousin, who he noted was quiet and modest.

I would sit there mesmerized by his playing of the guitar and watch the concentration on his face. The guitar was his life and sports were not part of any conversation. His main influence was Django Reinhardt and he focused on his style of playing when learning the guitar. Bert Weedon was very popular with anyone wishing to learn how to play and he took an interest in him too. Duane Eddy was also a favorite of his – he liked the twanging guitar sound that he played. Above those three was always his dad, my Uncle Jimmy, who played in a jazz band as Jimmy was growing up so he always had music around him from an early age. He wasn't pushed into taking up an instrument, in fact he asked for a guitar so he could learn to play.

McCulloch and his guitar were inseparable. "When they came to stay with my family in Derby, he always brought his guitar and was forever playing it," Adams recalled.

Jimmy McCulloch's entries in the aforementioned Thunderclap Newman 'Lifelines' piece in the *NME* reveal less about him than his bandmates, chiefly due to the fact that he apparently didn't bother to answer many of the questions, leaving nearly a third of them blank, unlike Andy and Speedy who answered them all. Height and weight for the 16-year-old McCulloch were listed at 5 feet 4 inches, 7 stone, a full ten inches shorter than Andy Newman and less than half his weight. Jimmy's first public appearance as an amateur was listed as 'Old folk's home, Glasgow', his first professional appearance 'Barrowland Ballroom, Glasgow.' He listed the Mothers Of Invention as his favorite band, and Bach and Frank Zappa as his favorite composers. But when it came to best friend: 'None'. Professional ambition: 'None'. Former occupation: 'None' (which was actually true).

The McCulloch brothers formed their first band, The Jaygars, reportedly named after the Jaeger clothing store, around February 1964, when Jimmy was 10 and Jack 15. "I was playing with a band at school and then I realized I had a better guitar player in the house than I had at school," Jack McCulloch recalled. "It made sense to work with him, plus there was the bonus of being able to rehearse every day." The group was originally known as The Jaegars, but changed the spelling to Jaygars after they found that the former spelling was too easily confused with The Jaguars, a name already in use by two American groups at the time. "At first the group played for charity, appearing at the Teen Canteen in Kildrum Parish Church," the *Cumbernauld News* reported in December 1964. They soon began branching out, playing alternate Sundays at the Kildrum and Sacred Heart chapel dances. "Gradually their list of engagements started to build up, and they played at such places as the Cragburn Pavilion in Gourock," the *News* continued. They also had a regular date in a Paisley bingo hall where they entertained the audience during the interval." By October 1964, in addition to the McCulloch brothers, The Jaygars consisted of Billy McGowan and Robert Ross (vocals), Frank Quin (bass) and Norrie Gilliland (guitar). "I was the old man in The Jaygars at the age of 16," said Gilliland, adding that Ross, Quin and McGowan were all between 13 and 15 years of age.

McGowan pointed out to Paul Salley the importance of the influence and guidance of McCulloch's father on the young group of musicians: "We were talking about forming a group and ended up at the McCullochs' house and meeting Jack's mum, Jimmy, and his trumpet playing dad who took this all very seriously. We were astonished by the size and age of Jimmy, but his dad made us practice, practice, practice, teaching us how to sing harmonies, tune up properly, and how to act on stage." McGowan recalled that

Jimmy's guitar "looked huge on Jimmy, and he could hardly get his right arm over the body, but he never complained and could play it fine."

"As a musician himself, James Snr knew the critical importance of hard work, and was quick to bring us to order if he caught us larking around instead of rehearsing," Norrie Gilliland recalled. "His trademark rebuke was, 'I'll shoot the boots off you!', although it was always delivered in a lighthearted way."

By late 1964, Jimmy had bought a Hofner Futurama guitar, a cheaper version of the fiesta red Fender Stratocaster played by Hank Marvin of the Shadows. "I really wanted a Strat but couldn't afford it," he recalled. "I settled on the Futurama 'cause it looked a bit like a Strat. It was kind of salmon-pink and had a tremolo arm. Great for doing the old Shadows stuff which everyone was into at that time."[21]

The 'first professional appearance' that Jimmy listed in the *NME* as taking place at the Barrowland Ballroom in Glasgow was a gig secured by Jimmy's father, where The Jaygars supported The Pretty Things on December 7th, 1964. The Jaygars were billed as "Scotland's Youngest Beat Group" in the newspaper ad. "There is no shortage of dates for the group," James Sr. told the *Cumbernauld News* a few days before the show. "I have never had to look for anything for them; it has all come to us. This date in Glasgow's Barrowland Ballroom on Monday evening is an example of this. Promoter Billy McGregor heard of the lads and got in touch with me, asking if they would play with the Pretty Things."

By this time, Jimmy's father was working as a production engineer at the Burroughs Factory, built in 1958

---

21 Jimmy later gave this guitar to his friend, Track Records office employee Dana Wiffen, who still has it today.

and already Cumbernauld's largest employer. The plant produced accounting machines, a mechanical precursor to calculators and computers. He was also managing The Jaygars. "Mr. McCulloch himself is a musician and used to play regularly in bands in leading Glasgow dance halls," the *Cumbernauld News* reported in December. "That was before The Jaygars started." The elder McCulloch told the *News* that due to his time commitments with his full time job and managing The Jaygars, he'd given up playing. "We are taking our time with the boys," he said. "There is no rush, and I want to make them musicians, not just guitar plunkers as a lot of modern groups are."

The Jaygars' appearance at the Barrowland Ballrom in late 1964 led to a six-week residency there which was, by all accounts, a resounding success. "The reaction the boys have been given is absolutely fantastic," Jimmy's dad told the local press, recalling that the fans had a particular affinity for Jimmy. "You would have to see it to believe it," he said.

On the first Saturday they appeared at Barrowland there was a crowd waiting outside the door for them. The boys were chased when they left the ballroom, and we had great difficulty getting Jim out. I sent the bigger boys out first, thinking the crowd would follow them, and leave the door clear. But some of the crowd chased the boys while others waited. Eventually an agent and I had to force our way through the crowd carrying Jim between us. We managed to get him into the van, but we had to drive off without our equipment, and wait till the crowd had broken up before we went back.

One can only imagine what was going through 11-year-old Jimmy's mind at the time.

"Three weeks ago, two girls approached us and asked if they could start a fan club," Jimmy's father said. "I agreed and they now tell us there are over 700 members. ...Of course when people see them walk on to the stage, they do not expect much. My wife and I help the boys set up equipment and then stand back to watch the faces of the audience. They do not usually pay much attention till the boys start playing, when they realize that The Jaygars really can play, the bored looks disappear to be replaced by looks of amazement."

The typical Jaygars set "would include some soul/Tamla/R&B, mixed in with a few Stones, Beatles and other U.K./American pop stuff and usually two or three new chart hits from the previous week or two," Norrie Gilliland recalled, citing some of the group's mainstays as: 'Mr. Tambourine Man' (The Byrds), 'Don't Let Me Be Misunderstood' and 'House of the Rising Sun' (The Animals), 'Land of a Thousand Dances' (Wilson Pickett), 'Under the Boardwalk' (The Drifters), 'Do Wah Diddy Diddy' (Manfred Mann), 'You Really Got Me' (The Kinks), and 'A World Without Love' (Peter and Gordon). "We were the archetypal covers band," he said, "and probably never thought about writing our own stuff, in comparison with many Scottish and U.K. bands who were writing their own stuff at the time. I did pen a couple of completely forgettable songs, which we played a couple of times. I remember one of them was based on a typical Bo Diddley rhythm and style."

The increasingly popular and in-demand Jaygars were all still attending school, with the exception of Gilliland who'd recently begun working, oddly enough, as a telephone engineer with the GPO. The rest of the older boys attended nearby Lenzie Academy while Jimmy was still at Kildrum Primary School. "We are taking things easily at the moment," McCulloch Sr. said at the time.

The boys' education always comes first, and because of that we have refused many offers. We only accept weekend bookings, because nearly all the boys are still at school, and have exams to pass. This week we play our last Saturday afternoon date at the Barrowland, but the management is talking of giving the boys a short lay-off and then asking them back. Meantime we will be playing at the Greenock Palladium. Big name groups are being brought to Greenock by the new management. Next month we will be appearing with Tony Rivers and the Castaways. An agent is coming to hear the boys on Saturday. We will let him hear four numbers the boys have written, and if he likes any of them he has promised us a recording date.

The Jaygars supported a host of well-known acts including The Hollies and Manfred Mann in between school commitments. They played a gig with Dean Ford and The Gaylords, later known as Marmalade. "We also played several times with Chris McClure, a staple of the Scottish scene, and a couple of times with the Beatstalkers," Gilliland recalled. "There was also a really brilliant, tight funky band called the Dream Police who we played with several times at Kirkintilloch Miners' Welfare Club and other local venues."

"Many of our gigs with the aforementioned bands took place at obscure venues, including Miners' Welfare Clubs, which were pretty good venues because they had decent lighting and sound, and usually good crowds," said Gilliland. "They were played by a lot of the upcoming acts. One of my favorites was a venue in Greenock, a barn-like place with the highly unlikely name of The Greenock Palladium. ...We played there a lot and also at the Cragburn Pavilion, an Art Deco dance hall in Gourock. Part of the entertainment at these two venues was watching the U.S. Navy Police when they turned up near the end of the night, wearing their white helmets, with riot sticks at the ready to keep the Holy Loch sailors and local lads from trying to kill each other."

The group were scheduled to support The Kinks at Greenock Palladium on March 27th, but the gig was canceled when one of the Davies brothers came down with the flu.

"Although these were the 'wild' '60s, we saw very little trouble at the gigs we played," said Gilliland. "We did have a fight spill onto the stage one night at Kildrum Church Hall in Cumbernauld. Jackie had to keep rattling away at the cans while the rest of us scrambled to move his kit plus mic stands, and keep playing, singing and smiling. It ended when the proponents punched and kicked each other down the back steps into an anteroom... James McCulloch Sr., our manager, always insisted that the show must go on."

During the summer of 1965, with school commitments easing, The Jaygars began another six week residency at the Barrowland. "We were regulars at the Barrowland for well over a year, playing alongside the resident big band Billy McGregor and the Gay Birds, mainly afternoon gigs on the weekends for teeny boppers just like us," Gilliland recalled. "We also played alongside several good Scottish bands including the Pathfinders, who became White Trash, or Trash as they became known."[22]

Part of McCulloch Sr.'s plan to 'make the group musicians' was to ensure that they were never lacking top of the

---

22 The Pathfinders' keyboardist, Ronnie Leahy, went on to play with Jimmy in Stone The Crows and The Dukes. During these early days, though, he only knew McCulloch from a distance. "I knew him, but only as an acquaintance," said Leahy. "We didn't play together; we were in different bands in Glasgow. I was in the biggest band in Glasgow at that time, and Jimmy's band were just doing covers and things like that. Nothing really... but you could see that he was a good player then."

line equipment. "Jimmy and Jack's parents must have put a lot of trust in us at that time," said Billy McGowan, "as lots of new gear kept appearing – a Marshall 50-watt head for Jimmy, Jack had the best Ludwig drum kit, Frank, the bass player, had a fantastic Vox Foundation rig." MacGowan also recalled the group having "Vox AC30s and a 100-watt Selmer PA amp with Vox column speakers and Shure mics… and let's not forget the Rickenbacker. Up until then, we had been ferried about [in] the family Vauxhall estate car, but having this gear now necessitated a van, and sure enough, one appeared, old with a roll-top rear door." Most of this equipment was stored in the McCullochs' compact home on Kyle Road. "…Space was at a premium," said Gilliland. "We did have quite a lot of stuff lying around – amps, stands etc. – given that our regular practice sessions took place there."

James Sr. and Lily's support of their sons' musical ambitions was a constant through Jimmy and Jack's formative years. "They were always supportive of their sons and encouraged them all the time," Steve Adams recalled. "Never pushy, they showed the boys how to behave and NEVER take anything for granted." Lily also appears to have designed and created the group's stage outfits in early 1965. "Our excruciatingly crap sparkly stage gear was conceived, I think, by Jimmy and Jackie's mum, bless her," Norrie Gilliland said. "I think she actually ran them up on her Singer in the front room. We soon rebelled and began to style ourselves as the Mods we thought we were."

"There is still a lot more equipment we would like to get for the boys," McCulloch Sr. told the *Cumbernauld News* in 1965. "At the moment anything they earn goes towards paying for their equipment. We had already bought them £1000 worth of equipment, but there is still more we would like to have." To aid with this effort, Lily began working on an assembly line in 1965 – presumably at the

Burroughs Factory where her husband also worked. "The group has become a way of life," she told the local press. "Jim is the centre of it, he is the one teenagers go wild about. I like to be on hand in case things get rough. Last week after appearing on the same bill as Sandie Shaw in Ayr, there were tense moments when they slipped through crash barriers. Sometimes the others in the group have to pass him over their heads to get him clear." Her husband added: "He's quite philosophical about it all, and he gets quite upset if the girls become too mushy. He also gets upset when they pull buttons off his new shirts. I'm sure he thinks the girls are mad." Lily began collecting press clippings and other items related to Jimmy and Jack's musical accomplishments in a scrapbook.

In addition to drawing attention because of his good looks and tender age, Jimmy was also gaining a reputation as a capable guitarist. "I had the luxury of meeting him one Saturday morning when I worked in J.T. Forbes' music shop in West Nile Street," Bill Henry told Paul Salley. "We had just taken delivery of a nine-string Framus electric guitar, and the guys asked if wee Jimmy could have a shot. The guitar was about the same height as him and we plugged into a Vox AC30. The next five to ten minutes stopped time. He was going places."

The Jaygars, meanwhile, continued to support popular acts, playing the aforementioned gig with Sandie Shaw in August 1965 at Ayr Ice Rink and appearing in Edinburgh with Adam Faith around this same time. The group's second residency at the Barrowland Ballroom was again a huge success. "Cumbernauld beat group, the Jaygars, stopped the traffic in one of Glasgow's busiest streets on Saturday, or rather their fans did!" read one report.

The Jaygars were playing at Barrowland Ballroom
on the third of their six dates there. As they left

they were mobbed by a huge crowd of fans. Jackie McCulloch (16), 7E Kyle Road, drummer with the group, said: "We were not expecting any scenes, although we had been mobbed when playing at Barrowland earlier this year. When we came out the front door, however, there was a tremendous crowd, and we had to fight our way through to the van. I had my shirt ripped, and another member of the group had his jacket torn. We had to smuggle my brother Jim (12) – the youngest and smallest member of the group – out of the back door. Traffic was held up in the Gallowgate, and as we drove away we could see everyone was wondering what the crowd had gathered for.

That same month, the Jaygars would perform in Glasgow with Jimmy and Jack's father's band, an unlikely combination indeed. "One of Scotland's oldest silver bands and the country's youngest "beat" group are to share concerts in two of Glasgow's parks," the local news reported. "Mr. Archie McLivain, 66, conductor of the Duntocher Silver Band has invited the "Jaygars" from Cumbernauld (average age 15) to play two 12 minute spots at Kelvingrove Park next Wednesday, and Queen's Park the following Tuesday. Mr. McLivain, who admits that brass bands have lost their appeal, said so many people had left the city centre for housing schemes that they would have to try and tempt them back. "Only young people are likely to make this effort, and they'll only come to hear the young group. But when they do so they'll have to put up with the 'squares' as well." One of the 'squares' will be the silver band's cornet player, James McCullough, of Kyle Road, Cumbernauld, who is also the "Jaygars" manager, and father of their drummer and lead guitarist."

However, the organizers appear to have underestimated

either the popularity of the Jaygars, or the enthusiasm of their fans, or both. As a result, the Jaygars' performance scheduled for the following week was canceled. "A band, out to get 'with it', booked a beat group to appear with them at one of their concerts," the *Cumbernauld News* reported.

> Now the band's leader has been told: "Don't do it again." And the announcement has meant disappointment for hundreds of pop fans. Trouble hit the six strong Jaegars [sic] beat group after they appeared at a concert in Kelvingrove Park, Glasgow, with the Duntocher Silver Band. When the show was over the boys were besieged by autograph hunters. Next day, Archie McLivain, conductor of the Silver Band, received a letter from the Corporation[23] telling him the group was not to appear again. He said last night: "The Jaegars [sic] were booked to appear with us on Tuesday in Queen's Park. They can't now. It seems the group's supporters spoiled things for themselves. I booked the Jaegars myself to try and attract more people to the park shows. I have written apologizing to the Corporation."

On Friday, August 20th 1965, The Jaygars (minus Billy and Frank – "I don't know why Billy and Frank weren't there," said Norrie Gilliland) met with Muhammad Ali's sparring partner Jimmy Ellis at Peter Keenan's boxing gym on the outskirts of Glasgow. Ali was in the midst of an international tour and later that day participated in an exhibition bout against Ellis at the nearby Paisley Ice Rink. He had been set to meet The Jaygars but backed out, citing

23 District Council

85

exhaustion. "When we got there, we found out we were actually meeting Jimmy Ellis and not Cassius Clay," Norrie Gilliland recalled. "Somehow James Sr. had arranged to set up a publicity shoot at Peter Keenan's gym. Great thinking, the theme being along the lines of Wee Jimmy Meets Big Jimmy. I'm not sure what publicity it got, apart from a photo in the *Evening Times* showing Roscoe sitting on Big Jimmy's shoulders. I'm sure there was also one taken of Wee Jimmy perched up there, which was the main purpose of the exercise."

Around September, The Jaygars auditioned at STV Studios in Glasgow for *Stramash – The Big Noise From Glasgow*, a television program which first aired in October 1965. It was "a poor man's version of *Top of the Pops* complete with dancers the Stramashers and the Lindella Movers," Gilliland recalled. "I thought we performed well at our audition, but someone in STV took cold feet and said he couldn't put us on a broadcast show as Jimmy was too young."

Not long after this audition, the *Cumbernauld News* reported that The Jaygars had broken up, or as they put it: "The Jaygars beat group is to be re-formed. This is the shock news announced this week by manager Jimmy McCulloch, 7E Kyle Road, Kildrum. After a few months of disquiet among the group, rhythm guitarist Ronnie [sic] Gilliland left. Then on Monday came the moves which left only two members to carry on the Jaygars name. Robert Ross, Frank Quin and Billy McGowan and their manager "agreed to part company." This leaves Mr. McCulloch's sons Jack (16) who plays the drums, and lead guitarist Jim (12) to carry on with the group."

According to Gilliland, the McCulloch brothers' bandmates lacked the desire to advance their musical careers. "Apart from Jimmy and Jack (understandably encouraged by their parents) I don't think any of us particularly wanted to move up in the music business," he said. "We were just having fun, playing for little more than fish suppers and ice cream, meeting some nice girls – and wondering what the hell was happening."

"Things had not been going as well as they might for a few months," Jimmy Sr. told the *Cumbernauld News*. "We decided to part on Monday. But the Jaygars are by no means defunct. I will audition any new town boys between the ages of 15 and 17. I am looking for a good bass guitarist and a singer. I shall try to keep to our Barrowland dance contract. If I can find boys good enough before Saturday the Jaygars will play. It all depends on the dance hall management." And he appealed to the fans: "Bear with us for a few weeks. In no time at all I believe that the Jaygars will be even better than before."

Sure enough, a new Jaygars lineup soon emerged, with Alan Young (vocals) and Billy Scenters (bass) recruited from other local bands to occupy the recently vacated roles. "We continued as The Jaygars, playing around various venues in and around Glasgow until one day we were asked by an agent to think about moving to the London area," Young told Paul Salley. The group had already begun performing gigs further afield, taking weekend trips to London and requiring Jimmy to begin working with a tutor in order to keep up with his work at Cumbernauld High School, particularly in the areas of English, French and mathematics. "I enjoy the pop world – it's really exciting," he told the *Cumbernauld News*. "Particularly in London. But, on the other hand, I want to do well in school, too."

A full move to London was no small thing for the McCulloch family to contemplate. Jimmy was only 12 years old, and both of his parents worked in Cumbernauld. For a move to London to happen, the entire family would have to uproot and find work in that area. Andy Newman's recollection was that James Sr.'s job actually led to the move to London. "It turned out that this little lad was coming down to London with his family," Newman recalled, "and of course there was a subplot behind this, which was that his father was actually working for a Scottish engineering firm that was making the transmission for the transporter that moved the Saturn rocket at the NASA headquarters for the moon shot. So although he couldn't say anything about it 'cause it was top secret, that's the reason why he came down to London."

It's not clear whether it was James Sr.'s job, or The Jaygars wanting to further their prospects, or both, that drove the move to London. Regardless, the McCullochs, along with new recruits Young and Scenters, found lodging in Potters Bar, Hertfordshire, just north of London. The move took place around late spring or early summer 1966, perhaps after the conclusion of Jimmy's school year. "After lots of discussions, we eventually did move and changed our name to One In A Million, based on Jimmy's ability on guitar at such a tender age," Alan Young said. The group's first gig in the area took place that summer at The Nutty Club, Leytonstone. "At this stage, we started to get gigs all over the country in England, Wales and Scotland," Young recalled.

"I was only twelve when we came to London," Jimmy told *Melody Maker*'s Chris Welch in 1971. "We stayed above a china shop and the room was stacked up with stock. We had to make a space on the floor for our sleeping bags. It was mostly down to pub gigs but people said we were too loud and they were very prejudiced because we were Scottish and we had to get over that barrier." In an effort to help overcome this bias, the band decided to use stage names. "We'd just come down from Scotland, and the others had this idea that calling themselves by common English surnames would somehow make them sound more hip and less provincial," Young recalled. "I was happy with my own name, but Bill Scenters called himself Billy Fisher, and Jack and Jimmy plumped for the surname Collins."

By the end of 1966, a year filled with dates in pubs, clubs and ballrooms, One In A Million connected with entrepreneur and promoter Mervyn Conn, who had staged The Beatles' first Christmas tour in 1963 and had promoted Johnny Cash's first U.K. tour that same year. Conn arranged for the group to record a single. They weren't thrilled about the choice of A-side, the Artie Wayne composition 'Use Your Imagination', which had been recorded by The Guess Who the previous year. "We were really pissed off about that because we wanted to record original material, but we had to do one of the publisher's songs," Jack McCulloch told Paul Salley. The single, released on January 6th, 1967 by CBS Records, failed to chart. The fact that the group refused to play 'Use Your Imagination' onstage certainly didn't help matters.

One In A Million were still in demand, though. In 1967, they performed regularly around London and further afield, and supported such acts as Pink Floyd and the Jeff Beck Group. The group's performance at the massive '14 Hour Technicolor Dream' took place in April. Jimmy, who turned 14 years old that summer, continued to accrue an impressive amount of experience. "When we were going out with One In A Million, we were doing 150 shows a year," Jack said. "We were together as One In A Million for about three years, so we'd have played at least 450 gigs. We were pretty tight; we could scan the audience and know exactly which set to play."

In addition to gaining a reputation for his developing musical prowess, McCulloch remained a hit with the size-able contingent of teen girls within the One In A Million fan base who continued to seek locks of his hair, buttons from his shirts, or even old guitar strings. "Jim is the star and the one the girls go for, but the rest of the boys don't mind," Jack told the *Cumbernauld News*. It was doubtless Jimmy's popularity with the girls that led to a two-page feature on the band in the August 1967 edition of teen magazine *Boyfriend and Trend*. The quotes the band gave reporter Penny Weston appeared tailored for maximum effect, painting the band in a rebellious hue. "All the pirate stations have banned us now because we insisted on playing for money," said Billy Scenters. "We rubbed the pirate stations up the wrong way," Alan Young told Weston. Jack and Jimmy apparently weren't as comfortable delivering this nonsense: "Meanwhile, the other two members of the group, brothers Jack and Jim Collins, sat in the corner sipping a milkshake," Weston wrote.

By this time, One In A Million had begun working with both the Harvey Block agency and promoter Harvey Goldsmith, which led to a recording deal with MGM Records. During August sessions at Southern Music's studio on Denmark Street, the group recorded their own composition, the Alan Young/Billy Scenters-penned track 'Fredereek Hernando', with the Jack McCulloch/Billy Scenters song 'Double Sight' as the B-side. The distinctly psychedelic single, complete with backwards guitar track, was released in December. An ad in *Melody Maker* in late November proclaimed One In A Million were a "tremendously exciting group now on MGM records, look out for fantastic new release."

It was at this point that Jimmy McCulloch and Pete Townshend's paths crossed again. "I met Pete Townshend in Denmark Street and I laid a copy of my record on him," Jimmy told Chris Welch in 1971. "Pete Townshend had always been very supportive of us, and I remember we went over to visit him in his flat in Victoria when we were about to release the single," Alan Young later recalled. "I'm sure he was also there when we played live at a press reception for 'Fredereek Hernando'." This press reception coincided with their appearance on the children's television programme *Come Here Often*. "Jim Collins, 15-year-old [he was actually 14], four-foot-nine inch guitarist with One In A Million impressed at [the] group's reception," *Melody Maker* noted on January 13th. "Pete Townshend shared a ride with Jim on a mini-hovercraft." The group also performed their new single on *Come Here Often*, reworking the slightly macabre lyrics for their young audience: *He's a dead man now* became *He's a big man now*, and a reference to a *graveyard* was altered, rather comically, to a *barnyard*. Despite these promotional efforts and the fact that John Peel played the song on his BBC Radio 1 programme *Top Gear*, 'Fredereek Hernando' failed to break into the charts.

The disappointing performance of 'Fredereek Hernando' soon resulted in the departure of Billy Scenters from the group, and shortly thereafter, Alan Young. By March 1968, One In A Million had broken up.

Always working in the background to support their sons' musical ambitions, James Sr. and Lily McCulloch again stepped in to help find their children work, James Sr. bringing the boys to an audition for a drummer for the psychedelic group The Magic Mixture. "We'd just lost our drummer and when we were auditioning, Jack and Jimmy turned up with their father who was also their manager," Magic Mixture keyboardist Stan Curtis told Paul Salley. "Jack was a good drummer and the job was his when his dad said he came with a bundle of gigs he had booked for a band that no longer existed. Jack's dad asked if Jimmy could join for two songs at each gig, and we agreed. He was a great guitarist for his age but was very shy, although the girls loved him. He also had very lovely guitars, mainly Gibsons, and Jack said that they were all gifts from Pete Townshend, a mentor to Jimmy. The family seemed very well connected in the rock industry. ...We got on well with Jack, and his father wanted big success for both his sons."

The Magic Mixture released an album, *This Is The Magic Mixture*, in June 1968 featuring Jack McCulloch on drums. In a continued quest for work, Jimmy auditioned for Jethro Tull, traveling to the audition on the London Underground as he was still too young to drive. "I had to rely on cabs and public transport," he told *Record Mirror* in 1977. "I went for a Jethro Tull audition on the tube once. I had to struggle on the train with my guitar jammed upright," he later recalled. "Then it turned out I was too young." Jimmy's mother escorted him on another trip looking for work – the aforementioned foray to the offices of Track Records, the image of which has remained in Vernon Brewer's memory for the past five decades. The young guitarist's connection to Pete Townshend would soon lead to his next musical adventure.

PART TWO

CHAPTER 5

SOMETHING IN THE AIR

"Speedy, meanwhile, was not Pete's only protégé – for years he'd been nursing Andy Newman, surreal rag-time pianist, kazooist and Post Office engineer, and he now also came up with Jimmy McCulloch, hotlips pubertal guitarist. Three performers, three completely alien styles and no discernible outlets for any of them – in the end Townshend simply lumped them together, precisely because of their incompatibility, and named the resultant chaos Thunderclap Newman."

- Nik Cohn, *Rolling Stone*, 1973

On March 16, 1967, a Thursday night, The Who's management team of Kit Lambert and Chris Stamp held a launch party at The Speakeasy club in London for their new label, Track Records. Several of London's movers and shakers attended on this night: Michael Caine and his flatmate Terence Stamp (Chris's brother) were there, both busy actors, the former in the midst of shooting Ken Russell's spy thriller *Billion Dollar Brain*, the latter John Schlesinger's adaptation of the Thomas Hardy epic *Far From the Madding Crowd*. Accompanying them were Stamp's girlfriend, the model Jean Shrimpton, famous for causing quite an uproar at Australia's Melbourne Cup two years earlier when she showed up wearing a mini-dress – enough of an uproar to make the front page of the following day's newspaper, bumping the race winner to page two – and Caine's girlfriend, the actress Elizabeth d'Ercy. The American folk duo Simon & Garfunkel were there too, having arrived in London that week for a performance at the Royal Albert Hall on Saturday the 18th. The pair had a hit with 'The Sound of Silence' in 1966, and would gain further acclaim with the inclusion of their music in the film *The Graduate*, released in December, 1967. Football star Bobby Moore, captain of England's World Cup-winning team the previous July, was also on hand, along with all four members of The Who – dressed in dinner jackets, with Townshend sporting a bow tie – and a newly discovered American guitar phenom named Jimi Hendrix.

Track's first single, Hendrix's 'Purple Haze', was released the following day, ultimately reaching number 3 in the U.K. charts. The label, which added further releases by The Who, Hendrix and John's Children (featuring guitarist Marc Bolan, of future T. Rex fame) in the following months, took on the brash and uncompromising personality of its founders, an approach which helped gain them seven top ten records in 1967 alone, quite a feat for an independent label swimming in a sea dominated by majors. EMI and Decca were the big fish; the only other notable independent label in the U.K. at the time was Immediate, Rolling Stones manager Andrew Loog Oldham's label, which had launched in July 1965.[24] Sharing youthful enthusiasm and a disdain for the majors, both Track and Immediate blazed a trail of innovation, creativity and quality recorded output.

But it was Track that was better able to translate this into commercial success. "Chris Stamp and his partner Kit Lambert have together begun to revolutionize the recording industry by demonstrating that quality alone counts," observed Tony Palmer in a November 1968 article in the *Observer*. "With careful promotion and devoted musical production, quality can bring its just rewards." Palmer went on to note that the never-shy Track's future plans included an opera and a full-time orchestra. By 1970, the year Immediate folded, Track had captured 6 per cent of the U.K. market and were grossing nearly £500,000 a year.

An example of Track's 'careful promotion' could be seen in the efforts behind Hendrix's *Electric Ladyland* album, released in 1968: "As you know, the album sleeve is full of nude women," recalled Track promotions manager Vernon Brewer. "So we approached this big shop in Piccadilly Circus (the clothing boutique *I Was Lord Kitchener's Valet*),

---

24 Robert Stigwood's Reaction label folded in 1967.

and they had a huge window, and we plastered the whole window with the sleeve with all these naked women on it, except for a small square in the center, and of course inside we had very scantily clad females prancing around. And," Brewer added with a laugh, "people were clamoring to look through this square in this window and it just caused chaos, and brought Piccadilly Circus to a standstill."

Further exemplifying the label's unconventional approach, Kit Lambert told the press, "We're going to have an arm of experimental stuff; in fact, Pete Townshend is heading up a mysterious department called 'Jazz and New Sounds'." Townshend would be responsible for Track's jazz releases and also for discovering and supervising the recording of new talent. The 'jazz' portion of this role appears to have been neglected in favor of 'new sounds'.

In between his ever-growing commitments with The Who – which between March and August 1967 included the release of three singles, tours of Germany and Scandinavia, three separate visits to the U.S. for the group's first performances there, plus multiple U.K. dates and recording sessions – Townshend approached this new role with relish, and began scouting for talent at the UFO club, a basement hall under a cinema on Tottenham Court Road. "UFO was held in a location which for 5 nights a week was the Blarney Club, featuring Irish music," recalled the influential and flamboyant singer Arthur Brown, who performed there frequently. "The other two nights, it became the underground center of London. It was actually quite small, and could hold when bursting at the seams about 1,000 people. The advantage of this was its intimate atmosphere. Everyone in the club could see everything that was going on – and there was a lot going on. There were naked people wandering around. There were people who jumped onstage and spouted poetry. There was Mark Boyle with his amazing light show featuring the first oil-slides most of us had seen."

The stage was quite small in size but featured the cream of English performers: The Bonzo Dog Band, The Pink Floyd, The Pink Fairies, Hendrix, Soft Machine, and The Giant Sun Trolley. When we performed I used the fire helmet and finished with smoke bombs. There was sweat in the air. The audience were one hundred percent with whoever performed. That meant everyone could experiment to their heart's content. From the anarchic poetry of the early Soft Machine to the new electronic tones of the early Keith Emerson or the Floyd – to the stoned out humor of the Bonzos or the political savvy of Mick Farren it all flowed. It was the crucible in which was formed the future of English entertainment – from comedy to music to dance to club-formats to light shows to nakedness and sexual upfrontness, to political awareness, and poetry. It was where many people got the opportunity and courage and encouragement to explore the limits of their own minds.

Thus, the UFO Club was the perfect setting for Pete Townshend to frequent in his new role as talent scout.[25] He soon honed in on Brown, whose stage presence was quickly becoming legendary. In August 1967, Brown "stunned the Windsor Pop Festival by arriving on stage lowered by a crane and sporting a horn-shaped metal helmet ablaze with a sinister cow-gum substance," recalled Tony Palmer in his 1970 book *Born Under A Bad Sign*.

With his face smeared with hideous Red-Indian

---

25 There were other Townshend connections to the UFO: His girlfriend Karen Astley, a dress design student at Ealing Technical College, worked as a waitress at the club, and her face adorned its promotional posters.

daubings, his cloaked body writhing and squirming like an octopus in labor, his voice – at his own admission – a cross between Little Richard, Tom Jones and Maria Callas, it is little wonder that his act became the hottest property on the University dance-underground-prayer-meeting circuit.

Describing himself as the Prince of Eternal Dark, Defender of Omnipotent Forces, Keeper of the Leaden Key and Herald of the New Dawn, he was not likely to appeal to those who believed that pop music was intended as light entertainment. He tried London where he was seen and heard by Pete Townshend, leader of The Who. It was an ideal chance since Kit Lambert and his organization, Track Records, were about the only record company farseeing enough to cope with such as Arthur Brown.

"People kept coming up and saying why didn't I do something about him," Townshend commented later. "I thought he had great potential with a fantastic stage presence and a voice every bit as good as Hendrix's guitar, but he needed controlling because he was a bit of a lunatic!"

"It was a period when all the major record companies were rushing to sign any significant underground acts," Brown recalled. "We were royally wined and dined at some expense every night of the week. Along came Pete Townshend on behalf of Track Records. He said that Lambert and Stamp had just narrowly missed signing the Bonzos, and he was determined not to let them miss us as well. He invited me to Soho and took me for a drive in the first car I'd ever gone in that had electric windows. It was big and American, and pretty impressive. We decided that though Track was a small independent label, with less money than the majors, the fact that they had launched and handled

The Who was a good indication – we felt that they would be more likely to let us keep our musical integrity."

Townshend soon produced some demos with Brown and his band. "Pete was intrigued with the concept for a whole album I had come up with," said Brown. "He encouraged experiment and creativity both in form and content. For instance, with 'Spontaneous Apple Creation', I came in and said it was not finished. We recorded it with the verses spoken on the demo, and I said to Pete that I must come back again when I had written a tune for the verse. He insisted that actually it was fine as it was, and this is the version that made it to the *Crazy World* album. Everything was formed and shaped in the studio, so Pete had a hand in everything. We were all pretty new to recording, so in that regard Pete was a guiding light for all the technical possibilities. He also played guitar on some of the demos."

Townshend, who had begun writing his own concept piece (the song 'Rael', which was released as the final track on the album *The Who Sell Out* in December 1967), encouraged Brown to pursue his idea of a concept album. "He had let me read 'Rael'," said Brown, "and was convinced that my vision for the *Crazy World* album of a concept going through both sides – which I had come up with at about the same time as he came up with 'Rael' – was a good thing to pursue. Lambert, on the other hand, thought it was a stupid idea to have a whole album about 'Fire'."

Brown recalled that when the group recorded their debut album in early 1968, Townshend and The Who were on tour in the U.S. "Lambert and I had several heated discussions," said Brown. "It ended that he would not go into the studio unless we were going to record some of the numbers from our stage act, such as [Screamin' Jay Hawkins'] 'I Put A Spell On You' and [James Brown's] 'I Got Money'. So I was given artistic overseeing duties of the concept side, and Kit had charge of the other. Perhaps if Pete had been around it might have been different." Despite his absence from the album's recording sessions, Townshend was listed as associate producer "because of his formative influence on both the band and the production team before and after the actual studio work," Brown explained. Kit Lambert was credited as producer.

Townshend says today of Arthur Brown: "Kit stole him from me. I had already demo'd a version of 'Fire' with Arthur and his band." Townshend was convinced the song would be a hit, and he was right: 'Fire', released by Track in June 1968, became a million-seller, was number one in the U.K., number two in the U.S., and reached the top ten in several other European countries. Perhaps because of this experience, when it came time to record Thunderclap Newman, Townshend was the sole producer while Lambert appears to have had no involvement at all.

In addition to signing and mentoring Brown, Townshend planned to bring on more talent, and to even start his own label. "I had my own ideas," he said. "Kit Lambert and Chris Stamp had founded Track Records and I wanted my own label within it. My idea was to work with what today we might call 'outsiders'." Townshend, of course, was already familiar with three individuals who certainly fit that description: Andy Newman, Speedy Keen and Jimmy McCulloch. "Each of the musicians who made up Thunderclap Newman were going to have their own records," he continued. "Another band I wanted to record included Keith Emerson." At the time, the classically-reared keyboard virtuoso Emerson was honing his chops – and a reputation for onstage wildness equal to that of Arthur Brown – with The Nice. The animated Emerson would jam daggers between the keys to sustain notes[26] and would climb atop his instrument and knock it over while playing. Townshend had also entertained signing another bona fide outsider, the supremely odd ukulele-wielding falsetto Tiny Tim.

An early example of Townshend's efforts to develop the talents of some of these 'outsiders' can be found in his efforts to have Jimmy McCulloch record the Speedy Keen composition 'Accidents', which Keen had written not long after 'Armenia City In The Sky'. "Jimmy recorded a couple of versions of the song which didn't come out too well," Keen recalled a few years later, citing problems with McCulloch's pre-pubescent voice. "They sounded squeaky because he was so young." It's likely that these recordings featuring Jimmy were part of the first iteration of a band named Bent Frame, featuring Jimmy and Jack McCulloch, with vocalist Robbie Paterson and keyboardist Dave McDougal. Townshend reportedly planned to produce the group, but work – and life – kept interfering with his plans. He simply didn't have the time. The Who spent most of early 1968 overseas, embarking on tours of Australia, New Zealand, and the U.S.

On May 20th, the day after his twenty-third birthday, Pete Townshend married twenty-year-old Karen Astley at Didcot Registry Office in Oxfordshire. Speedy Keen was best man, an honor that he became aware of when Townshend picked him up on the way to the wedding. "[Pete] told me to be ready and waiting at the Dome Garage on the Great West Road, and along he came in a yellow Rolls Royce and immediately tells me I'm best man, but I wouldn't have to make a speech or do anything except

---

26 And not just any daggers – a pair of Hitler Youth daggers gifted by war memorabilia collector and future Motorhead frontman Ian "Lemmy" Kilmister, who at the time was working as a roadie for The Nice, as well as for Jimi Hendrix. We'll meet Lemmy again later when his and Speedy Keen's paths intersect.

be there," Keen recalled in his memoir. "…It was a nice wedding… I remember feeling a bit odd being best man but not really doing anything, but it was nice to be called best man, a great privilege. At the reception I remember we all got very drunk. Pete's mum was there, she and I got very drunk…"

There was no honeymoon, as Townshend was too busy. Two days later, he was back in the studio with The Who; the following month, they embarked on a nine-week U.S. tour, with The Crazy World of Arthur Brown as one of their supporting acts, although Brown's assignment was cut short when he broke two bones in his foot during the opening weekend in Los Angeles.

* * *

By the second half of 1968, Pete Townshend and The Who had reached a crossroads. Their last three singles, 'I Can See For Miles', 'Dogs', and 'Magic Bus'[27], had all been commercial disappointments. Townshend was feeling the pressure to come up with something good. "I was petrified that the band was going to finish," he recalled in 1977. "I felt strongly that I was being tied down too much to single records. I felt that if I had to say everything on a record in three minutes flat then I wasn't ever going to say very much. I wanted to find a way to stretch it a bit more without making it pretentious or pompous and without making it sound like classical music." He duly expanded on the ideas he'd started with smaller concept pieces such as 'A Quick

---

27 Track's typically over-the-top promotional efforts for 'Magic Bus' involved hiring an old open-top London Transport bus and, with The Who and some miniskirt-clad models aboard, driving it around London with the new single playing via loudspeakers. But that wasn't enough. "I thought well, it's a *magic* bus," recalled Vernon Brewer, by way of explanation before pointing out that a baby elephant and a lion were also on board. "Somewhere I've still got a photograph of me with my arm round this lion on the bus," he added with a laugh. "I wouldn't do it now!"

One' and 'Rael' and set to work on writing a full concept album, or, with the enthusiastic prodding of the classically steeped Kit Lambert[28], a "rock opera". When Townshend and The Who returned from their summer tour of the U.S. in September 1968, they entered IBC Studios in London to begin his most ambitious project to date: *Tommy*.[29]

Around this same time, Townshend's art school friend Richard Barnes remembers walking down the road in Ealing when a dump truck pulled alongside him and a familiar voice called out from the cab: "Barney!" It was Speedy Keen. "I knew him by then, and he was driving a lorry, delivering sand," Barnes recalled. Free spirit Keen had spotted Barnes and wanted to share his latest creative work with him, to such an extent that he pulled over on the spot. "This was the psychedelic period," Barnes said with a laugh, feeling it necessary to point this out before describing Keen's attire that day. "Speedy gets out and he's got really long hair, he's got a big nose, he looked like Sonny Bono or something, and he's wearing a tablecloth! Kind of a caftan thing – I can only imagine what the other drivers used to say to him."

"He left the lorry there and we sat on this bench at the side of the road," Barnes went on, "and he's talking about his songwriting and things, and starts singing to me."

Call out the instigators, Keen began.

---

28 Kit Lambert's father was the composer Constant Lambert, his Godfather the composer Sir William Walton. Kit's Godmother was Dame Margot Fonteyn, the *prima ballerina assoluta* of the Royal Ballet, of which Constant Lambert was musical director and conductor.

29 *Tommy* was, for a time, intended as an actual opera featuring none other than Arthur Brown on vocals. "At one time, I was studying orchestrations and listening to Wagner and all kinds of amazing things trying to get into full scale grand opera," Pete recalled in 1979, "and I was going to enlist Arthur Brown whose voice I thought somewhere between a Wagnerian tenor and Screaming Jay Hawkins and have him as the lead singer."

Because there's something in the air

We've got to get together sooner or later

Because the revolution's here...

Barnes remembers being puzzled as to why Keen was singing it to him. "I mean – I wouldn't know whether it was a good song or not," he said. "But the thing is, that's not the only time it happened! Another time, same thing: I met him somewhere and we were walking through this little park near Ealing Broadway and again we sat down and he sang it to me again, and I wanted to say well, you have sang this to me once, you know. And then he did 'Accidents' – explained this accident, milk float etc., and I thought, "that's a bit weird," but it didn't matter, 'cause those days, everything was a bit strange." Barnes remembers a total of three occasions when Keen sang these early – and arguably his best – compositions to him. "I think after a while I could have sung them back to him," he said with a laugh. "I really wasn't that interested, but I was very polite. It's amazing to think that it got to number one! It just occurred to me that his persistence paid off."

'Something In The Air', at the time titled 'Revolution', had begun life as one of Speedy Keen's many scraps of ideas and is a prime example of Pete Townshend successfully facilitating the realization of a song from Keen, who appeared not to know that it had been there, within him, all along. "I helped Speedy find the song," Townshend recalled later.

> I remember sitting with him and I said, "Have you got any ideas today?" And he said "No." And I said, "You must have something?" "No, nothing, absolutely nothing. ...not even a chord." I said,

"So you've got the guitar over there; you mean you couldn't pick it up and just play a chord?" And he went "Yeah, I could play a chord," and he played a chord, and I said, "Oh, it's an open tuning," – he'd tuned his guitar to E. He said, "Yeah, and if I play E, it goes… [Townshend imitates the chords resonating]," and he started to play, and I said, "That sounds like a bit of a song," and he said, "Yeah, okay, I've got a couple of chords, but they're nothing." And on it went. And two hours later I extracted this song for him, it was a completely, fully formed song with a beginning, a middle and an end. And he was so loath to let it out. I did the demo of it with him.

The arrival of Keen's promising new song around September 1968 couldn't have come at a busier time for Pete Townshend, with The Who's recording of *Tommy* getting under way at IBC Studios that same month. Townshend's idea of recording three separate albums with Messrs. Keen, Newman and McCulloch looked unattainable, as there simply wasn't enough time. Enter Kit Lambert, who made the unlikely but ultimately brilliant suggestion of merging the trio: "It was indeed Kit who suggested I put Andy, Speedy and Jimmy together so I could get on with writing and recording *Tommy*," Pete recalled. He decided to go for it.

Sometime in the latter half of 1968, despite being occupied with heavy touring activity and the writing and recording of his *magnum opus*, Pete Townshend wrote a letter to Andy Newman, inviting him to "record some songs with two guys he was working with," Newman recalled.

Townshend's initial invitation to Keen, Newman and McCulloch was ostensibly for music for a film, but the

(who directed Ready Steady Go! and The Rolling Stones Rock and Roll Circus) was a good friend of Kit's and they were always throwing film ideas around. Michael is Orson Welles son, and once in Paris Terry Stamp took me to meet Welles.

…It was a particularly whirlwind period, with a huge amount of activity squeezed in, both around The Who, and in my own private circle of friends and colleagues, and I was in a workaholic state. I was full of ideas, and so it seemed were all of my friends and colleagues.

There was also the Meher Baba[30] group. There were a lot of ideas flowing in that crowd about making films. There were many artists, musicians and poets in the group.

Robert Wyatt's partner Alfreda Benge edited *The Lone Ranger*. I vaguely remember her leading me to a few film ideas.

…It wasn't all about Richard Stanley; there were several other people I knew who were working with Tattooist International. I did write music for a couple of other films for people at the Royal Film School – 'Warm Thrill of Pleasure' was one song. It could be that I was planning for Thunderclap Newman to do film music for one of these people, but when I heard 'Something In The Air' decided it was too good to use elsewhere.

Whatever the initial justification, the first meeting of the three 'outsiders' took place at Pete Townshend's home in Twickenham on the day of the first session, in October or November 1968.

---

30 Meher Baba was an Indian spiritual master whose teachings influenced much of Townshend's work.

The studio in his family's home on the embankment of the Thames near Eel Pie Island was Townshend's sixth, his first being the setup he created in the flat above his parents' home in Ealing back in 1964, which consisted solely of two Vortexion mono tape machines and a single Reslo microphone. Each subsequent iteration was a marked improvement on the last. The quality of his demos followed a similar trend. "I always make a finished demo of numbers on which I play record producer's drums, record producer's bass and Pete Townshend guitar," he said in 1971. "I'm my own best backing group!" Townshend's meticulous technique was amazing – as was his equipment. "It started out as a hobby and now it's an obsession," he said. Glyn Johns, who later produced several albums by Townshend and The Who, said, "Pete's demos were always fantastic and were always a challenge. Very often I'd listen to the song that we were about to cut and I'd go, "How the hell am I going to compete with that?" Really, really brilliant demos."

Townshend noted that this most recent studio, set up in a converted upstairs bedroom shortly after he and Karen moved into the home in mid-1968, was "slap bang in the middle of the building and when I worked nobody slept." Andy Newman recalled that the studio contained "a couple of Revox tape recorders, and a Bechstein upright piano." In addition to these items, the studio featured two state-of-the-art Dolby A301 noise reduction units (one for each of the Revoxes), two organs, a cobbled-together drum kit courtesy of Keith Moon, bongos, and an assortment of guitars. In total, Townshend had spent about £8,000 equipping the studio, his first with a separate control room. "His studio grew to be exceptional – the equivalent of anything," Richard Stanley remarked. "It was small, but the control room part of it was amazing."

When I remarked to Newman that I had visited these premises and that it must have been incredibly difficult to get an upright piano up those narrow and winding stairs, he of course had a story: "Oh, that was alright," Newman began. "He eventually had a seven foot four Bosendorfer in there! It went in alright; there was plenty of room for it, amazingly enough." Once you got it up the stairs, I noted. "Well, that's the problem of the piano movers," Newman replied, adding, "they have to do some amazing miracles sometimes, and they have to know how to take windows in and out in order to get pianos in, you see."

> There's rather an interesting story about that premises. It's right by the river, and it's on the tidal part of the river. Now, normally, when the tide comes in, it just comes a little bit up the front sort of roadway of the house, and then recedes very quickly, but in the spring and the autumn, you get much higher tides, and when Pete first moved in there he decided to use the little cellar in the place as an echo chamber. So he set all this very expensive equipment up there to produce a really sophisticated echo chamber. Sadly, one day the tide came in and wrecked all his equipment. So… I think one Leslie speaker was written off, 'cause it doesn't do loudspeakers any good if you drop them in the water!

And so, here in Townshend's home on the banks of the Thames, a diminutive teenage guitar phenom met with a lanky hippie songwriter/drummer and a rotund, straight-as-an-arrow GPO engineer/throwback boogie pianist. Just like the trio's discordant physical appearance, their personalities and musical styles were an odd match indeed. "…All three of us were so opposite that in ordinary life we'd have hated each other and what we stood for," Speedy said the following year.

"Speedy and Andy Newman, talk about chalk and cheese; they really were different," observed Richard Barnes. As were Andy and Jimmy. "Andy and Jimmy were total strangers," Keen recalled of that first meeting in Townshend's house. "Jimmy I could immediately identify with – he was a rock guitarist although he liked my acoustic-type songs, but Andy, well he couldn't relate to us and we couldn't relate to him." Not only did Newman hail from the foreign world of working squares, but his musical tastes were completely alien to Keen and McCulloch as well. "Jimmy McCulloch and Speedy were very much into the music of the period," Newman said. "I was a complete stranger to it. I was mainly involved in traditional jazz… I was trying to fit myself into it."

Despite their numerous and varied differences, when the three began working together, they somehow clicked. "Something magical happened from the very first second," Keen recalled. Townshend recently used the same adjective when recalling this first meeting. "I just remember them playing together in my studio," he said. "It was sort of magical."

Newman recalled the trio working on three demos initially, two of which were 'Revolution' (later 'Something In The Air') and 'Accidents', and "some other song which I think was later on sort of revamped and changed around on a later record." Townshend served a multitude of roles. "I was of course the bass player and flew in sound effects from a third tape machine between bass notes," he recalled. "Mixes were made on the fly when working from machine to machine. And because of the Dolby A (I was one of the first people in the U.K. to use them) the sound was pristine."

The fact that the group meshed musically from the beginning seemed to take all of them by surprise, not least Townshend. "I thought, "impossible, three more unlikely people you couldn't get," he remarked to *ZigZag* a few

years later at the notion of the 'jamming them together' theory actually working. "But they got in a room together, they played together on some film music for a friend of mine and they were really great and I played them back the tapes and they said, "Yeah, seems to work," and they liked it and they were all enthusiastic about it as a concept, as it were." Despite the lack of any shared musical inclinations with Newman, both Keen and McCulloch "immediately loved the idea of working with Andy Newman," according to Townshend.

Encouraged by the success of this initial meeting, all involved wanted to pursue the concept further. "Pete thought it would be a good idea if we put this together," said Newman. "The guys in the band wanted to form it into a group anyway, 'cause Jimmy had come down from Scotland and he wasn't doing anything at the time, and Speedy wanted to get a band together, so they approached Townshend and he contacted me and asked me if I'd like to do it and I said yes.[31] So then sometime around Christmas, I think it was, in 1968, I suddenly got a phone call to go over to IBC Studios in Portland Place where we put together the basic tracks of the actual records that got released. Only three of the numbers – what later became 'Something In The Air,' 'Accidents', and 'Wilhelmina'."

Newman's agreement to join the band came with one rather difficult condition, which Richard Barnes remembers Townshend relaying to him. "Pete said, "We're having trouble getting Andy to join." I said, "Why?", and he said, " 'Cause he won't leave the GPO unless we match his GPO pension." And I thought well good on him – you see, we didn't have pensions in the music business. There's so many

---

31 "[Townshend] sent a letter about forming the group permanently," Newman later told the *NME*. "He said "I'm gonna make you a star," and I thought, 'Oh yes, I've heard that one before.'"

roadies that have worked with big bands all round the world and are penniless, they don't end up with a pension or anything. It's all kind of casual. Anyway, he wouldn't do it, and he wasn't going to be fobbed off or fooled with a fake promise, so I thought that was fantastic, so they had to set up a pension plan to match the one from the General Post Office – and *then* he'd leave his job, which is great!"

"The life of a GPO telephone engineer was secure, but unexciting," the conflicted Newman told *Melody Maker* in June 1969. "It took quite a bit of persuasion to get me to leave, and I'm really still thinking about it all." Townshend added at the time: "Track Records finally did give him a pension plan. He must be the first rock star to have a pension." He added prophetically: "Track Records will probably be long gone by the time he's supposed to get it."

Apparently this back-and-forth over pension benefits was ongoing during the recording of 'Revolution,' as Newman later admitted to Nathan Morley that the session took place when he was supposed to be at work: "I was in fact a telephone engineer when we made the original recordings and I have to frankly confess now that I did 'Something In The Air' in the firm's time. I was supposed to be working on the job and I was actually in the studio recording it, so please don't tell anyone, will you?"

The sessions at IBC took advantage of The Who's unused time from the recording of *Tommy* between November 1968 and January 1969. Pete's younger brother Simon, eight years old at the time, contributed backing vocals on *Tommy*'s 'Smash The Mirror' during a late night session and remembers seeing Speedy Keen "messing around on the drums" in the studio. Indeed, The Who's sessions reportedly took place quite late at night, freeing up studio time for Thunderclap during daytime hours – and requiring Townshend to pull extra duty.

"The majority of the sessions were at my home,"

Townshend recalls today. "The techniques I was using at the time were well-developed, and I got great results at home. We recorded a second (final) version of 'Something In The Air' at IBC (the demo is wonderful by the way). We also recorded two rather strained simpler versions of 'Accidents' which the folks at Track thought would make a good second single." Townshend recalls that the orchestral sections of 'Something In The Air' were recorded at either Dean Street studios, or De Lane Lea in Soho.

Following suit with Keen, who played Townshend's patchwork drum kit during the sessions, McCulloch utilized a similarly cobbled together instrument: A Fender Stratocaster given to him by Townshend… in pieces. "It was in five bits – completely smashed," McCulloch said. "So me and my dad got it, and stuck it together. [Townshend] also gave me a fabulous '57 maple neck to stick on." McCulloch used this guitar and a Gibson SG on 'Something In The Air'. "I double-tracked the SG and the Strat," he recalled. "They were slightly out of tune with each other and sounded a bit like a 12-string."

In addition to playing bass guitar and facilitating the recording of these first Thunderclap Newman tracks, Pete Townshend also had to assimilate the various contributions of the band members into a cohesive whole, which was not a simple task. But the payoff was endlessly satisfying. "The amazing thing about the way they work in the studio is that they've all definitely got completely different states of mind, but it's a kind of a catalystic thing," he said in 1970. "…They each give away to one another as a concession to playing with the other – practically 90% of their own musical personality."

For fifteen-year-old Jimmy, working up close with Townshend was an eye-opening experience. "Recording-wise, Townshend was a tremendous influence on that Thunderclap Newman record," he recalled in 1975. "He was working on *Tommy* at the time, and we were just three geezers who were thrown together. We didn't even know each other, we were thrown in the deep end. It was terrific, just seeing what could be done with two Revoxes or with an 8-track. At that time I was very young and that was great experience."

"He was a very good producer," Andy Newman said. "I didn't realize it at the time, but listening back to the recordings that were made, the whole virtue of them is down really to the hand of Pete producing them." While Townshend did not share composer credits, he certainly helped shape the songs. "He was managing the recording, and he made suggestions on the arrangement and the instrumentation that was going to be used and how the instrumentation was done," recalled Newman, "so I think he also arguably had a strong input on arrangement which was conceptual rather than written out. …the songs were written by the people who wrote them and Pete merely sort of finished them off and produced them. And injected a little bit of arrangement suggestion." Newman said it was also Townshend's idea to use a gong at the opening of 'Something In The Air'.

The unusual arrangement of 'Revolution' is particularly noteworthy. The piano is quite understated, if not completely inaudible, for the first two minutes of the song after which all other instrumentation comes to a halt and Andy Newman enters with a heavy piano part, more an interlude than a solo. After nearly a full minute of this, the orchestra's horns and strings bridge us back into the guitar, bass and drums. The piano all but disappears again. But somehow, the approach worked. "Perfect, it was, right down to those Andy Newman piano solos that seemed to have wandered in from a different studio," as Charles Shaar Murray put it several years later. "That, to me, was its value," Keen told Murray. "If it had been anybody else, it would just have been a piano solo that had nothing to do with the track. He'd use his own personal feelings towards the track and play it his way, whereas usually people bend into you and try and adapt, which he wouldn't do under any circumstances whatsoever." Or, as Andy put it: "I think this was all really down to the production genius of Pete Townshend, who had the songs of Speedy in his background, and also he apparently heard a lot of my music before that, and he sort of weaved it all in as a sort of a... I don't know – a mosaic?"

While Keen wrote the song's music and lyrics, "the arrangement is Pete," observed Jim Avery, who joined Thunderclap Newman as bassist in April 1969. "I mean, the key change – Townshend said we'll have a key change here and a key change there, I mean, Speedy wasn't playing guitar obviously. It was all Townshend's show, as you know – him putting key changes in there wouldn't have struck Speedy at all. I'm not having a go, 'cause Speedy was a good songwriter, but he wasn't that proficient as a guitarist." One final note regarding the arrangement of 'Revolution': Avery pointed out that the modulation in the song bears a resemblance to that in The Beatles' 'Dear Prudence', which was released in November 1968 and therefore certainly could have influenced the Thunderclap track.[32]

The key of the song itself was apparently difficult for Keen, as Newman later told friends that the high register of Keen's vocals on 'Revolution' was quite difficult to attain in the studio, something Townshend pushed him to reach. Newman later told Mark Brzezicki that Keen never actually reached the highest notes, and that the tape was slowed down during recording to achieve it instead. There

---

32 "This is very Beatleish in conception and in the arrangement," observed keyboardist Brian Auger in *Melody Maker*'s 'Blind Date' column in 1969. "Very well executed, well balanced."

were also apparently difficulties with Newman's timing during the piano break that required a tape edit. Some of Newman's later bandmates also attested that he struggled with adhering to a more 'rock' (and less 'orchestral') time signature. Despite these numerous challenges, Townshend was enormously happy with the results of these initial Thunderclap sessions. "I sit in the box, like freaking out," he said in 1970. "I've never been so satisfied with the way something came together."

Keen had written a dreamy call to arms – *Because the revolution's here / and you know it's right / We have got to get it together now*. And it was literally a call to arms, with Keen at one point sweetly imploring *hand out the arms and ammo / We're going to blast our way through here*, an odd mismatch with his delicate phrasing and the general innocently optimistic vibe of the song. It's all supported by simple but sublime vocal and guitar melodies, McCulloch's light, unadorned guitar matching Keen's airy falsetto. Newman's dissonant, jarring take on a barrelhouse romp (jarring enough that one critic wrote that it sounded like he was "playing whilst wearing boxing gloves") in the middle of the song sets it apart from all else. As a whole, it's delightful, melodic, and, arriving early in a summer of seismic cultural change, it was exquisitely well-timed.

In August 1968, the Beatles' single 'Revolution' had been released, prompting Townshend and co. to change the title of the new song to 'Something In The Air'.[33] The following spring, a completely unrelated single by Nina Simone, also titled 'Revolution', was released.

The B-side of 'Something In The Air' was 'Wilhelmina', a piano-based ditty sung by Newman about a "plump and round" dairy maid from Amsterdam who continually

---

33 Incidentally, Townshend's father's band, The Squadronaires, had a popular tune entitled 'There's Something In The Air'.

spurns her many suitors: *All she says is 'nein, nein, nein'* / *no wedding bells for me.* Newman's fittingly odd kazoo solo is followed by a wonderfully expressive guitar solo by McCulloch which should feel out of place but doesn't. Written by Cumberland Clark and Mark Strong, 'Wilhelmina' was erroneously credited to Newman on some pressings, much to his irritation.[34] Newman had probably heard the version played by English dance band leader Harry Bidgood's accordion band, known as Rossini's Accordion Band, who released it (titled 'Wilhelmina (She's Plump and Round)') as the B-side to their single 'When I Grow Too Old To Dream' back in 1935.

As 1968 drew to a close, Track Records hosted a Christmas party at their offices on Old Compton Street, Soho, attended by The Who and the Small Faces along with various staff and media. It's not clear whether Newman, McCulloch and Keen attended, but if they didn't, they missed quite a party. "We were all upstairs and they had food all laid out on the table – they had loads of food and drinks," *Melody Maker*'s Chris Welch recalled. "And someone picked up an olive or something and flicked it across at somebody else, and somebody flicked it back." Within seconds, an all-out food fight ensued, which *Melody Maker* reported as "leaving the floor, ceiling, walls and guests coated in inches of sausage, pastry and cake." And it escalated from there. "Pete Townshend and Keith Moon started ripping everything off the walls," Welch recalled. "They had all these gold records and posters and framed portraits and things, and they were tearing everything off the walls and smashing it up. And Pete and Keith were shouting, "Destroy! Destroy!" I don't think Kit was actually in the room at that moment, but the rest of the management were all standing aghast and couldn't stop them."

34 Track also misspelled the song's title on some pressings, omitting the second 'L'.

With 'Something In The Air' nearly complete by this point, various names for the fledgling group began to be floated about. A distribution agreement had been reached with Track and Polydor, but there was no name under which to release the recordings. "They had terrible problems thinking of a name," Andy Newman recalled. Thankfully, Kit Lambert's suggestion – 'My Favorite Freaks' – was abandoned. They eventually settled on 'Thunderclap Newman,' Andy's nickname. "They didn't consult me," Newman said later. "I thought it was most peculiar. I was just playing piano. I felt a big burden of responsibility." Indeed, the naming took him by complete surprise. "I was never notified that they'd decided to call the band we were playing in Thunderclap Newman until about a week after they'd made the decision," he said. "So they never asked me if it was alright to use my name. But I didn't mind, 'cause I didn't think the thing was going to succeed anyway."

The first public mention of the new group appeared on the back page of the January 11, 1969 edition of *Disc & Music Echo*, along with a photograph of Townshend, McCulloch and Keen gathered around Newman, who was seated at a piano. The piece, titled 'Spotlight on new faces being tipped for fame', listed names and ages of each of the three band members (misspelling 'Keen' as 'Kaene') and describing the group's style as "as yet unheard, but described as completely new, a sort of cross between Big Pink and Bix Beiderbecke, the jazzman, slowed down – and very light-hearted!" It reported that the group were currently in the studio with Townshend and listed the group's chances as "Excellent. Mainly because Townshend is a shrewd talent-spotter. He found Arthur Brown. Also because pop is in dire need of a big new force, funny or not, and this might well be it."

CHAPTER 6

LIFTOFF

"It was electric, the way they came together: Andy's old-time 1920s piano, but with a difference somehow, with a sinister difference, and Speedy's incredibly straight, functional kind of drumming, and Jimmy's amazing young guitar."

- Pete Townshend, 1970

The Spring of 1969 was a monumentally busy period for Pete Townshend. Final recording and mixing of the most important album of his career, *Tommy*, took place in March, ending more than a year of painstaking work. Track released the project's first single, 'Pinball Wizard', on March 7th. That same month, his first child, Emma, was born. The Who spent eight days in April rehearsing the new *Tommy*-centric live show at a community center in west London, after which they went on a short tour of Scotland which served to both tighten up the new act and provide a small amount of relief to their dire financial situation.

May was equally hectic. The month began with The Who's heavily anticipated press showcase of *Tommy* at Ronnie Scott's tiny jazz club in London, an excruciatingly loud event that according to *Melody Maker* "left scores of people literally deaf," the power of which helped pave the way for mostly ecstatic reviews. A week later, the group embarked on a six-week tour centered around the Eastern U.S.: Boston, Detroit, Chicago, New York, Philadelphia. Track released the *Tommy* double album in the U.S. on May 17th.

Townshend's absence meant that Thunderclap Newman was without a bassist, an issue that was rectified in early 1969. The new member was Speedy's friend Jim Avery, a 20-year-old from Ealing who was also known variously as Jim Avory and Jim Pitman-Avery (or Pitman-Avory). Avery claimed not to know how 'Pitman' attached itself to his name in some circles for a time – he didn't have a hyphenated last name ("at the time, back in in 1969, people would get the wrong impression – they thought I was a member of the aristocracy," he said), and his middle name was Peter.

The brusque but endearing Avery was a working musician with various local groups, notably pop group The Attack and the more psychedelic-oriented Mosaic. He'd also performed with Irish show bands at American air bases. "The reason I was doing that is that they actually paid you good money," Avery recalled. "And a lot of these other gigs, you'd get fuck all, you know. And it was really tough, because everybody wanted to be a pop star in the '60s, 'cause it was better than being a footballer or a criminal. What else are you going to do in life if you're a working class boy?"

Avery had recently joined the music publishing company Writers Workshop after sending demos to producer Denny Cordell. "I went there because Denny Cordell was the producer of 'A Whiter Shade of Pale', and I personally thought he was the best producer in England at the time," said Avery. "I sent him demos and he said, "Come up and join Writers Workshop," so I was there, writing songs. Rick Wakeman was there, and we sometimes had heavyweight folk guitarists, it was quite a collection – and of course famously we had Joe Cocker."

It was Speedy, who referred to him as 'Pitman-Avery' to the bassist's mild annoyance, who had seen Avery perform at Ealing Town Hall and various other local venues.[35] "He heard of me and he tracked me down," said Avery. "He was saying that he writes songs and he had written a song for the Who, 'Armenia City In The Sky',

---

35 Avery, incidentally, had been in a group with Les Elliott, lead singer of The Cat, a few years before the formation of that group. "I remember Jim in the early days, asking me to sort of help him learn bass," Chris Thomas recalled.

and eventually he took me round to where he was hanging out. He had a beat-up piano and a guitar he was learning to play. I was with this psychedelic group and basically I was living on floorboards, and living with girls who fed me. We'd sort of split up and I thought, 'Why don't I just go along with Speedy?', 'cause Speedy's saying, "I'm working with Pete now, I'm with this band, we're gonna be big, man, really big!" and all this."

Keen colorfully explained to *ZigZag* magazine that he'd brought in Avery "after auditioning over a hundred people… some of them were good bass players who just got freaked out when they saw Andy and Jimmy, some were really bad, some weren't bass players at all but just wanted to join a group, and I just couldn't find anyone who was suitable. …I'd come into the office and there'd be about 10 cats waiting to see me and I'd say, "OK – let's hear you," and they'd play a bit and then I'd show them a photo of the band and they'd say, " 'Oo's that geezer, I ain't playing with 'im – he's around 50!" And the whole thing was a drag – you couldn't tell how good they were or anything."

Once on board, Avery joined Newman, Keen and McCulloch at the Old Corn Mill, a beautiful secluded stone structure on the banks of the River Wey in Bordon, Hampshire.[36] Kit Lambert had rented the property and sent Thunderclap Newman there in March 1969.[37] "He sent us out there to prepare our stage act," Speedy later explained.

So we got out there and set about doing just that, but it was so hard to get started… there was Andy

36 The Old Corn Mill was just 1.5 miles from Headley Grange, which Led Zeppelin began using as a rehearsal / writing retreat the following year.

37 In order to free up the requisite time for this rustic adventure, Andy Newman told the GPO that he needed six months off to "sort out some personal problems," *Disc & Music Echo* reported.

playing his 1928 blues, Jimmy would be playing like Led Zeppelin and I was in the middle trying to balance it out. Like Andy is a fantastic pianist, but he had no idea what a 12 bar was, or what a middle 8 was, or things like that and once he started up you had to either turn him off or blow him out; and it was very frustrating.

Then Andy would come up with complaints about Jimmy, and Jimmy would come up with complaints about Andy, and we got to the point where we held a sort of board meeting every week to sort out the troubles. It was always little things – like I'd be playing records about midnight and Andy'd come in wearing pyjamas saying "Here, how am I going to get any sleep?" We solved that one by him deciding to live in a tent about half a mile from the house, which enabled him to record the dawn chorus and talk to the birds, because he'd bought a load of birdcalls. And he used to practice his bass saxophone at dawn, walking around the house.

At first, Jim Avery's arrival on the scene further compli-cated this dynamic. "First of all I had a friendship with Speedy, and Andy and Jimmy were a little bit wary of me – they were thinking like, why is Speedy bringing in his old pal?," Avery recalled. However, Newman and McCulloch both soon warmed to the charismatic and talented bassist. "As for Andy, he once caught me rehearsing by myself – I was doing 'Johnny B. Goode', playing the guitar and sing-ing, and he came in and he said, "Oh – I thought it was the record player! Very good!"

"Little Jimmy always called me 'Jim Bass', and I always called him 'Little Jimmy'," said Avery. "I had a sort of musi-cal relationship with Jimmy; he was giving me lessons, and he was knocking about with me – not copying me, but…"

Perhaps McCulloch looked up to Avery a little, I suggested. "A little bit, yeah," said Avery, adding with a laugh: "Not musically – he was *miles* ahead of me musically. He gave me lessons – he taught me how to play 'Classical Gas' on acoustic guitar. He was amazing – absolutely amazing." But in all other aspects, 15-year-old McCulloch's head must have been spinning. "I knew him when he was just trying to learn the ropes," said Avery. "It was very bewildering for him – it was bad enough for me! So for him, it must have been like, what the hell's going on? …he was thrust in the deep end straight away."

Thunderclap Newman's television debut took place on Friday, April 11th, just a few weeks after Avery had joined. It was the first time any of the group had been on TV, with the exception of Jimmy McCulloch, who'd first appeared with One In A Million on *Come Here Often* in early 1968. The group performed 'Something In The Air' on the BBC television program *How Late It Is*, a full six weeks before the single's release – a rather ill-timed promotional effort, suggesting that the single's release was perhaps delayed for some reason. The following week's episode featured a clip of this performance, after which host Angela Huth commented, "That was Thunderclap Newman when they played for us last week 'Something In The Air,' their new record. We had so many letters asking us to invite Thunderclap back for more that what could we do but happily grant the requests, so here they are again, this time with the B-side of their record, 'Wilhelmina.'"[38] The group's performance of the song featured a model dressed as the song's titular fraulein, standing alongside Newman and stroking his beard and hair as he sang, sufficiently distracting

38 Avery said Track had arranged for two weeks' worth of performances from the beginning, and that the notion of the second appearance being tied to the popularity of the first was a "bullshit story."

133

him that at times he was glancing amorously at the model instead of singing his lines into the microphone.

Track Records released the 'Something in the Air' single in the U.K. on Friday May 23, 1969 – precisely the same day that The Who's *Tommy* album finally underwent its U.K. release on the same label. Accordingly, the May 24th editions of the U.K. music weeklies contained ads for both releases, the Thunderclap Newman ad featuring a fish-eye lens photo of the grinning band with WE WERE SENT FOR printed across the bottom, as if this were some group from another dimension. It wasn't far off.

That same week, news broke of The Who encountering a spot of trouble whilst on tour promoting their new album in the U.S. where it had been released a week earlier, earning a rave review by Nik Cohn in the *New York Times* as the album's first single, 'Pinball Wizard', climbed the charts. The problem occurred at the Fillmore East in New York during The Who's performance on May 16th when a plain clothes police officer took the stage and lunged for the microphone in an attempt to alert the crowd to a fire which had broken out in a nearby building. For his trouble, the officer received a punch from an aggrieved Roger Daltrey and a kick in the groin from Townshend which, unsurprisingly, prompted the wounded man to retreat, jumping off the stage. Townshend and Daltrey were both charged with assaulting a plain clothes policeman and faced a maximum penalty of £420 or a year in jail. A court hearing was set for May 27th, at which the pair pleaded not guilty. Townshend later told reporters, "We mistook the policeman for some kind of heckler. We very much regret the whole thing."

Meanwhile, back at Track HQ, while Lambert and Stamp were dealing with this latest distraction, Vernon Brewer was working his magic to promote the label's new releases. During the lead-up to the release of the

Thunderclap Newman single, Brewer had sent a different item each week to DJs, music journalists and producers, all in keeping with the 'Something in the Air' theme: A can of air freshener one week, a plastic dog turd the next – each with a note: 'There is Something In The Air.' The final week, a small envelope was sent, labeled as follows: 'This packet contains three original Thunderclap Newman GO Pills. Dosage: Take one pill with a glass of water and you will GO like the Thunderclappers.' Andy Newman later insisted that some DJs did take it, "and it turned out to be a very powerful laxative, which wiped the DJs off the air for about a week." He credited the idea to Kit Lambert. Track's promotional efforts for 'Something In The Air', aided by Tony Hall Enterprises, the U.K.'s first independent promotions company, also included a promotional film for the single, filmed in Maidenhead city center, showing the group emerging from a photo booth as if arriving from another planet and handing out balloons to often bemused passers-by before performing the song in public.

Soon, the reviews started coming in. "Stand by for sensation! Pete Townshend's proteges are about to be unleashed [sic] on the public," proclaimed *Melody Maker*'s Chris Welch. "A new group, they feature Andy 'Thunderclap' Newman on piano and 15-year-old Jimmy McCullogh [sic] on guitar, making their single debut with a song by their drummer Speedy Keene.[39] Thunderclap is the phantom pianist featured in a cliff-hanging boogie-type break sandwiched between the straight vocals. They make a weird team that will blow several minds. Townshend did the production and it's a strong chart contender, once their image is established."

---

39 Keen's name was often erroneously spelled with the extra "e" in media reports, a trend that began when Track misspelled his name on the label of the 'Something In The Air' single.

"Driving guitars and drums power this number along with some very intriguing and exciting instrumental work going on behind the vocalist," wrote John Wells in the *NME*. "There's also an instrumental break in the middle which alone is well worth listening to. A Pete Townshend, of the Who, production who has certainly come up with some fascinating sound combinations. But if it's going to reach the charts it's going to need an equally fascinating number of plugs."

Several reviewers mentioned that the song grew on them after repeated listens. "Hear this a couple of times before making up the mind, because it seems to grow in stature with each spin," *Record Mirror* observed. *Rolling Stone*'s John Mendelsohn's offered a similar assessment when the single was released in the U.S. in October:

> Happily, it all begins to make sense after a few listenings, and, as a decidedly teenage expression of the desire to revolt, starts to come across as an unqualified delight. I've begun to find that wonderfully freakish lead voice (which belongs to drummer Speedy Keene, who wrote the song as well) telling me and us to get it together because the revolution's here endlessly charming in its pimply earnestness. And Thunderclap's bizarrely honky-tonk piano, backed by very quiet strings, has so little to do with the rest of the song that one can't help but dig it, can one? Simply, 'Something in the Air' knocks me out, as does its flip, the Newman-Himself-composed 'Wilhelmina', a polka-based drinking song in which T. Clap proves to have a marvelously clumsy Ringo Starrish voice and sense of humour.

Pete Townshend agreed, commenting at the time: "It

is a record in actual fact, that has to sink in. It has a couple of eccentric passages in it that take a while to grasp. You need to anticipate them in the record."

Townshend's production also received high marks: " 'Something In The Air' is a majestic piece of music, sweeping through Keen's fantasy of revolutionary Utopia with a hard-edged rock beat," wrote Dave Marsh in his Who biography *Before I Get Old*. "The recording is a model of spaciousness, and the suggestions of orchestration are beautiful and expansive. It makes the pinched, muddy sound of *Tommy* that much more difficult to bear." *Crawdaddy* reported in 1970, "Pete as producer gets better and better and his single with Thunderclap Newman is a technically perfect achievement."

At the end of May, Track published an ad in the music weeklies which touted their new signees' readiness for live performance: "MARSHA HUNT[40], THUNDERCLAP NEWMAN now available for engagements." In reality, the group were far from ready. "They could just barely do the stuff that's on the LP," Jim Avery recalled of the group's state when he arrived at the Old Corn Mill. "I learned all that stuff; Jimmy showed me what it was all about." But rehearsals continued to present a challenge, with a distinct lack of the focus and cohesion that the retreat was supposed to bring about. Near the mill were a riding school and a pub, The Robin Hood – two distractions the group didn't need. "In the end it was great and we really got to dig living out there," Speedy later recalled, while highlighting the fact that far more time was spent on pursuits other than actually rehearsing. "Andy had bought a rubber dinghy and 2 air guns (an hour's rehearsal then 2 hours target practice, an hour's rehearsal, then down to the river),

---

40 Track had released the former *Hair* musical star's version of Dr. John's 'Walk On Gilded Splinters' in April.

and we were getting £25 a week each and altogether it was so cushy that it's amazing we ever got anything together." It's not clear that they ever did.

Chris Welch visited the Old Corn Mill in early June after being intrigued by Thunderclap Newman's new single. "I was the weekly singles reviewer at *Melody Maker* and that record stood out for me," Welch recalled. "Everybody at the office was saying, "Have you heard this amazing pianist?", and he seemed such a remarkable character; bizarre – although we were used to bizarre characters at *Melody Maker*. We wanted to do a piece and the editor of *Melody Maker* at the time, Ray Coleman, said, "You've got to go and interview Thunderclap Newman." We set it up and it involved quite a long journey out to the countryside to track them down. I went with my photographer friend Barrie Wentzell."

The resulting article provided further evidence that little focused work was actually getting done. "The team have been living and rehearsing for some time in a beautiful country cottage in Surrey where a mill stream trickles through the garden and geese wander at will," Welch wrote. "As I arrived at this idyllic scene, Mr. Keene was drying himself off after falling in the river, and Andy was wading about attempting to find some valuables that had been dropped. After they had finished their aqua show, Andy joined me in the low-beamed dining room to talk about the strangest group to hit pop in years…"

The group say they are sincere and honest in their aims. Speedy is their composer and says, "We want to play music and we've been working hard on building up an act. Playing with a piano, I have had to adapt my style, and we've had quite a bit of trouble finding a piano to amplify." …"I'm really excited about the band," says Tiny Jim. "Originally

I was going to go solo, but this came along and it's completely different from any other type of group in the country."

A drummer himself, Welch watched Thunderclap rehearse and was particularly struck by Keen's work, commenting, "by God, his left hand is a bitch. Rumbling boogie shattered the peace of the countryside, and I was so amazed by his ferocious technique." During another rehearsal, Welch sat in on drums. "It was quite fun," he recalled later, adding that Newman even asked him to join the band at one point, "because I had the jazz feel." But rehearsals soon gave way to other pursuits, as Welch wrote:

> After playing some of Thunderclap's record collection which included such priceless 78 rpm items as 'Ali Baba's Camel,' and 'The Prosperity Song' by the Connecticut Collegians on Eclipse, the group decided to take me horse riding. At this Speedy proved as skilled as the Lone Ranger, galloping enthusiastically o'er lea and dale, Jimmy seemed to have been born in the saddle, and Andy trotted carefully around the paddock. Jim the bass player, however, managed to fly over the head of his horse and land on his cranium[41], while my beast totally ignored all suggestions and cantered into his box there to eat oats while I sat contemplating the stable roof from what seemed an extremely dangerous height. A stable lad led me out into the fields,

41 Avery was indeed thrown and dragged by the stirrup. "For ages, I couldn't lift my neck – like, I should have worn a neck brace," he said, marveling at the resilience of his youthful bones. "I'll tell you what it doesn't say in that article is that we were all *severely* smashed out of our heads. And Chris Welch wasn't too keen to get on a horse, let alone with all these lunatics [laughs]." Indeed, Welch later noted that he was "terrified", and that this was the only time he ever rode a horse.

and as I watched Thunderclap Newman and his merry men disappear across the downs, my steed settled down to an afternoon of shuffling about in cow dung.

The group's time at the Old Corn Mill was clearly not well spent, lacking focus and discipline – precisely the qualities which were always present when Pete Townshend was on site. Townshend, however, was in the U.S., on tour with The Who, performing the new *Tommy* set to rave reviews. "The truth of the matter was that we didn't really rehearse that much in the countryside," said Jim Avery. "This was down to Speedy, really. It was his fault. [Townshend] was nowhere to be seen. He would have come down and maybe rehearsed us. That would have been good. That would have been *very* good."

"I think they all thought it was a bit like a camping expedition," Chris Welch recalled. "And they were having fun, but yeah, I don't recall much heavy concentration on 'getting it together in the country'."

That was the big phrase – all bands were doing that, like Traffic – the record company or the manager would send them all off into the country. The idea was that they would all be away from distractions in town, concentrate on rehearsing and recording and writing new songs. I didn't see [Thunderclap] doing a lot of that, I must say. But they were bonding together as friends, and I think they all found it a unique experience, and the thing was that because they had Pete Townshend in the background, not actually there physically, but they were all sort of aware that somehow if Pete had faith in them then they had to do something seriously good to reward his faith in the project. They wanted it to be a success, there's no doubt about that, but I'm not sure if they knew which way they were supposed to be going. 'Cause it was a big recording production wasn't it, and what would they do on stage? So that's what they had to really work out. Whether they actually achieved that or not, I'm not sure. A tall order, really.

Ready or not, the group were quickly drawn into the fray when 'Something In The Air' entered the charts on June 17th, 1969. Two days later, a slot on the popular national television program *Top Of The Pops* followed[42], with the band performing in the studio along with The Kinks and The Tremeloes. Thunderclap Newman's live debut took place at the tiny Kirklevington Country Club in North Yorkshire (capacity: 375) on Saturday, June 21st. A chart entry, a major TV appearance and the group's first live performance, all within six days. "We didn't think it was going to go anywhere, but we were told just before the gig that it was in at number 27, which really scared us," Newman told Nathan Morley, adding: "Which is the reason why the place was absolutely packed and we did our very best to try and live up to the recording, but I'm afraid we weren't quite that well-rehearsed." The group's ill-spent time at the corn mill was already beginning to show.

The following week, The Who flew home from the U.S., having had to extend their stay on American soil for Townshend and Daltrey's court case in New York related to the Fillmore incident. Free to go after agreeing to a reduced charge and paying a $75 fine (Daltrey's charges were dismissed), Townshend was welcomed home to a three-month-old baby and the news that his pet band's

---

42 Maddeningly, due to the BBC's practice of recording over old film to save money, none of the footage of Thunderclap Newman on *Top Of The Pops* has survived.

first single was now in the top twenty. Meanwhile, The Who's *Tommy* album had proved a huge success, reaching a million dollars in U.S. sales in just two weeks.

On June 28th, the day after The Who's return, the weeklies reported that 'Something In The Air' had continued its rocket-like ascent, vaulting twenty places in the charts to number 7. Thunderclap Newman, unknown just days earlier, didn't know what had hit them. "It was like going from a peaceful monastery to a loud, noisy nightclub with lots of people intruding in," Andy Newman recalled. "I don't quite know if that's a fair description of it, but I can tell you, for me it was a bit sort of traumatic, except for having been a civil servant, and being used to dealing with the public [laughs]. ...Playing in front of very big audiences – I mean I'd never had more than about 20 or 30 in an audience before that – the first two or three were a bit of a surprise, but in the end we just got used to it."

The group's second live gig took place at Loughborough University that same evening. Keen was reportedly recovering from what the *NME* reported as "an attack of laryngitis". This may have been a euphemism for sheer nerves – stage fright would become a major issue for Keen in the coming weeks as the single climbed the charts and the pressure increased – or for a problem that had quickly become apparent during these first two performances: Keen couldn't sing and play the drums at the same time. "The problem was," Andy Newman explained, "the first two gigs, Speedy led on the drums, which was difficult 'cause he was at the back and, you know – flailing away on the drum kit is not conducive to singing. I mean, before that, he either sang, or he played the drums." Speedy explained to *Melody Maker*: "Because I was busy playing the drums, I couldn't get my breath to sing, and I sing lead vocal on the record. I was just squeaking."

Another problem for the fledgling act was a dearth of

original material. Because of this, in addition to the obvious 'Something In The Air', their setlist was an unsatisfactory hodgepodge of contemporary and original selections, including a cover of the Beatles' 'Lady Madonna', a Newman-composed piano instrumental called 'Water Music' which, complete with wood blocks and bird calls, proved rather plodding in a live setting, and a jam around a 12-bar blues theme. Add to this the fact that the material was being performed by an under-rehearsed and unfocused group, and it's not difficult to understand why Thunderclap Newman struggled to find their footing onstage.

Despite the growing list of problems with the group's live act, the attention garnered by the new single meant that Thunderclap Newman's calendar began rapidly filling up with bookings and recording sessions, the latter materializing now that Townshend was back in town.[43] A free open-air performance on the grounds of London's Goldsmith College was announced for July 1st, as part of the school's 'Golddream' summer festival, although the lack of any media reports renders it doubtful that the group actually performed, again probably due to Keen's "laryngitis". "Offers are flooding in for the group to join several British package tours this autumn, although no decision has been taken," the *NME* reported. "Also planned for Thunderclap are a lengthy European tour in September and an American visit late in the year."

A single in the top ten also led to increased media scrutiny, with the June 28th editions of *NME*, *Disc & Music Echo* and *Melody Maker* all featuring long pieces on the group.[44] "Andy Newman is a big, fat, jolly man without too much hair on his head, with owl-like specs, a middle-aged

---

43 By this time, Andy Newman was sufficiently confident in the group's prospects to formally resign from the GPO.

44 The weeklies also announced the death of Judy Garland that same week. Garland had died on June 22nd in London, age 47.

spread despite being only 26, baggy grey trousers held up by braces and red carpet slippers which look quite cosy," was *Disc & Music Echo* scribe Bob Farmer's rather unflattering appraisal of the pianist.

He drones rather than talks, grins sheepishly as he pounds his honky tonk piano and likes to be thought of as something of an intellectual. He has been worried about his pension. Jimmy McCulloch is a tiny tot in comparison. He is 16, stands five foot on tiptoes, weighs seven stone and surely risks death by drowning every time he takes a bath since he could probably slip down the plughole. He used to suffer an inferiority complex and has had to drink fizzy lemonade in pubs. He also wears braces but with boots which have bright yellow laces. Speedy Keen has the countenance of a fairhaired Pete Townshend with a prominent hooter to match. He freaks out fairly often and is the prototype of a pop group roadie. He used to think McCulloch was a snotty-nosed little kid and can only communicate with Newman by being straight to the point and not messing around in the manner roadies have. Jim Avery is Speedy's friend and, if he wasn't so slapdash about shaving and the other chores of life, would look strikingly handsome… The gentlemen just summarized all live in a lovely country cottage near Liphook in Hampshire which they keep very tidy to the amazement of the lady who used to live there – and they are all in a pop group to the amazement of all who have seen them.

The *NME*'s long piece, written by Richard Green, provided a further colorful description of the group's lineup: "The contrast between 26-year-old Andy Newman, who resembles a cross between Burl Ives and the mad professor from a Hammer film, and Jimmy McCulloch, who stands five feet nothing and is ten years younger, is the biggest surprise," Green wrote. "Then there is John Keen – Speedy to all and sundry – who wears a scarf round his long hair, is an original looner and who writes most of the group's material."

The *NME* piece went on to further illustrate the group's lack of focus during their stay in the country. "We drove in Andy's battered Volkswagen to the stables where an all-day gymkhana was in progress," wrote Green. "Alan, the group's roadie, was entered in a couple of events so the others had turned up to watch him. Or, more precisely, to laugh at him. Andy and I were greeted by Jill, the girl from the local grange, and her groom, appropriately named Miss Dobbin. They showed us where the refreshment tent was and in there we found Speedy propping up another girl."

Interestingly, these reports reveal that the group did contemplate how their live act would be received by the contemporary rock crowd – it just seems that they didn't translate this concern to making a concerted effort to improve the act itself. "Andy was sitting in the back of a van playing piano to a bunch of small girls," Green went on. "He was immensely enjoying himself and he broke off only to attempt to psychoanalyse me. He became serious again and talked about the group's music. "On a gig, people will wonder why we don't sound like our records. The only way to get over this is to say 'One policy for records and one for live performances.' You get a rapport with an audience, but you don't get it on a record. The thing to remember is a recording studio is an entirely different medium to a live performance. We've all got different ideas on this."

Keen shared his ideas on the subject with *Disc & Music Echo*: "We are going to be playing to 600 heavy mods, and they'll either boo Andy offstage, or accept him," he told

Farmer, who added: "At present they think the odds are in favor of the immense Andy being booed so their rehearsals include practicing how to stand in front of him to shelter him from flying missiles. Andy himself appears quite calm at the prospect."

The 'girl from the local grange' was Gil Woodley, 20 years old at the time the strange group arrived at the Old Corn Mill, which was situated only half a mile from Standford Grange, where she lived with her parents and her 15-year-old brother Martin. They first met Thunderclap Newman at The Robin Hood, which was situated directly across the street from their home. "There was a piano in the main bar and Andy used to play there," Woodley recalled. Gil's brother attended military school in Scotland at the time, traveling home during holidays. He and Jimmy quickly became friends, not only because of their closeness in age – just a week apart – but for other reasons as well. "I didn't really have a childhood," said Martin, who attended Gordonstoun school from age 6 to 17. "I went home at holidays, but my dad was never there."

> My mum was there doing things, but I spent most of my time with my dogs, by myself. And I think that's probably why Jimmy and I hit it off so well, was because we were both kind of loners. I had some friends who went to grammar school and they went home every night and they had a family environment, and they did so much better than I did. And I think that was probably what happened with Jimmy, although he did have the family, because he got into music as early as he did, I think it was pretty lonely, I really do.

"Jimmy was just a little kid," Gil Woodley observed. "I'm sure he was a lot more experienced and a lot more worldly than I ever thought he was at the time, but I think when he was with us, he just kind of reverted to being a kid. And I think that's what he liked about it. That's why he liked being in the country and just hanging out with me and Martin and doing stuff at the farm. No pressure. I know he loved to play, but I think it was a lot of pressure, too, for him."

The two boys decided to go shooting one day, wielding heavy double-barreled shotguns. "I said whatever you do Jimmy, don't pull both triggers at the same time," Martin recalled, "and that's what he did. I think it knocked him back about four or five feet. He was like, "*Ooohh* – I've got a gig I've got to play tonight."

Martin Woodley sometimes traveled with Thunderclap Newman in their Ford Transit van and helped them with their gear. "I'd help them set up and do the roadie thing," he said, remembering "just how good Jimmy was, and how strange Andy looked in that format. It was like everybody else around fit the mold and then there was Andy, who looked like he should have been working in a restaurant or something."

Gil Woodley's 21st birthday had taken place back on May 21st and was commemorated with a big party at Standford Grange, complete with live band. Later in the evening, Jimmy grabbed a guitar and sat in with them. "We left a name list on the door because my parents didn't want a whole lot of gatecrashers coming," Woodley recalled. "We left Speedy's name as 'Speedy Keen'." Keen, typically not averse to parties, didn't show up for some reason. "The next day when I saw him, I said, "What happened Speedy?"," said Gil. "And apparently they wouldn't let him in because he'd given them his name as John Keen and not Speedy! So he just gave up and went home."

Meanwhile, although he had been unable to attend any of Thunderclap Newman's distinctly underwhelming live performances, Pete Townshend was being apprised as to what was going on. "Pete Townshend's spies were down there," said Avery. "We were using some of the Who equipment – the PA, you see. The roadies would come down. They reported back to Pete." What happened next presumably took place in late June, after the group's first two gigs, both of which were decidedly unsatisfactory. "Pete heard about it and drove his Lincoln Convertible full pelt down to the Old Corn Mill," said Avery.

> He just came in the room, he said "I hear you were shit; I hear…" blah blah blah, this, that and the other, we're all going, "Oh my God!" I mean, I thought we were all in for the sack. And he had a real go at Speedy saying, "I could have got it together, why couldn't *you* have got it together?" And – Andy was in a daydream; he was thinking, well I've got *nothing* to do with any of this. Jimmy was a bit nervous, but I was sitting next to him saying, "Don't worry," and then Speedy's going "Oh man, it's because of this, it's because of that…" The truth of the matter was we didn't do any rehearsals 'cause Speedy was too busy going to the stables to collect a horse and going horse riding around the countryside, things like that. You may laugh, but it was very heavy.

Townshend's frustration was probably partly due to the fact that he knew that the plans being made for the group likely wouldn't reach fruition, because at the time it was becoming increasingly evident that they simply weren't capable of attaining a satisfactory standard of live performance. "Thunderclap Newman, the Who and former *Hair* star Marsha Hunt are being lined up for an eight-week American tour during October and November, which will also include several other British attractions," the *NME* reported on July 5th in an article headlined NEWMAN AND WHO CO-STAR IN BIG BRITISH PACKAGE FOR AMERICA. "The package, promoted by Track Records and consisting of that label's artists, will visit most major U.S. cities and is expected to include several TV dates."[45] One can only imagine Townshend trying to reconcile the stories he was hearing of the group's live act with visions of them performing in front of thousands at the Fillmore East or Carnegie Hall, two venues which were being considered for the proposed tour.

With Townshend back in the U.K. and being apprised of Thunderclap Newman's lackluster stage debut, changes were made. By the time the group returned to *Top Of The Pops* for an in-studio performance on July 3rd, they had a new member: Jimmy's older brother Jack McCulloch on drums. Jack, now 20 years old, had recently been working with Bent Frame, a group that had been rehearsing and writing under the watchful eye of Roger Daltrey at his cottage in Berkshire. "Speedy decided he couldn't do both jobs – sing and play drums," Townshend told the press, adding, "and I think his voice has a nice sound and was instrumental in the record being a hit. So we've brought in the new drummer. It will give the group a bit more stability. Anyway, Jimmy needs a friend – to help his confidence. It's nice that it's his brother!"

The angle that the move would not only resolve the issue with Keen's live vocals but would also provide needed support to the younger McCulloch, barely 16 years of age at the time, was something Keen agreed with. "They've brought Jack in on drums now which will help us a lot, especially Jimmy," he told *Melody Maker*. Jimmy's friend

---

45 One such TV date was The Who's planned performance on *The Ed Sullivan Show* on October 5th, an appearance that never took place.

Chris Hunt concurred: "[Jack] looked after Jimmy and took him under his wing, like: 'This is my younger brother, don't mess about with him.' Jimmy was so talented; he was just streaks ahead of everybody else. Jack was very protective of him."

For his part, Townshend had long insisted that the group weren't suited for live performances anyhow, regardless of the disposition of the drumming duties. "I said always, right from the beginning, that they should never play live," Townshend said in 1971. "But – Jimmy desperately wanted to play live. You can imagine, he's a good guitarist and he was brought up in the tradition of loud, young, arm-swinging guitarists and he was into Clapton and Hendrix and The Who – groups of that ilk, guitar groups, and he wanted to play and so I suggested that he got his own group and that Andy got his own group, but Speedy, for a start, should never, ever, ever have got on stage because he's not constitutionally built for it, he's incredibly nervous."[46]

It appears that Keen's move to the front had been brewing for some time, regardless of the ergonomic drumming/singing issue that had recently come to light. "After Speedy watched [Thunderclap's performance on *How Late It Is*], he decided he wanted to be a front man," said Avery, who pointed out that the camera primarily focused on Newman, Avery and McCulloch, and not Keen. "He didn't want to be the drummer anymore. After he decided he wasn't going to drum, he was going, "We need somebody heavy up front, man," and all that, and what he meant was *he* was going to be up front." Avery remembered Keen seeing a photo in *Disc* magazine after the *How Late It Is* performance that

46 In the July 5th edition of *Disc & Music Echo*, Townshend was asked: *If you were asked for advice by someone wanting to become a musician or singer, what would you reply and why?* His response, perhaps not coincidentally: "You've got to have self-confidence and faith in yourself and in the future…"

also fueled a touch of jealousy. "They chose a picture of me, and this upset Speedy," Avery recalled. "He was saying, "It's my group, my song – I should be in the front." But I didn't pick the photo. And that really – 'cause we were quite good friends before that. I think it's just down to jealousy I guess."

In retrospect, Townshend says today, "Speedy should never have stopped drumming. Jack was a good drummer, but Speedy would have been a clumsy front man." At the time, Townshend told an interviewer, "We're not sure a big record this early in the group's career is so good. The demands may be bigger than they can handle." And bigger than Townshend had time for. Today he adds, "I was far too busy then dealing with the massive success of *Tommy* to take any more time with them. I absolutely loved working with them, and wished I'd been able to continue."

* * *

Jimmy's friend Martin Woodley was back at military school in Scotland when Thunderclap Newman appeared on *Top Of The Pops* on July 3rd. "I remember watching it with my buddies, thinking I shouldn't be here," said Woodley. The group's appearance that evening was a triumphant occasion marking the arrival of 'Something In The Air' at number one, bumping The Beatles' 'The Ballad Of John And Yoko' from the top spot, and holding Elvis Presley's 'In The Ghetto' at number two, a remarkable feat. "THUNDERSTRUCK!," proclaimed the headline on the cover of *Melody Maker*. "The pop world was amazed this week when Andy 'Thunderclap' Newman, ex-GPO telephone engineer from Shepherds Bush leaped to number one in the MM Pop 30 with his first record, 'Something In The Air'." Newman, too, was amazed at the song's success. "It completely surprised me – I just couldn't understand why it had gone that far," he said in 2010.

Pete Townshend was at the studio that evening. "I thought, at last, justice!", he recalled. "It was great to be in the *Top Of The Pops* TV studio in the third week with *Tommy* in the charts and my first serious production at Number One."[47]

Andy Newman took the stage dressed in a policeman's uniform. "The reason behind that was simple," Townshend later explained. "How can you dress Andy on stage? If you try and freak him out he looks stupid, so we thought what a gas to have him look like a fuzz, which is what he did look like because he's so straight." Newman fully embraced the role, wandering around the studio imperiously and periodically offering, "Excuse me sir, but you can't do that here," or "'Ello, 'ello, 'ello – what's going on 'ere, then?"

Chris Thomas bumped into Jim Avery backstage at *Top Of The Pops* and remembers seeing Speedy, one of the very few times he saw Keen after their work together with The Cat. "I remember chatting to Jim in the bar afterwards," said Thomas who, perhaps still sore from the 'Club Of Lights' experience, didn't talk to Speedy. Andy's friend Rick Seaman also attended. "I went there with the group," Seaman recalled. "Speedy seemed very, very nervous but Andy was just... couldn't care less, you know. It was a breeze to him; he was always like that."

Robin Newman also remembers the night his brother was on *Top Of The Pops* with a number one hit. He and his family had no idea that Andy had left the GPO and moved to the Old Corn Mill to rehearse with Thunderclap Newman, nor that the group's single had been rapidly ascending the charts. "He had never told us anything about the pop music, so it was a complete surprise to hear this,"

---

47 While he was there, "an old friend took me aside and told me of the rumor that Brian Jones had been found dead," Townshend wrote in his memoir. Rolling Stones founder/guitarist Jones had died that same day, the coroner's verdict ultimately that of "misadventure". "I just sat there in stunned silence," Townshend recalled.

said Robin. "Our family didn't watch *Top Of The Pops*; they weren't interested – *I* wasn't interested." On that Thursday evening, the Newmans received a hurried phone call. "It was my cousin ringing up from Chiswick, and she said, "Quick, quick – turn on the television – Andrew's on!", said Robin. With this being the 1960s and televisions needing a few minutes to warm up before displaying any image, "by the time of course we turned it on, the item had gone," Robin recalled.

Jim Avery's sibling was a little more in tune with his career. "My little sister was copying out the pop charts in the *New Musical Express*," he recalled. "It was a fantastic chart, 'cause just coming up was 'Honkytonk Women' by the Rolling Stones, going down was the Beatles, and there was even Elvis Presley, they were all there in the top ten and we were number one. My sister was so proud of the fact that I was in this band."

And while he may have kept his family in the dark, Andy Newman, too, was documenting his group's meteoric rise, recording chart positions and tour dates in a notebook. "I've got them somewhere; I'll have to dig them out when I've located them," he told me in 2009.

> I've probably put them in the wrong file, that's the problem. All I've simply done is I've taken them out of the copies of the *Melody Maker* and the *NME*, the *Record Mirror* and the *Disc & Music Echo*, which were the four top music papers of that time, because I couldn't photocopy them, they won't let you do that, so I had to sort of pencil it all down...
>
> There was some uncertainty about some of the actual dates, as to exactly when they took place, 'cause sometimes they don't give all the details of dates, or they often put dates in that you didn't work... And sometimes, the publicity department

gives a whole load of gigs which they say we're going to do but they haven't booked them and they couldn't come to an agreement with the promoter, so they got pulled, you know? It's rather interesting.

It's similar like that with old jazz recordings, where they give you a list of all the people that played on the record, but when you check it through you discover in actual fact half the people that were supposed to have played on it didn't, because the ones that were supposed to be at that recording session had got themselves gigs and couldn't make it so they'd put a dep in! [laughs]

The group's rapid ascent proved difficult to process. "Suddenly I'm in this pop group with still no money[48], and we're messing about in the countryside and I'm riding horses, being interviewed by the likes of Chris Welch, meeting all these wonderful people like that, and then suddenly we're number one and we're being flown all over the place," said Jim Avery. "And we were having these ridiculous interviews – in those days if you were in a pop group, they would ask you these stupid questions, like "What is your favorite color?" It was so stupid, the fakeness of it all." Avery recalled a group of teenage girls who won a contest, the prize for which was a visit to the Old Corn Mill. "They all turn up at the Old Corn Mill and they're all in love with little Jimmy – they're about the same age – and we let them in, their eyes are popping out of their heads, you know? We didn't know what the fuck to do with them – what do you

---

48 Avery learned how to save on equipment by leaning on his famous counterpart with The Who, John Entwistle: "I was always borrowing equipment off him and not paying him," Avery recalled. "He was a superstar – like, if it was me, I had to save up to buy bass guitar strings, which cost a fortune, like 15 quid, which to me was a week's wage. And he'd get like a caseload of them free as long as he used one of the sets when he was on TV. So I used to raid his box of strings. He knew I was at it."

do? "Well, this is the Old Corn Mill, here's the stream that they use to turn the mill…" It was unreal. I mean, personally on my own trip, I'd gone from like Louis Armstrong and psychedelia and all that to showing little girls round the Old Corn Mill!"

"It was like absolute bedlam," Newman told Nathan Morley of his newfound success. "Suddenly the whole world all round us was going crazy and we were being lauded left right and center and people would come up to me, this is a person who'd never been really in the professional music business before, as though I was the person who knew how to pull hits out of the stratosphere. Which just wasn't true."

Collectively, Thunderclap Newman's response to the news of their hit record was one of excitement, but with the knowledge that they had work to do. "We're very excited about being number one," Speedy said. "Sincerely – it's a gas. But we've really got to get down to writing numbers for our album."

"The fact that 'Something In The Air' is such a hit has knocked us out," Andy told *Record Mirror*. "It has put a tremendous responsibility on us and has had a very sobering effect. Now we have to work hard to keep up the status."

* * *

The day after Thunderclap Newman's victorious number one appearance on *Top Of The Pops* marked another memorable performance, this time for all the wrong reasons: On July 4, 1969, the new five-piece Thunderclap Newman played their first live gig (the *TOTP* show was mimed) at the Wellington Townhouse, near Telford, Shropshire. This was to be Speedy Keen's first show at the front of the stage, singing and playing rhythm guitar. "One of the roadies produced a big lump of hash," Jim Avery recalled.

"Like, little Jimmy's only 16, being exposed to all this and of course I was used to it by then, I was like 19 or 20, and Speedy was practically living on the stuff, and we all got out of it, and then we're about to go onstage and Speedy realized he didn't know any of the chords!" This is quite hard to believe, but Speedy's account corroborates the story: "Five minutes before we were due to go on I realized I didn't know the chords to any of the numbers," he told *Melody Maker*. "So it was all down to a 12-string with no amplifier and my back to the audience."

Avery, however, remembers it a little differently: "We suggested, 'Just, like, go on – make sure you're not plugged in, so nobody'll hear you,'" he said. "You may laugh, but this is it: Here we are, rising up in the pop charts!"

So we get up there, and he's such a bag of nerves, he's got a guitar lead and I'm going, "Why are you bothering with a lead?" He says, "They're gonna suss me out, man! If I'm not plugged in, they're gonna suss that I can't play the bloody thing!" So he's got the other end of the plug, and he's gone to the amplifier stack, and he's messing about with the knobs and everything, and he's really got what's known as *The Fear*. And he's like – he's vomited in between the stacks, and with that, rushes off stage. And the audience think it's part of the act. This is at the very beginning of the show. So me and Jimmy had to take over, singing and playing, getting through it like that. Andy didn't know what was happening. So it was like a trio, the two McCulloch brothers and me. And we just about saved the day, because Jimmy was an *excellent* guitar player, he was an absolutely fantastic guitar player, 16 years old. A wonder. And that's what saved us.

The following evening, Thunderclap Newman had somehow sufficiently recovered from this fiasco to be able to perform at Van Dyke's in Plymouth. Perhaps this is where Speedy recalled performing with his back to the audience, an unplugged 12-string slung over his shoulder. Regardless, it would take a long time before he recovered any semblance of his shattered confidence. "They dragged me off drums and put me on guitar," Keen said the following year. "I couldn't play and they made me sing in a key I couldn't reach. It was pathetic. The hype was bigger than us. In fact my guitar playing was so useless I wasn't plugged in half the time, and the first three songs I wrote were done on one string. I was scared to death at the responsibility. After playing drums, my fingers just wouldn't work on a guitar. It's like being a blacksmith and then being told you've got to be a brain surgeon instead."

The next day, July 6th, further recording sessions commenced at Pete Townshend's home studio, spanning four days. All involved were doubtless bleary-eyed: Newman and co. having just completed a long drive back from Plymouth; Townshend having performed two shows with The Who at the Royal Albert Hall the previous night, part of the 'Pop Proms' lineup with Chuck Berry. The sessions were complicated by the presence of Townshend's three-month-old daughter Emma. "I think occasionally his wife sort of wagged the finger about keeping the baby awake," said Newman. "We'd do a recording and get something done to a certain point, and he'd say, 'Right, we're going to have to stop now because baby's got to get some sleep!'" Accordingly, Townshend did not hesitate to apply some sorely needed discipline to the proceedings. Keen later told *ZigZag* that Townshend "used to come out yelling, "Fucking get it together!,"'" which is not at all hard to believe after hearing Jim Avery's account of Townshend's tirade at the corn mill, even though Townshend later denied that he resorted to such practices in the studio: "That's not me. Glyn Johns does that to The Who, mate. It's not making a creative contribution."

One item of discussion during the sessions was the group's next single. "Speedy has written so many great numbers that are musically much better than the hit and we have one recorded already which might be the follow up," Jack McCulloch told Chris Welch. "But we want to re-record it as we aren't happy with the arrangement." McCulloch is presumably referring here to 'Accidents,' which the group had recorded at the beginning of the year. "The next single might be called 'Accidents,' a number which Speedy composed, or one of several which Speedy, Jimmy and I wrote together," Andy said at the time. "Or it might be a fusion of several which we may take and orchestrate or arrange. We'll be putting several tracks down during the month and starting an album for late summer or autumn, depending on what is decided and knowing how things tend to get delayed." Interestingly, *ZigZag* reported that same month that "at the moment, Bent Frame are at IBC in Portland Place (where the Who and Thunderclap record) producing their first single – 'Accidents', written by Speedy Keen. If Pete Townshend and Roger Daltrey are both satisfied with the result, it will be released by Track in August."

On July 10th, the day after the group's four-day stretch of recording sessions had concluded, Thunderclap Newman again performed on *Top Of The Pops*, their single perched atop the charts for a second straight week. "We just watched ourselves on *Top Of The Pops*," Andy Newman told *Melody Maker* the following week. "We followed the Rolling Stones and I'm afraid Mick Jagger's performance showed up all our iniquities. For example, I was told to move around and smile and I have a feeling

I rather overdid the moving and smiling.[49] Also, I didn't know they were going to do a close-up of my hand while playing the piano, which filled the entire screen, otherwise I would have manicured my fingers. Still, one mustn't let success go to one's head."

Meanwhile, Thunderclap Newman vacated the Old Corn Mill, whose owners had returned from a trip overseas. Chris Welch paid the group a visit on their final evening at the cottage. "The first part of the evening was spent imbibing considerable quantities of ale in the Robin Hood," Welch wrote in an article which appeared in the July 19th edition of *Melody Maker*. "Andy drinks only Coca Cola but manages to loon as heavily as any beer head. While a ferocious game of bar football was in progress, involving Jim and a team of locals, Speedy, Jack and Andy managed to conduct a conversation above the racket. "Little Jimmy has been abducted by a girl in a Simca[50], who I believe has carried him off to the woods," chuckled Andy, and indeed there was considerable mystery as to his whereabouts. Speedy was anxious to return to London on business..."

"...The fantastic success of their first record, which has proved to be Track's fastest and biggest selling single, has taken the group unawares," Welch went on. "The most they had hoped for initially was a healthy showing in the lower regions of the chart. They have been working daily to prepare an act and get used to playing in public together. They are excited and nervous. Above all they are

---

49 "I do not go in for the gyrating antics as do other members of the popular music profession," Andy told *Record Mirror*. "I try to concentrate my efforts on the production of music rather than the curious sideways-kicking actions which other performers carry out with great efficaciousness, with the obvious intention of distracting the audience from their musical disability."

50 The Simca belonged to Gil Woodley. "Yeah I had a Simca," she recalled, "but for my 21st birthday I got a convertible Mercedes, a 190SL. They shot a video, just Andy, Speedy and Jimmy sitting up on the back while I was driving. What it was for I don't remember – I've never been able to find it."

determined to succeed as a valid musical contribution."

Welch's account of this period revealed a renewed focus, presumably the result of Pete Townshend's motivational visit and the group's daily interactions with him during the recent recording sessions. "We've been working all day – and now we can play a programme that lasts well over an hour," Jack McCulloch told Welch. "We're trying to get a really full sound. Very few people use our kind of line-up so I think it's a very original sound. …I did my first gig with them last Friday and it was mainly a teenybopper crowd. Then we did the Van Dyke Club, Plymouth and Andy freaked them out. He was doing his 'Water Music' with bird call effects which breaks into rock and roll."

Welch asked the elder McCulloch whether he thought the group would be able to retain the attention of their initial audience. "I'll tell you in six weeks' time," Jack replied. "It will either be a great success or a disastrous flop." The answer would become evident in half the time.

Welch's account of the group's final evening at the Old Corn Mill (or, more accurately, at the Robin Hood) continued: "…Andy heaved a way through the crowd, beaming, in a combat jacket. "A young girl recently came to me for an autograph and as she had come a long way, I decided to give her a lift home. When we arrived the entire street came out to meet us and I had to sign the wallpaper in every room of her parents' house!"

> At this moment two of Andy's greatest admirers arrived in the pub, proving that he really has become a fantastic hit with teenage girl fans. "Ah, ha! Here comes the Blonde Bombshell and the White Tornado," he exclaimed as the girls rushed over to exchange greetings. Other greetings came by post, for Andy had received several telegrams from old colleagues and even the staff of the local

newspaper who had enjoyed discovering Thunderclap in their midst. This reminder of his past caused Andy to relate some of the dangers that face the telephone engineer about his daily duties. "You know, the trouble with some of the point boxes in the City are that they often accumulate gas. And if you are incautious enough to go down one with a cigarette on, without first having tested the gas content, there is a big flash and you see the manhole lids blowing off all down the street. The sound resonates to the frequency of the pipe." And here Andy performed an amazingly life-like impersonation of a series of gas explosions fading into the distance.

At this point somebody broke in to ask Andy, the acknowledged fountain head of all knowledge in Liphook: "What is a balalaika?" "It's a three-stringed Caucasian harp," said Andy without need of a second to ponder.

…We strolled back to the cottage from the pub down the silent, dark country lane, Andy arm-in-arm with the Blonde Bombshell and the White Tornado, who later confided that they thought Andy was "lovely" and "ever so intelligent" and were sure he would never become big-headed. While the group's roadies Alan and Keith were loading up a Ford Transit with tons of equipment for an impending tour of Scotland, Thunderclap regaled me in the cottage with the sounds of Bix Beiderbecke, Jabbo Smith, Louis Armstrong, Romeo Nelson, Lionel Hampton, Gene Krupa and King Oliver.

On Friday, July 11th, Thunderclap Newman returned to the road, playing what was billed as their FIRST PUBLIC

CONCERT at Leeds Town Hall, with the Scottish group White Trash supporting, among others.[51] This was clearly not the group's first public concert, but one can't fault them for looking for a fresh start. The event was promoted by Pleasure Machine Enterprises, a mobile discotheque outfit operated by Doug Smith and a partner.[52] "What I did was I hustled record companies for records, so we had the records for free, and we were able to promote their artists," Smith recalled. "I started sort of pushing Thunderclap Newman's record. I wasn't paid for it, and as a payment from Track, the management gave me a date. And in July 1969 at Leeds Town Hall, I promoted Thunderclap Newman."

> So anyway, this partner of mine, not only was he an old masters art dealer, he was also an accountant. And he was a little bit of a wide boy, but a well-spoken wide boy, if you understand my meaning. If he saw an opportunity, he dived in, and one of the opportunities was a friend of his in France owned a vineyard and asked him if he'd like to import champagne. So we went up to Leeds with a couple of boxes of champagne, and I mean *boxes*, as well. And we got to the gig, and …we marched into the band's dressing room and gave them a box of champagne. So by the time they went onstage… [laughs]. The gig was terrible. It just was a real disappointment.

Fortunately for Smith, Thunderclap Newman were

---

51 White Trash were a Scottish band signed to Apple which featured keyboardist Ronnie Leahy, later of Stone The Crows, the group Jimmy McCulloch would go on to join in 1972. Leahy had been a member of The Pathfinders, contemporaries of The Jaygars in Glasgow in the mid '60s.

52 Smith would later become Motorhead's manager and would cross paths with Speedy Keen in the late 1970s.

booked for two performances, and this was after the matinee gig; there was a chance for the group to redeem themselves later that evening. "At the end of the matinee, all the audience marched out and said, "Fucking awful – we want our money back!," Smith recalled. "It took a bit of negotiation, but in the end I persuaded them, because they all went on about the fact that White Trash were "bloody great" and all this. And I said I tell you what, why don't you come back and see White Trash in the second show, and I won't give you your money back [laughs]. And they did. And as it happens, on the second show, Thunderclap and the band smartened up a bit."

After Leeds, the group continued north for three shows in Scotland, at Kilmarnock Town Hall (July 12th), Kinema Dunfermline (13th) and Glasgow's Electric Garden (14th). Coupled with the news that 'Something In The Air' remained at number one for a second consecutive week, the presence of native Scots Jimmy and Jack meant that the group was in for an enthusiastic reception. "Every time we did a gig up north or in Scotland we'd get half murdered," Speedy told Nik Cohn in 1973. "The local heavies would come swarming up onstage and we'd disappear out the bog windows." Glasgow, being the McCullochs' home turf, was particularly raucous. "[The audience] thought we were a Scottish band because of the two McCullochs in the band, and they went berserk so we didn't have to do much," Jim Avery recalled. "It was like – screaming and shouting. In those clubs, it was just like a sweat shop – we just sweated onstage. It's like stepping into an oven, and you come out and it's as though you've been swimming with all your clothes on. I have a newspaper, the center page of the *Daily Record* and the whole of the center page is just girls screaming. And you could see the band in the background all disheveled with sweat – it looked like we'd just come out of the pool."

Avery recalled he and Jimmy being mobbed in Glasgow. "We were staying in the hotel, and they said, "Do not leave the hotel." Which to me meant that I was going out. And Jimmy said, "I'm going with you." So we went out and I suppose it was Jimmy who got recognized, and all these girls ganged up on us and they got pairs of scissors out – they were going to cut bits of clothing, bits of hair. Suddenly it was getting very frightening, so we had to make a big dash to the hotel, and Jimmy was frightened out of his mind – I don't think he went out again for about a year!"

Upon their return to London[53] on July 15th, Thunderclap Newman undertook three more days of recording at both Pete Townshend's home studio and IBC. Another slot on *Top Of The Pops* followed on July 17th, the group's fourth and final appearance on the program. 'Something In The Air' remained at number one, but the Rolling Stones were now nipping at their heels, 'Honky Tonk Women' having climbed to number 3.

The following day, Thunderclap Newman appeared at the Coatham Hotel in Redcar, on the bill with Deep Purple, the group's second performance with new lead singer Ian Gillan. Though Deep Purple were reportedly paid £150 – more than double the £60 received by Thunderclap Newman – it had been decided that Thunderclap Newman should headline the gig based on their current number one hit. However, as Jack McCulloch later explained, "We realized the problem and turned round to Deep Purple and said, "Look, this is fucking stupid," …it

53 "When they went back to London and the lease was up on the house, Jimmy actually moved in with us because he didn't want to go back," Gil Woodley recalled. "I mean, he obviously had to go back to London to do appearances and everything, but he stayed with us." Sometimes Martin Woodley and Jimmy would thumb a ride or take the train into London. "We just got to hang out and do things like normal teenagers," Martin recalled. "We went to Battersea fun fair I don't know how many times."

was all Deep Purple's crowd. We said, "We'll go on first because you're the bigger band," and they thought that was great." Thunderclap therefore took the stage first, to a hostile crowd: "We went onstage and as soon as we got on, people were throwing coins at us," Jack recalled. "We had to come off after about a quarter of an hour because it was too dangerous."

Jim Avery remembered things a little differently – "[Deep Purple] were shit hot – we could not compete – but luckily our extremely loud screaming fans drowned out our inadequacies," he recalled.

"I believe they were mainly Deep Purple fans," Andy said a few months later. "But after three numbers only one bloke was left booing, and after the fourth number he was cheering! The booing never upset me, in fact I remember with great pleasure the occasions when we changed an aggressive, hostile audience by playing something they had possibly never heard before. I prefer a cheering or booing audience to a quiet audience that doesn't react at all."

On Sunday, July 20th, the day after a performance at Nantwich Civic Hall, Thunderclap Newman performed at The Place, in Hanley. "Every up-and-coming band wanted to play The Place club because it was one of those places that had a reputation of being a good gig," Jack McCulloch recalled in 2008, appearing alongside Andy Newman on the television program *Those Were The Days*. "The place was heaving. There was a buzz about the moon shot; everyone wanted to be a part of it, this was a worldwide special event, something that would never happen again." The world was anxiously awaiting news of the lunar landing, as the Apollo 11 mission was due to touch down on the moon that very evening. "We were informed by – I think it was the owner – that he was going to give us updates," Jack said, "so every now and again when we were playing, in the middle of the set, he would come up like a bad bingo caller." Andy

Newman recalled that the group extended their set at the promoter's behest. "We went on to do our set, and the promoter came up to us and said look, would you please stay on because I want to announce when they land on the moon," Newman said later. "…and so we carried on."

The buzz about the moon landing was made more meaningful for the McCullochs due to their father's connection to the event: James McCulloch, Sr. worked for the engineering firm that made the transmission for the crawler-transporter which moved the Saturn rocket from its assembly building to the launch pad. "At the time it was the biggest vehicle that had ever been built," Andy Newman explained. "So the McCulloch brothers had a personal sort of stake in that moon landing."

Thunderclap Newman's set that evening was their longest ever, extending well into the early hours, as the moon landing didn't take place until nearly 4am. After their standard set was complete, ending with 'Something In The Air', the group went into extended jams to fill the time. Afterwards, the five exhausted musicians collapsed into the dressing room – but not for long. "We'd just come offstage," Newman recalled. "We were in the dressing room and some of the members of the band actually smoked that terrible thing called marijuana, and there was quite a lot of this going down, and then suddenly one of the roadies came back and said, "Get rid of that stuff, there's four coppers coming this way across the dance floor!" And anyway, absolute trauma, "We're all going to get arrested!", and all the rest of it, so they said, "They're looking for you!" – me, you see. So I said okay, so out I went. All they wanted was me autograph for their kids!" Later, at the hotel, the landlady forced Newman out of bed. "The money which was supposed to have been spent on the hotel had been spent on other things, shall we say recreational drugs," said Newman. "Certainly nothing to do with me, and I had to put my hand in my pocket and give this woman every penny I had so we could stay in the hotel and get a night's sleep."

On the following night, the group performed a set of more conventional length at the Bath Pavilion. Although they didn't know it at the time, it would be Thunderclap Newman's last live performance that year. It would be another eighteen months before they'd perform onstage again.

The Apollo 11 mission came to an end with the crew splashing down in the Pacific Ocean on July 24th. A few days later, Thunderclap Newman's three-week ride in the stratosphere also ended when the Rolling Stones displaced them from the top of the charts with 'Honky Tonk Women', which would hold the top spot for five weeks. 'Something In The Air' remained in the top ten for another three weeks.

The group flew to Germany for an August 2nd appearance on the TV show *Beat Club*, where they performed 'Something In The Air'. "When we got to number one, the biggest pop show in Europe was *Beat Club* in Germany, and we got flown there to do that show," Jim Avery recalled. "Same again – basically miming, we had the backing track, we tried to play our little bits on top of it, it's a procedure, like in Britain on *Top of the Pops*, they had to have a vocal track, but Speedy got round it because he double-tracked the vocal on the single, so he could sing along with a vocal track in the background. Jimmy wasn't allowed to play in a foreign country," Avery said of McCulloch, who had celebrated his 16th birthday in June. "And Kit Lambert, he went to public school and all that, and his father was Constant Lambert – he was a big deal in the aristocracy world, so he phoned up somebody who ran the passport office and suddenly Jimmy had the ok to go to Hamburg."

Although they had dates booked through the end of July and into August, Thunderclap Newman's brief 1969

U.K. tour mercifully came to a premature end. "It ended up at the Bath Pavilion, and they pulled us off because all the gigs after that had been negotiated when they thought we weren't going to do any good," Andy Newman recalled. "And so they were like, literally for peanuts. And so effectively, what they did, they told these people, if they paid more money they'd get us, if they didn't they wouldn't. They wouldn't, so they didn't." Newman, who later told Chris Welch that the reason they were pulled off the road was "because the cost of lugging my piano around became a handicap and the vibration of moving it put it out of tune," was avoiding the elephant in the room: The group's live act remained an utter mess.

To begin with, Speedy's voice often would be reduced to a squeak by the end of the night. "I mean, half the time when it came to the ending number, I think me and Jimmy were singing 'Something In The Air', you know: 'Call out the fumigators,' et cetera," Jim Avery recalled.

> 'Cause he couldn't be heard – he'd go up to the mike and just *eeehhh eeeehhh*. A singer who couldn't project his voice, a pianist who was out of time… eventually on that first tour, it got so bad, Jimmy said he didn't want to do it anymore, and Speedy didn't want to do it anymore. And that was the end of that. That's why Track took us off the road. It was laughable; it was unbearable, I mean there was Andy Newman, he introduced something called… was it 'Water Music'? And he was using bird calls and standing up there and blowing his whistles and things. And of course the guys in Deep Purple were on the floor! And me and Jimmy are so embarrassed, 'cause we'd both been in rock bands. It was a complete fiasco.

"We didn't want to do an on-the-road-band thing," Keen reflected to *ZigZag* in September 1970. "We just wanted to record mine and Jimmy's songs – a nice relaxed sort of thing, using this guy Andy, who was very strange. I knew it would be hard to work with him because he's so, how can I put it, straight." But when 'Something In The Air' began rapidly ascending the charts, everything changed. "Everyone was saying "Where's the band then, bring out the band." So Track sent us to the country to get it together, which was a total disaster, and then we went on the road, which was an even bigger disaster."

> Getting us on the road was very expensive, because I was into everybody having 4 cabinets, 36 cabinets for the PA and Track laid it all out, which was very good of them because I'd been laying blagues on them for two years and they knew that… but they also knew that under pressure I finally came up with a song. Anyway, we went on the road and did a tour of England which as I said was a nervous wreck of a disaster. There was always this reaction by the audience of not knowing how to act – they wanted to scream at Jimmy, but they didn't know what to do about Andy. It was successful, but not musically successful… I mean I couldn't ask Andy to play rock'n'roll when he'd never heard any because if you just play it mechanically from sheet music it sounds dreadful. So we didn't really have time to work things out because we had to capitalize on the record before people forgot about it.

"We were forced to go on the tour really, because of the success of the record," Speedy told Dutch Radio host Wim Noordhoek in 1975. "The tour really was the killer in it because it was put together in a very loose, friendly, social level and to suddenly have the pressure of backing up a single really was very difficult. ...It was very hard work when you ...play a gig and it'd be like: The Electric Jackplugs, with 30,000 watts, followed by the Inflamed Earholes, with 50,000 watts, followed by The Golden Sparkplugs with 100,000 watts, and then Thunderclap Newman, right, with like a seven foot contrabass saxophone and a 30 watt amplifier."

When Noordhoek offered that the band "wasn't really fit to go on tour," Speedy agreed. "Not really, no," he said.

"We were hoping to bang the whole thing into some sort of shape but what it actually did was destroy us," Speedy told *ZigZag*. "Andy for one wasn't equipped to play in front of big audiences at a big rock venue. I just really wish we could have just recorded because it put me through so many changes I couldn't believe it. I really felt strongly about 'Something In The Air'...obviously I didn't foresee it being a huge success, but really and truly it was a reflection of what I was seeing at the time. ...It backfired on us really because we weren't in a position to follow up its success... it's especially difficult if you're not equipped, and I definitely wasn't. On the first four or five gigs I played a 12-string that wasn't even plugged in, and when you're doing that in front of 2,000 people it takes a lot of nerve... you've got to have a lot of front – more front than Selfridges in fact. After ten or so gigs like that you come off like scrambled eggs because you're lying to yourself and to all those people. I think it was really heavy for all of us."

CHAPTER 7
HOLLYWOOD DREAM

Thunderclap Newman with Jim Avery and Jack McCulloch, summer 1969. Courtesy of Pr4vte Records

"I think it's an incredible album."
– Speedy Keen, 1975

"I love it all. Recording it is one of my favourite experiences. People that know and love that record are very special people in my eyes."
– Pete Townshend, 2022

On August 16th 1969, the day after Thunderclap Newman's canceled appearance at the town hall in Torquay, capacity 1,500, Pete Townshend and The Who navigated the mud at Max Yasgur's farm in Bethel, New York as they prepared to perform in front of nearly half a million at the Woodstock Music and Arts Fair. In the middle of The Who's set, activist Abbie Hoffman, apparently unaware of the incident that had occurred onstage at the Fillmore a few months earlier, decided to hijack the microphone to make a political speech. A furious Townshend bayoneted him with his Gibson SG, and, like his predecessor, Hoffman leapt offstage, leaving The Who to return to a glorious performance of *Tommy*, augmented by the world's best light show: Just as they reached the end of their set with 'See Me, Feel Me', the sun came up.

Meanwhile, back in the U.K., the August 16th editions of the music weeklies reported the Thunderclap Newman shakeup in their various ways. The *NME* ran two stories, with the headlines NEWMAN: U.S. TOUR OFF TILL SPRING, TWO MEMBERS QUIT and ROCK MADE JIM AND JACK QUIT. *Melody Maker* went with the slightly less sensational (and lower case) "Thunderclap Newman Split." The weeklies reported that Jim Avery and Jack McCulloch, ages 21 and 20 respectively, had left Thunderclap Newman as of Friday August 8th, and would not be replaced. The group would continue as a trio. "The reason there was discontent was because Thunderclap

Newman are coming off the road to concentrate on an album and the next single," a Track spokesman told *Melody Maker*. "Kit Lambert is sifting through some new Speedy Keen compositions for the single and the album will be started as soon as Pete Townshend returns from America."

With the *NME* reporting that the six-week American tour set to begin in October with Track labelmates The Who and Marsha Hunt (with Arthur Brown "being considered for inclusion") now delayed until April 1970, it appears that the plan was for the recording of the album to be complete by then, and for Thunderclap Newman to be back on the road. Interestingly, the article also noted that "no decision has been reached regarding the release of 'Accidents' as the follow-up single to 'Something In The Air', according to the group's recording manager, Pete Townshend." As *ZigZag* had reported back in July, Bent Frame had recorded a version of the song at IBC studios that month. In September, *Beat Instrumental* announced, "Look out for Bent Frame and keep your ears open for the very good and very commercial single 'Accidents'. We have the feeling that you are going to be hearing an awful lot of it if Track have their way." Clearly there was momentum towards Bent Frame releasing their version of the song.

Perhaps Track wanted 'Accidents' released by an active band, one that could promote the song via live performances, hence letting Bent Frame run with the single. But perhaps Track then deemed the Bent Frame version of the song unsatisfactory. Or perhaps all involved were distracted with the myriad other things going on at the time – the writing of the next Who single, the writing and recording of Townshend's Meher Baba tribute album *Happy Birthday*, plus a scattering of live Who gigs – the result being a lack of clear direction for Thunderclap Newman. Whatever the reason, all of this back and forth with 'Accidents' contributed to Thunderclap Newman's follow-up to 'Something

In The Air' being delayed for another ten months, finally seeing release in June 1970. The Bent Frame version has never surfaced. Meanwhile, all future booked live dates for Thunderclap Newman – and there were several, including their planned appearance on Friday August 22nd at the Humberside Pop Festival which was reported in the very same editions of the papers that announced the breakup – were canceled.

The headlines stating that Jim Avery and Jack McCulloch 'quit' the group were a little misleading, as Avery said their hand was forced. "We were taken off the road, so you don't need the augmented musicians," he said. "Chris [Stamp] more or less said to Jack, "We can keep you on as house musicians," and Jack said, "Will you pay us?", and of course Chris said no. I pushed off straight away."

"Speedy didn't want me writing songs," Avery added. ""I'm the songwriter," he said. And yet somehow later on, Jimmy and Jack stepped in and wrote a few things, which was acceptable, but me – no." Perhaps Keen, suffering from a chronic lack of confidence, viewed Avery, with his Writers Workshop background, as a threat. "Speedy sort of turned against me, which was weird," said Avery.[54] "I mean, he had nothing to complain about because I was playing what he wanted on the stage. Speedy wanted to get rid of me – and he succeeded."

Avery and McCulloch, frustrated at their former band's impotent live act and the lack of creative input, set out to form a new group with the working name of Wild Country. "We were very discontented with the way things were going," Jack told *Melody Maker*. "We had no individual freedom. Everything we played was laid down to us, and

---

54 The following year, Keen told *ZigZag*, "For the road, we had to augment the group, so we got in a friend of mine called Jim (who's now an enemy of mine)…" By 1972, the pair were again on friendly terms.

we had to do it." The pair quickly enlisted 18-year-old guitarist Terry Keyworth (who also played trumpet, trombone and piano) and 16-year-old keyboardist Stuart Whitcombe and began writing and rehearsing in the Woodley's cottage on the grounds of Standford Grange. "One reason why Jim and I split from Thunderclap was that our songs weren't accepted," Jack told the press. "Everyone in Wild Country writes material and this is what we'll play. Terry and Jim will do most of the vocals, although we'll switch around a bit. Our sound is a bit like Creedence Clearwater and a little bit like the Band. Country-based with a definite rock feel." The group, yet to sign a recording contract, were planning a debut single for release in the new year, soon to be followed by an album. "We want to work on the road – which Thunderclap didn't," said Jack. "We've already done a few local gigs and reaction has been very good. We're planning a Scottish tour soon."

Since Jimmy McCulloch also wanted to work on the road, and with his current band sidelined from touring as they focused on studio work, he lived with Wild Country at the cottage and sometimes joined them on stage. "Jimmy would come down and play with us," said Jim Avery. "Of course the crowd were really into the blues thing in those years, and there's Jimmy playing the blues. And they loved it." Unfortunately, the presence of the younger McCulloch proved to be the group's undoing. "The record companies and management that were looking into us – that would be Enthoven and Gaydon, who managed King Crimson – they looked at us and said, 'Yeah, we'll take you on, but we have to have Jimmy'," said Avery. "And Track weren't letting go of Jimmy, the golden boy." Wild Country soon folded.

During the month of August, 'Something In The Air' gradually descended the U.K. charts, but made its first appearance in the U.S. top 100. By the end of the month, the single was number 26 in the U.K., and 82 in the U.S. The song peaked at a disappointing number 37 in the U.S. for a week at the end of October. By December, Thunderclap Newman were awarded a gold disc for 'Something In The Air' having reached world sales of over a million.

While Pete Townshend was in the U.S. with The Who in August, he visited Atlantic Records' New York office in connection with Thunderclap Newman[55] and conducted an interview which was published in the *Detroit Free Press*. The subject of Thunderclap Newman's live challenges came up. "They are definitely a cabaret act if they do appear," Pete told Mike Gormley. "Concerts or one-nighters just wouldn't be possible with this group. Other musicians had to be brought in to duplicate the sound they had on the record. They didn't like doing that so they just don't appear anymore." Townshend also discussed recording plans. "The album isn't too far away," he said. "It will be out in September or October. We're going to try to get some famous-ish musicians to play on the tracks. People we've talked to are most of the Small Faces, Ron Wood and some other members of the old Jeff Beck group." It's unclear what transpired with these plans, if anything, but none of these musicians were credited on the finished album, nor are there any accounts of them recording with Thunderclap Newman. And Townshend's timeline proved hopelessly optimistic: The album would indeed surface in October, but it was October *1970* – a full year later.

Recording work resumed at Townshend's home within days of The Who's return from the U.S. around August 20th. Ten days later, *Melody Maker* reported that Thunderclap Newman would have "a new single out in six to eight weeks' time. The group have recorded several tracks under the supervision of Pete Townshend, and the new

55 Atlantic would handle the group's distribution in the U.S.

single is likely to be chosen from these." On the same page was a report that Keith Moon had broken his foot when he fell down the stairs at his home. Moon's injury didn't prevent The Who from flying to Hamburg, Germany from August 26-28 where they mimed to a selection of songs from *Tommy* for the *Beat Club* television program. Moon required pain-killing injections in his ankle before The Who's performance at the Isle Of Wight festival on August 30th. Further scattered live dates for The Who in England, Scotland and Holland over the next thirty days rendered any Thunderclap sessions very much a stop-and-start affair.

During the down time between sessions, the group members went their separate ways. Speedy worked on pulling together finished demos from the fragments of songs he'd composed, while stories regarding the activities of the ever-restless Jimmy soon appeared in the music weeklies. In early September, the *NME* dropped a tantalizing one-liner reporting "Sensational: Thunderclap Newman's jamming with Love Affair at Dunstable recently." A report in the *Record Mirror* the following week provided more details and made it likely that "Thunderclap Newman jamming with Love Affair" was probably Jimmy McCulloch jamming with Love Affair, although perhaps Andy Newman accompanied him. It soon emerged that McCulloch's involvement with the group was deeper than that. "Although Love Affair's next single is expected to be a Phillip Goodhand-Tait number, Steve [Ellis] himself has recently been composing along with the 16-year-old wonder from Thunderclap Newman, Jimmy McCulloch," *Record Mirror* reported in mid-September. "I started writing with Jimmy a few weeks ago," said Ellis. "We've finished a couple of numbers and they are both completely different. One is kind of Trafficky, and the other is rather like Fairport Convention. I think they're

180

great. ...Thunderclap Newman might be using some of the things that Jimmy and I write, but it depends on whether Pete Townshend likes them. He's so talented, I feel embarrassed even to give him the tapes. For me he's the ace pop writer, he does more for me than Paul McCartney."

Ellis soon left Love Affair and began working with others. Jim Avery recalled performing with Jimmy and Jack McCulloch and Steve Ellis a few months later. "[Ellis] wanted to form a group with Jack, Jimmy and me, and we did this gig at the Marquee," Avery said. "But Track, the management, suddenly they realize that we're doing this gig at the Marquee and they put their foot down and said no way. And, if we had Jimmy with us, the band was going to be called Blue Glue."

Andy Newman, meanwhile, was spotted at the *Melody Maker* awards in late September at London's Waldorf Hotel. Thunderclap Newman had landed at number two in the poll results for BRIGHTEST HOPE, second only to new supergroup Blind Faith. *Melody Maker*'s report, accompanied by a photo of Andy "sporting a curiously-shaped wooden pipe," with "young lady escort" sitting in his lap[56], reported, "...there was a happy if unlikely drinking team which included Eric Clapton, Thunderclap Newman, Peter Green and Keith Moon. In fact, a great deal of alcohol was consumed during the proceedings – which ran from midday to three in the afternoon – and afterwards ...much of the mob went to the Cottage Club, a haunt of musicians and journalists, where Roy Eldridge won a who-can-down-a-half-the-quickest contest. Keith Emerson had to rescue his girlfriend from Denmark, model and dancer Elinor Lund from certain *MM* staffmen, while

---

56 This image of Andy was perhaps less uncharacteristic than one might otherwise think. The following July, he served as a judge at the 'Miss Model Girl 1970' contest at the La Valbonne Club. The winner, incidentally, was Rachel Storm, daughter of chaplain to the Queen, Canon Peter Gillingham.

Thunderclap cheerfully chatted on about Bix Beiderbecke."

Newman needed some time to decompress after the blur of TV appearances, recording and rehearsal sessions and live performances that occupied June, July and August. "I look at the tour schedules and everything we did in that very, very short period of time," he said, "and I think well, how did I manage it? I mean, it was amazing, but I'm not sure I could go through that again." When asked if he enjoyed it, Newman responded, "Umm, well... some of it was enjoyable, some of it was not so enjoyable. It was going so fast, you didn't really have a chance to sort of enjoy it or not enjoy it. You just got it done, and then got on with the next one. It's rather like the stories you get from people in war zones where they had so much happening that they just had to get on with it, and hope that they would not be the one that would stop the bullets. And I must admit, when it was all finished I felt the effects of it, when we finally sort of stopped working and had a bit of a break."

In early October, as The Who were departing for a six-week tour of the U.S., *Record Mirror* reported that "The new Thunderclap Newman single will not now be 'Accidents' as previously reported. It will be 'Hollywood' and is in the McCartney vein and very funky[57] according to reports from Track Records. ...A spokesman for Track said: "Thunderclap Newman will be going on the road as a trio. If the sound of piano, lead guitar and drums doesn't work out, they'll be aided by session musicians." From the outset, this plan was unworkable: Keen had already demonstrated that he couldn't sing and play the drums at the same time. The group stayed off the road. It had been five months since the release of 'Something In The Air,' and two months since the group's last live performance. With no live act, their single fading from the charts and nothing

---

57 'Funky' was not a term often used to describe a Thunderclap Newman song.

to follow it up, Thunderclap Newman were becoming a commercial nonentity.

In late December, Chris Welch sat down with Andy Newman and discussed the group's recent work. "The band that soared to number one on the *MM* chart with 'Something In The Air' last July has practically vanished from sight," Welch wrote, adding that Newman was far from being disillusioned or disappointed. ""Fed up? Oh Lor' no!" said Andy, eating a toasted sandwich in a Fleet Street toasted sandwich bar this week." Newman told Welch that "Thunderclap Newman has been working on an LP which should be out in January or February, about the same time as a new single. ...Apart from some TV we have made no 'live' appearances since we came off the road last August, but we have been busy recording and trying things out," he said. "...The next single will probably be called 'Hollywood,' a tune written by Speedy, but we are having trouble selecting a B side. It should have a contrasting musical structure."

"It was a shame the full musical potential of this strange, unlikely group was not fully realized at the time of their hit," Welch lamented, "but there is still the chance for Thunderclap, Jimmy and Speedy to show the world they were not a one-hit wonder."

A few weeks later, on New Year's Day, Welch interviewed Pete Townshend over breakfast at Townshend's home. "...Despite a New Year's Eve hangover, Peter was happy to answer pressing questions," Welch reported. "One of the causes Townshend wishes to champion most is that of Thunderclap Newman, who Pete describes as a genius. And having heard several of the hundreds of tapes that Pete possesses of Andy's work I am bound to agree. ...A number one hit single last summer was the result of their first collaboration. "But I had to go away to America with the Who in the middle of it all and that number one was so unexpected," Townshend told Welch.

I never even got to see them play a gig, although I hear it was a disaster and the audiences were fantastically disappointed. Andy enjoyed the tour, but people thought they were going to be a rock group, which wasn't the idea. I came back from the States and found they had been contracted to make a lot of appearances. So I thought the best thing would be to let them forge ahead. Then we found we had to take them off the road. We want them to concentrate on recording, but Jimmy badly wants to work and make appearances so he is going to form his own group while remaining with Thunderclap, to do an album and singles. Jimmy will go on the road and may record on his own as well. Of course financially it didn't do them any good at all, despite having a number one single. There was nothing to follow it up and I feel very guilty about it.

Work continued on the album in January and February 1970, the majority of the sessions taking place at Townshend's tiny home studio, known as Eel Pie Sound. In January, Townshend and the group had about two weeks to work together before The Who embarked on a short tour of European opera houses, during which they also found the time to record their next single, 'The Seeker', at IBC studios. In February, Townshend issued the Meher Baba tribute album *Happy Birthday*, and The Who played two live dates, both of which were recorded. The album *Live At Leeds* was the result. During off days, Townshend and the members of Thunderclap Newman would gather at his home studio.

The recording equipment used during the majority of the Thunderclap Newman sessions consisted of the same pair of Revox model G36 stereo tape machines that had been used to record the first handful of songs in late 1968/early 1969. It was a simple setup, expertly operated by Townshend, who'd been multitracking demos for years. "This is just a two-track tape recorder, but it's got self-synching on it," Townshend explained to *Rolling Stone*'s Jonathan Cott a few months later. "I can put something on one track and then put something on the other directly parallel to it. Then I can get those two tracks, which were in this case voice and acoustic on one track and drums on the other, mix them together adding a bass guitar and put it onto one track of another tape recorder. Then on the other recorder I've got guitar, voice, drums, and bass together and I put a piano on the next track of that recorder. And then I mix those two tracks down onto the *other* recorder again in stereo, adding a guitar."

"We always recorded more than one person at a time, so sometimes we only needed three passes," he told Paul Salley. "'Accidents' is a good example. On that, I played bass, mixed the other musicians' levels, and also flew in the sound effects from a pre-made tape."

"This is where Pete excelled himself – playing bass, mixing it down, and recording it all at the same time," Speedy told *ZigZag* in 1975. "He used to make all his own demos for The Who," Keen told Dutch radio that same year, "…and on my life, I mean they were incredible as they were… before The Who even did them. He'd always done that, so that part of the hill was already overcome. But, like, to play bass and mix down all at the same time, because once you do it, it's done – you've either got to re-do it or – do you understand what I mean? When you mix things down and add things as you're recording, it's straight on to tape, and most of them were done like that," he said, marveling at Townshend's ability to multitask. "The production on it, to me, is superb, and the quality is superb."

"Most of the stuff we did on the *Hollywood Dream* album was done in his studio at the Embankment, Twickenham, initially with the two Revoxes bouncing between each other," recalled Andy Newman. "He also had one of the earliest Dolby A systems, which was a noise eliminating compression system to get rid of background noise on tape. I think he probably was one of the first people to have it." Townshend indeed had two of the first Dolby A machines available. His studio would become truly state of the art in the coming months. "As time passed, my home studio equipment got better and better, until, in some ways, it was better than some of the studios we worked in," he later told *Guitar Player*. Sessions for an EP by The Who would take place in this studio in the coming months[58], and the iconic synthesizer tracks which are prominently featured on the *Who's Next* album were recorded here.

Townshend's embrace of technology, though, was carefully considered. "Pete Townshend is a little worried about the advancement that is being made with musical equipment and recording studios," *Beat Instrumental*'s Steve Turner wrote the following year. "The technology is beginning to overtake the musician," Townshend told Turner. "The infinite possibilities presented by technologies makes me want to capture the present in a far more simple way." The accolades for Townshend's production of *Hollywood Dream* reflect this ideal, and his description of The Who's music could quite easily be applied to that of Thunderclap Newman: "It's an economy of musical statement," he told Turner. "It's quite simple music directed at the young at heart."

In keeping with this theme of simplicity, most of the band used the instruments at hand in the studio, Keen

---

58 "The success of the Thunderclap sessions gave me the confidence to invite The Who into my home studio," Townshend later wrote. "Absurd really, but we had fun."

playing the Ludwig drum kit, McCulloch playing Townshend's Gibson SG electric and J200 acoustic guitars, and Townshend using a Danelectro bass. Aside from his use of Townshend's Bechstein upright piano, Newman was the exception. The variety of instruments he used – all manner of saxophones, flutes, cymbals, etc. – came mainly from his own collection, although the glockenspiel Newman used on 'Look Around' belonged to his grandfather, a plumber who had died in 1938. "Andrew was very interested in that glockenspiel – he borrowed it, and I think it came back; I can't remember," said his brother Robin.

Given the differences between group members, finding common ground musically was a continuous challenge. "Recording the *Hollywood Dream* album was an incredibly painful experience," Speedy told Charles Shaar Murray in 1975. "Usually in a group you get four guys who get together because they're all from the same neighbourhood and they try and work something out because they're all the same kinda guys, right? Whereas we'd *all* be thinking, 'Why am I working with this bunch of guys?'"

Keen found working with Newman particularly difficult. "I don't want to put them down," he told *Sounds*, "but I'll rush in with great ideas in my head and by the time Andy has solidly told me he won't start anything until he's written all the chords down on a piece of paper I've lost a lot of that initial enthusiasm."

"As it is, I take the song to the studio and have to write down all the chords for him, starting on a piece of paper this big (stretches arms) then a piece of paper this big (stretches arms wider) and end up on a fucking great enormous board bigger than the house and he finally learns the chords," he told *ZigZag*. "But it's still difficult because if you play G, he plays an Andy Newman version of G, which is completely different. But he's a bloody good pianist and he's got a good way of speaking to the papers – they like him."

"We all had to compromise greatly when it came to recording – that shows on our album," Keen said in 1975. "In actual fact the majority of the recordings were really difficult...we had to really concentrate on what we were doing. We knew it was good, but we couldn't go like, 'Hey man, that was heavy'; We'd think, 'Well that track was really hard work'. But two years later we'd suddenly realise how good it was. And we realised at the time that it was all very opposite...it was hard to relate to each other in terms of what we wanted to do and say."

Townshend appears to have been able to facilitate a creative and collaborative atmosphere during the sessions. "He's really fantastic," Speedy said. "We're not one of these groups that comes into the studio, gets stoned and fumbles around for some sort of sound... we go in straight and work hard, and if it's not going well he comes out and bawls "FUCKING GET IT TOGETHER"...he puts a lot of pressure on us because he's either just about to go to America or he's just come back... It was very difficult for Jimmy in the early days, because Pete was Jimmy's idol, but it's OK now." But it didn't appear to be a dictatorship or an oppressive environment: Recall that Townshend referred to these sessions as the most enjoyable of his entire career.

"We composed some of the songs in the studio," said Townshend. "I contributed when necessary but did all the arrangements." He had to coax songs out of Keen at times, as he told *ZigZag* in 1971. "I mean, Speedy very much needs me to tell him that he's written a song. He doesn't know until I've told him. That doesn't mean that I've written it. I mean, he will stand in front of me and I'll say, "Well, what have you got?" and he'll say well, nothing." So I say, "We can't record then, can we. You must have something – what's on that bit of paper there?" "Oh, that's just a few lines I wrote down the other day." "Well, has it got a tune?" I ask... "Yeah – a bit of a tune, but it's not very good." "Well, play us that," and it's a great song like 'Something In The Air'."

But he was emphatic that it was the group themselves who did the bulk of the creative and musical work. "There was an incredible amount of misunderstanding, because I suppose they did look like a manipulated group, or a dreamed-up group," Townshend said. "But a lot came out of the top of their heads. Stuff like 'Hollywood Dream'. ...I gave them a process to work in. ...Thunderclap Newman did the fucking playing. All I did was play engineers. They played. I came up with the arrangements. Jimmy played every solo on that album straight off. Some of them are fantastic, spontaneous chipped solos, considered solos."

Speedy Keen's writing formed the bulk of the songs recorded for *Hollywood Dream*: 'Hollywood #1', 'Hollywood #2', 'Look Around', 'Accidents', 'Something In The Air', 'Wild Country', 'When I Think', 'The Reason', 'The Old Cornmill' and 'I Don't Know', of which Andy Newman said: "I think it's the best song that Speedy wrote." There was one cover song: A version of Bob Dylan's 'Open The Door, Homer', an unreleased track which Dylan had recorded with The Band in 1967 as part of what would eventually be released as *The Basement Tapes* in 1975. Thunderclap Newman recorded the song at IBC studios. "I think I chose that," Townshend said. "It wasn't one of the more successful songs on the album but... it was a song that Speedy and I have always mutually liked and we had the 'basement tapes' before they were released as an album. ... Arthur Brown had 'em, that's right, so they were at Track. There was a good quality version there and we listened to them and liked them. It was the only unreleased one of the basement tapes, so we figured we'd put it out as a single. So it was recorded as a single." Despite these plans, the song was not released as a single.

"'Accidents', "...was one of the very early songs I did,"

Speedy later recalled. "I used to drive a truck, and I used to sort of like get these incredible emotional upsurges... Just suddenly, as I was driving down the road, I would see these ...like four year old kids just marching around, you know. And that's what sprang it up." This also helps explain why Speedy would impulsively pull over and sing his new composition to Richard Barnes and likely others he spotted along his route.

Clocking in at more than nine and a half minutes, 'Accidents' relays the story of various children meeting their demise – not exactly uplifting subject matter, but Keen's delivery and lighthearted melodies render it a beautiful, innocent, heartfelt ode to life. "The kids equally could have been killed in all the instances described in the song, or they could equally have gone home," Speedy said later. "But the onus is on us to make sure that they don't get killed... It was very sincere; sincerely meant."

"Basically, the track that's on the *Hollywood Dream* album is – the first part is their accidents, right – the description of their accidents, and the second part is them presumably going to heaven, which Andy did, right?", Keen explained.

> ...And the last part is the fulfillment of the total song, the meaning of what we were trying to portray in that particular song. And I like that, the accumulation of... it's like breaking the sound barrier, that's the effect we tried to make. Going from one extreme to another really, which it does do, as soon as Andy begins, you don't forget the song that's come before. For some reason it worked incredibly like that with him – because normally, if somebody starts playing the piano like that, under normal circumstances you forget the song that's gone down before, or what's happened previous to

it. But he had that sort of quality of playing things which, though they didn't fit in rock & roll terms, they fitted in in *sense* terms...

'Accidents' in particular made perfect sense to Townshend, who told *Rolling Stone* in 1970 that "the original demo's just a guy with a twelve-string going and someone was hitting a cardboard box in the background. But I mean the first time I heard it, it completely blew my mind. I just knew it was incredible." Today he says, "the version on the album is a masterpiece."

One advantage of the *Hollywood Dream* sessions taking place at Townshend's home was that there was very much a community vibe there. Through a local network of artists and their families, the group became acquainted with Townshend's filmmaker friend, Richard Stanley. "I got to know Speedy and all of those people quite well," Stanley recalled, "because it was quite a large social group that met together, partly inspired by Pete and Karen and their house." Stanley remembers chatting with Andy Newman about such subjects as music, and of course the GPO. "He always called me 'Mr. Stanley' – old-worldy polite," he said.

At one point during the sessions, Townshend enlisted Stanley's creative assistance. "I had been doing so many different types of promo films and working with different artists that I had a reputation for doing interesting stuff," said Stanley. "I had been talking with [Townshend] about the possibilities of this band, and I'd talked to Pete about some stuff that I'd been doing... We'd talked about this before, about music and images, and when we wrote *Guitar Farm*[59] – when we were working on it, idea sessions, we

59 *Guitar Farm* was a 1971/72 film project involving Townshend, Stanley and others. Townshend describes it as "a Utopian rock music idyll based partly on an update of *The Wizard Of Oz*." The project reached full script stage and drew the interest of *Star Trek* executive producer Herb Solow before ultimately petering out.

were again talking about music and film – how can they work together."

One experiment that I persuaded Pete to carry out with Thunderclap Newman when they were going through a sticky patch of creativity was where I suggested that we should do some sessions in which Thunderclap – who was just this amazing jazz improvisational pianist – would play, and I would put photographs in front of him on the piano, which were meant to replace musical notes, and to change his playing, as it were. So I got a whole bunch of color photographs of weird stuff: Crocodiles, horses, a chestnut. Jimmy was sort of vamping on the guitar, Speedy was clapping or something, and then Andy was playing based on a tune, and after he'd started a bit, I would put these photographs right in front of him on the music stand on the upright piano to try and inspire him, or push the needle on his brain. It was just a kind of Rorschach test, to see what happened, and it was quite effective, and I think it sort of freed up the block a bit.

In addition to the quasi-Rorschach, Stanley said he and Townshend spent hours discussing the creative process with the group. "It wasn't all with the pictures," he said. "It was also just talking about the thing in general, Pete doing most of the talking, not me, because I didn't know maybe the whole story. And I think we had a couple of sessions of that."

Stanley's recollection is that "Andy was kind of stuck in this certain type of piano playing, and Pete wanted to get a bit more out of him, not use necessarily these '20s kind of choppy chords and whatever, which came from the whole

Dixie period and trad jazz and all of that stuff." Townshend says that the experiment was driven more by Newman's desire to fit the group dynamic than any wish by the others to change the way he played: "I would never have tried to force Andy to change, or even divert," he said. "I think he wanted to be more useful in the "rock" band that Speedy wanted. Speedy loved Andy's style, but they all wanted to rock out and get groupies etc. Not Andy!"

"I was focusing on Andy," Stanley recalled. "I mean, Jimmy was a fantastic guitarist; that was clear. For what Pete had in mind, Jimmy was perfect. The problem was Andy with the other two. He was stuck in this kind of downtown, syncopated kind of music, and Pete did try and explore a wider version of that, and I can see why, because it's – in a way, when you listen to 'Something In The Air', it really works, this kind of solo piano thing, but if every song's going to have that, it works, but it's not a formula for many hits, you know. Certainly Pete called me in because it wasn't working as he wanted, and he thought that, you know – some shock treatment [laughs] was maybe necessary." The experiment provides an example of the creativity at play during the sessions. "I loved brainstorming with Richard Stanley, as I had once done with Speedy," Townshend observes today. "We were both ex art school so probably loved trying to create an 'installation' around Andy."

Stanley noticed a distinct pecking order during the Thunderclap sessions, starting at the bottom with the youthful McCulloch deferring to his elders. "Jimmy did what he was told – didn't speak very much, a bit shy. He was very young then," Stanley observed. "Speedy had his own views – he was the driving force, in one sense. Andy was quite philosophical and so forth, but in the end, he kind of didn't get it, if you know what I mean; he wasn't quite of this world which he was entering." Hence the attempt to better assimilate him. "So I would say in the pecking order," Stanley said, "Pete was definitely in control, or knew what he wanted to get, and of course he and Speedy were old friends, so I think they had a nice sure hand to work together. Then Andy, and then finally Jimmy."

Which is not to say that McCulloch didn't make his presence felt in the studio – quite the opposite. The young Scot's melodic influence can be heard loud and clear throughout Thunderclap Newman's recorded work. And Townshend was blown away by McCulloch's prowess in the studio. "I've never come across such a disciplined studio musician," he said. "He never played a bum note. His solos were practiced to a tee (like George Harrison). His songs were developing well too, I was surprised he didn't get really good as a songwriter, but guitar was where he excelled."

It's still incredible to think today that about 80% of the guitar tracks on *Hollywood Dream* were recorded by a 16 year old – and the other 20% by a *15* year old. The blazing solo at the end of 'The Reason' is a great example. "All three of those guys were terrific in the studio – disciplined and brilliant," Townshend said in 2021. "Jimmy was an amazing acoustic player and I taught him a few of my tricks[60]. But his lead guitar could be really fierce; he had some inner demons that came out. Jimmy was on top of his game. He was a well-rounded player, hugely talented and inventive, and able to take suggestions really well. A joy to work with."

Another member of the social circle around the Townshend household at the time was photographer and musician Chris Morphet, who had met Pete when his band The Contacts opened for The Who in Leicester in 1965. "I was the singer and harmonica player and maracas shaker and tambourine hitter," Morphet recalled. "I used to have long

---

60 One 'trick' was that McCulloch's acoustic guitar tracks were recorded in a booth at Eel Pie Sound, or more accurately "a tiny cupboard with a glass door," according to Townshend.

hair and wear a polka-dotted shirt." Morphet, a photography student at Leicester College of Art, became friends with Townshend. "My other half, Johanna, is American, we were friends with Pete and his wife Karen at the time, and we used to go and stay with them and things," said Morphet. "The wives were friendly. It wasn't necessarily an artistic sort of thing, and when Pete had his kids and we had ours, it was more just like a couple of families, really... But I'd take photos and things, and I loved to hear him playing." In addition to taking a series of photographs during the *Hollywood Dream* recording sessions, Morphet is credited with playing harmonica on two songs, 'Look Around', and 'Accidents', and although uncredited, is likely playing the instrument on 'The Reason' as well.[61] Morphet's photos from the *Hollywood Dream* recording sessions, the originals of which he says are now "all lost," were used in the album's center spread.

The *Hollywood Dream* sessions stretched into March, when Townshend received a new piece of recording equipment: A 3M M23 model 8-track tape recorder. As with the Dolby noise reduction units, Townshend's 8-track machine was one of the first to be delivered in the U.K. – or perhaps the very first. "He got the first 8-track 3M tape recorder in the country," said Andy Newman. "He put his order in a long time before anybody else. I know for certain that he was the first person, 'cause no other studios could see the point in it, and all the other manufacturers thought 3M were mad, and they were going to lose a lot of money out of it," Newman went on. "But then the boot was on the other foot within a year. Suddenly the studios wanted 8-track and they couldn't damn well get them – 3M weren't

---

61 Morphet's short film about the harmonica, Playing The Thing, was released in 1972 and includes a short clip of John Sebastian playing the harmonica in Townshend's home studio.

making them fast enough."

The 8-track recorder "made a heck of a lot of difference," Newman recalled. It immediately made the recording process simpler for the group, but Townshend's assessment of the overall quality of the sound was perhaps not as enthusiastic as one would expect. "Technically things were indeed a little easier with 8 track," he said. "But the songs that recorded from stereo Revox to stereo Revox (via Dolby A) had something very special. The 8-track stuff was less risky and less adventurous."

Before Townshend could use this new equipment, he had to overcome an initial problem: "I had no way of playing back the eight tracks while recording, and was still using a valve (tube) mixing desk built by my friend Pepe Rush," he recalled[62]. "It was tricky to set up earphone mixes. So I spent a weekend building (and wiring) a small, passive, eight channel stereo mixer with volume controls and pan pots that sat in my equipment rack."

The 8-track machine arrived during the final week of recording *Hollywood Dream*, in time to be used on Jimmy McCulloch's two compositions: The instrumental 'Hollywood Dream', and the song 'I See It All', which featured Jimmy on lead vocals and ultimately wasn't included on the finished album. "'Accidents,' which is the best track on there, was done on two Revoxes," Townshend said in 1971. "The other ones – 'When I Think' and 'I Don't Know' – were done on Revox, and 'Old Cornmill' and 'Hollywood #1'. The ones that were done on Revoxes have a sound – I don't know what it was – they have a sort of silky sound. I can't explain it. The ones that were done on the 8-track had that typical rock hardness, but 'Accidents', for example, has got an incredible spacious hi-fi stereo feel about it. I dunno what it is."

---

62 Townshend later gave this mixer to Andy Newman.

On the track 'Hollywood Dream', Townshend played a Sho-Bud pedal steel guitar, giving the track a laid-back western feel. Newman recalled Townshend's playing being "very, very good – I was quite impressed by that. I'd heard these on records, but I'd never actually seen one. It's an instrument that I think in America was very common on the country and western circuit. We'd seen Hawaiian guitars, which are different, but we'd never seen these pedal steels. I think he'd been over to America and he'd seen it, and he'd bought one, and he'd learned how to play it, and thought he'd put this nice sort of west coast sound on the recording."

By late March 1970, Thunderclap Newman recording sessions wound down, while The Who's calendar became busier. Keith Moon's massive black Premier drum kit was squeezed into the cramped quarters of Eel Pie Sound as The Who began recording there. "I was lucky to have tolerant neighbours," said Townshend. The Who toured the U.K. in April and May, and in early June departed on a month-long tour of the U.S. By July 10th, only two days after his return, Townshend had completed and mixed *Hollywood Dream*. Finally, the album was complete.

'Accidents', the follow-up single to 'Something In The Air', was finally released on 27 June 1970, more than a year after its hit predecessor. The single's B-side was 'I See It All', the Jimmy McCulloch composition which had been left off the album. Unfortunately, by this point, any momentum gained by the band's hit single had long since dissipated. "When 'Accidents' came out, I was trying to promote it at the BBC, and of course the BBC had almost forgotten 'Something In The Air'," recalled Dana Wiffen, who began working in the Track offices in 1970.

"I think timing is important, isn't it?," offered Richard Barnes. "I mean, The Who did it brilliantly with their singles, bringing them out at the right time every three months or so when they were a singles band. But I think also – I don't know – if you're not really that great [live], word does get round. To see a band play 'Something In The Air', that would be a great draw, I would think." Or, as was the case with Thunderclap Newman at the time of the release of 'Accidents', the group was not actively performing live – at all. "It didn't have a band to back it up," said Jim Avery.

It's not clear why the single version of 'Accidents' – less than half the length of the album version, and with Jimmy singing several lines – took so long to emerge. "Nothing to do with me," Townshend said recently. "'Accidents' was ready to go as a single while 'Something In The Air' was still in the charts," he said, although it's not clear whether he's referring to the version which finally saw release, with Jimmy singing some of the verses. "I have a feeling my absence may have been felt to be a problem by the folks at Track," Townshend added. For his part, Keen said the pressure created by the first single caused considerable problems following it up. "'Something In The Air' was very hard to live up to because it wasn't done under any pressure," he said in 1975. "It was very hard to get that same feel when we knew we *had* to produce another single."[63]

"The problem was we didn't follow up 'Something In The Air' until over a year later, and you've really, in that business, got to follow up very, very quickly," Andy Newman said in 2010, unsure of the reason behind the delay. "You've got to have the follow up ready to release as the first one is going up the charts. But unfortunately for some reason

---

63 Keen cited this same pressure when he spoke with *ZigZag* in September 1970, recalling that he'd begun composing a song inspired by the May 4th shootings at Kent State University in the U.S. "I mentioned it to Chris Stamp that I was thinking of a song on those lines a couple of days after it happened, and he leapt off shouting "Rush release, rush release, bring it to me finished in the morning" and things like that, and it threw me for weeks." Keen's song never materialized.

it never got done. We were out touring, we were doing all sorts of things, and the record company, for some reason, didn't follow up. I've no idea what was going on behind the scenes there, but it's one of those mysteries."

Vernon Brewer had the difficult task of promoting the song, and applied his usual creativity. "I thought, 'Right – what can we do with this one?'," he said. "I thought about the name 'Accidents' and had this sort of vision of a St. Bernard dog, brandy barrel around its neck." St. Bernards had famously been used to rescue travelers in the snowbound St. Bernard Pass in the Alps between Switzerland and Italy. "I put adverts in all the national newspapers – I got fifty St. Bernard dogs," he recalled with a laugh. "We paraded them from Track Records all the way to Bond Street, which is where one of the BBC studios were, but unfortunately the record didn't do too well." A photo of BBC DJ Alan Freeman surrounded by St. Bernards appeared in the *Evening Standard*, with Speedy, Jimmy and Andy standing in the background.

Reviews of 'Accidents' were generally positive, with one assessment reading: "With a stack of la-la-lahing hoo-haa vocally, this gets off to a very good start. Dramatic beat is added, some authoritative guitar work, and it moves smartly into a sure-hit category. Main point is that it is different, almost all the way, with imaginative lyrics – not too heavy, not too pure-commercial. And the production (Pete Townshend) is clean, tight, controlled. It's a shade monotonous on the main melody line, though. Maybe that could cause a hang-up."

"One would have to listen to Wagner in a funeral parlor for something even more morbid than Thunderclap Newman's 'Accidents', which chronicles the deaths of various hapless children who all meet a very nasty end – Poor Mary falls in a river whilst waiting for the Queen to sail by and little Johnny is killed by a speeding car," read one review, credited to Nathan Morley[64]. "That said, the song, orchestration and performance are simply brilliant. It is captivating and without doubt their best recording."

On August 28th, just two months after the release of 'Accidents', Thunderclap Newman released another single, the Speedy Keen composition 'The Reason'. "...a startlingly fast follow-up single this time," read the review in *Record Mirror*. "But the ingredients are there. Good vocal arrangement, some hearty piano, a rather plaintive quality somehow despite the actual heaviness. Bit ragged, melodically, maybe. But in with a chart chance." Chris Welch gave the song a rather lukewarm thumbs-up in *Melody Maker*, calling it a "groovy LP track."

The single's B-side was 'Stormy Petrel', an Andy Newman-penned instrumental featuring piano and kazoo. The track, credited as 'Produced by P. Townshend and R. Cardboard', was recorded in Hammersmith Town Hall. "I suppose I did produce it, for want of a better word," said Rick Seaman, A.K.A. 'Richard Cardboard'. "It was only me and Andy at the Hammersmith Town Hall," he said. "We used it because it had some decent acoustics basically – that was the reason we were there." The pair used a mobile recording setup that Newman had assembled with the help of Pete Townshend. "He got this old GPO van and converted it into a recording studio, with a couple of Revoxes," Seaman recalled. Newman and Seaman would drive around in this van, visiting various locations and making sample recordings. "We were constantly trying to find different places to record," said Seaman. "Andy would want to go and record the dawn chorus... birds singing or some nonsense like that."

Always yearning for live work, around September

---

64 I was unable to find this review in print. "I have no recollection of ever saying it or writing it," says Morley.

1970 Jimmy worked with his brother and Robbie Paterson (rhythm guitar/vocals) and Dave Struthers (bass) to form the rather predictably named McCullochs, Struthers and Paterson, a band that was formed solely for live performances. "I can have the best of both worlds," Jimmy told the press. "It won't affect us in any way with recordings, well, certainly not at the moment. We're trying to write most of the music ourselves. It's not going to be pop music or even bubblegum but just a pleasant kind of noise. This is what we hope to achieve." McCullochs, Struthers and Paterson flamed out after about a month.

That same month, Speedy sat for an interview with *ZigZag* in the offices of Track Records, previewing tracks from the new album and talking about Thunderclap Newman's future. When asked if the group were going back on the road, Keen responded: "Well, no, not yet. What I've got to do is write some more songs, which I don't find particularly easy." Speedy hinted that he was already eyeing a second album when responding to a question about Newman's importance to the group. "Well, I reckon if we didn't have Andy to pin us down we'd just be another 2 album group who split up," Keen said, before offering more thoughts regarding the band's future. "...The band's still very young, and Andy's got to get into playing rock more, and Jimmy's got to get into singing more – he sings a bit on the album," Keen said. "But we only see each other when we arrive at the studio now." Keen said he preferred to play drums onstage, "but you need the stamina of a wrestler if you're gonna sing too."

CHAPTER 8

LOOK AROUND

Thunderclap Newman with Roger Felice and Ronnie Peel, 1971. ©Muziekkrant OOR / Gijsbert Hanekroot

"In this country Thunderclap Newman had a number one hit with their first record, it took everyone unawares, but with the highest ideals in mind they went on to make an album which very few people bought over here. That is a kind of failure. It's not too hard to bear because in my opinion (I produced it, so my opinion isn't worth much) it's a bloody good album. An incredible first album.

...In the States it's a totally different story. Not only did they not have a number one hit with their first record, 'Something In The Air,' but neither did they with any of the others. Big deal, you say, but you have to talk to the kids in the streets to get the feeling that exists around them in the States. ...They are a myth. They make records, that when reviewed in a batch, have a mysterious and dreamlike quality about them. They have an album which, on the strength of the myth, and a lot of Atlantic plugging is beginning to sell. It will probably sell many more after their second album emerges. That is usually the way. If they took a walk together in the street over here, they would arrive home feeling like it was all over. If they took a walk in the street in New York, they would feel like it was all beginning. I know, the WHO did that very thing about three years ago."

- Pete Townshend, *Melody Maker*, April 1971

Thunderclap Newman's album *Hollywood Dream* was finally released on October 2, 1970, the day after their labelmate Jimi Hendrix's funeral took place in his home-town of Seattle. The world had lost a singular, phenome-nal talent who changed the musical landscape; Track had lost a star.

It had been 17 months since the release of 'Something In The Air,' and 14 months since Thunderclap Newman had performed live. They'd shown some signs of life over the summer, finally releasing 'Accidents,' but it was too late. The single peaked at number 46, spending only a week in the charts. 'The Reason' followed two months later, failing to reach the charts at all. There was still no band to back it up.

This was the situation Vernon Brewer faced when trying to promote *Hollywood Dream*. "I don't remember an awful lot about the promotions for the album," he said. "I think by that time, they'd come and gone, as it were." Track did release a seventeen-minute promotional record featuring an interview with Pete and the band, conducted by former Pirate radio DJ Roger Keene and interspersed with clips of songs from the forthcoming album. The single-sided album was packaged in a plain white sleeve and hand-stamped with A SPECIAL RECORD FROM PETE TOWNSHEND AND THUNDERCLAP NEWMAN. The hand-stamp approach had first been used by Track six months earlier for The Who's *Live At Leeds* album, enlisting all comers: Office staff, band members, even visitors to the office.

The *Hollywood Dream* album came in a gatefold sleeve, the cover photo by Graham Hughes[65], and most of the interior photographs by Chris Morphet. Townshend is credited as producer. On some editions of *Hollywood Dream*, the bass guitar work is uncredited; on others, it's credited to 'Bijou Drains', a name Townshend dreamed up, inspired by the oddly named Bijou Guest House just off Ealing Common which he and Richard Barnes walked past on the way to Ealing Tech during the short period that the pair lived at Townshend's parents' home on Woodgrange Avenue in the early '60s.[66] Townshend later used the name on other projects: The 1970 Mike Heron album *Smiling Men With Bad Reputations* featured the song 'Warm Heart Pastry', credited to 'Tommy and the Bijoux' (Townshend, Moon, and Ronnie Lane). On Townshend and Lane's 1977 album *Rough Mix*, the credits for the song 'Misunderstood' include: 'Bijou Drains: Gulp.'

Speedy is credited with drums and vocals on all tracks on *Hollywood Dream*, and acoustic guitar on just

---

65 Hughes, Roger Daltrey's cousin, designed and photographed album covers for The Who, Daltrey, John Entwistle, Pete Townshend, Andy Newman, and Speedy Keen, among many others.

66 Barnes and I retraced their steps in 2022 and were surprised to find that the Bijou Guest House is still there.

two: 'Accidents' and 'I Don't Know'. Jimmy is credited with all other guitar work. Andy's credits are voluminous, for example: 'Piano / Oboe / 3 Soprano Saxophones in harmony' on 'Open The Door, Homer', and 'Cor Anglais / 3 Bengali Flutes in harmony / Oboe' on 'Wild Country'. The credits for 'Hollywood #2' help to illustrate the extent of Andy's exotic collection of instruments:

Andy: Piano / Vocals / Japanese Battle Cymbal / 3 Soprano Saxophones in harmony / Hand Bells / Indian Finger Cymbals / Chinese Temple Block / Sleigh Bells
Speedy: Drums / Vocals / Glockenspiel / Gong
Jimmy: Electric/Lead Guitar / Wood Blocks

Keen was immensely proud of the twelve-track album, ten of which were his own compositions. "I think *Hollywood Dream* – and I know it's the writer saying this – I think it's really very special," Speedy said in 1975.

It was a very difficult period with the Thunderclaps when they tried to put us out on the road. Anybody with enough insight would have seen that the best thing to do would be to make another album and then another one, because it was such a unique experience, playing it as well as listening to it. Pete was the guiding force there, he put it together. He's amazing – well he's amazing anyway – but he's amazing because he must have seen it all before it was even brought together, which is incredible, I'm proud of that... not only 'Something In The Air' but the whole *Hollywood Dream* album. I know there are millions of brilliant albums out, but there aren't that many with that kind of twist to them.

Townshend did have some regrets about the

album's construction at the time. "As an album, I feel that my biggest mistake was the way I put the tracks together," he told *ZigZag* in 1971. "I don't think I really did it correctly, I was far too into the group: like, putting two versions of 'Hollywood' on was daft. I should have made a choice. A few other things like that. It could have been shorter. It's about 22 minutes a side and it could have been shorter and tighter." Today, he remains incredibly fond of *Hollywood Dream*. "I love it all," he said recently. "Recording it is one of my favourite experiences. People that know and love that record are very special people in my eyes."

Townshend still has all of the tracks he recorded with Thunderclap Newman in his possession. "The only thing I don't have are the final masters for the album because I wasn't able to make copies," he said. "Polydor have a very good copy master though, and that has been digitized with decent remastering. I also have Speedy's original words for 'Something In The Air' scribbled on a tape label. Maybe some for 'Accidents' too somewhere in my personal files. ...There aren't any outtakes I don't think."

It appears that not all of the music weeklies bothered to review *Hollywood Dream* – for example, a review of all editions of the *NME* from September and October 1970 revealed no mention of the album. But the reviews that did appear in the press were largely positive, if not a bit confused. "At last – the long-promised Thunderclap Album has emerged with a fanfare of kazoos and Japanese Battle Cymbals," wrote Chris Welch in a *Melody Maker* piece entitled 'Thunder: Mixing Problem' on October 10th, the review accompanied by a photo of Andy wearing a blonde wig and smoking a cigar.

But isn't it a trifle late? More than a year has elapsed since they first took the singles chart by storm and public enthusiasm for all kinds of musical delights waxes and wanes with fearful irregularity. The main problem with Thunderclap Newman the group, was mixing in the talents of Thunderclap Newman the pianist. Andy Newman is a unique pianist and exponent of kazoo and saxophones, who can be nearest compared to Ron Geesin[67]. The group features the song-writing talents of Speedy Keen and the guitar work of Jimmy McCulloch, but despite the good intentions of producer Pete Townshend, the twin artistries don't quite mix. Perhaps one day the pianist will be able to record a solo album which will fully illustrate the ideas hinted at in 'Hollywood Dream' and 'Accidents'. Speedy's tunes are quite attractive in an old-fashioned style, and one of the best numbers is the driving 'Wild Country' with the mysterious Bijou Drains on bass and Andy on Cor Anglais. 'Something In The Air' is included in this slightly schizophrenic set.

Disc & Music Echo's assessment of the album also arrived at the same term: "Thunderclap Newman on Hollywood Dream are a bit schizophrenic," read the review.

On one part heavy psychedelic sounds, broken by Andy Newman's "jolly" pub-type piano, over an incredibly commercial melodic song. ...Keen's

67 Geesin is a Scottish musician and composer who performed as pianist with The Original Downtown Syncopators, a throwback Dixieland jazz group who performed in the UK in the early '60s. A prolific composer, Geesin later co-wrote Pink Floyd's 'Atom Heart Mother' and contributed the instrumental 'With A Smile Up His Nose They Entered' to Pete Townshend's *Happy Birthday* album.

lyrics are explicit and socially aware, sung in the manner of a puzzled young man, and time and again the piano cuts across the heavy backing with a backing and/or solo that belongs on an old 78 r.p.m. record. Andy Newman is credited with an amazing number of instruments through the track notes. ... Exciting, new and different (FOUR STARS).

Rolling Stone's John Mendelsohn's praise for the album was effusive and lacked the qualifiers that his British counterparts had enumerated. "How anyone will manage to remain a nasty narrow-minded jade in the presence of this unremittingly delightful album defies the imagination," Mendelsohn wrote.

There's simply no exaggerating the pimply splendor of Speedy Keen's lead voice, a reedy, breathless, disarmingly earnest affair that resides in the No-Voice's-Land between little-boy soprano and grown-up falsetto. There's simply no describing the charm of Andy Newman's keyboard-tickling, which takes the form of a dazzling assortment of boogie-cum-piano-bar chops laid down with unerring clumsiness only in the least likely places (and there without accompaniment, as there's apparently no keeping up with it). Nor could one exude excessively in behalf of wee Jimmy McCulloch's precisely lyrical lead guitar.

Put alternatively, nothing in Thunderclap's music has anything much to do with anything else in Thunderclap's music, the result being that Thunderclap's is at once unexaggerably bizarre and a mightily refreshing rock and roll sound. That sound couldn't in a month of Halloweens be better suited to Speedy's imbecilically catchy little songs, which abound with surreal, nostalgic, surreally nostalgic, and other wonderful lyric sentiments.

Try on for size 'Wild Country,' in which he glorifies the great outdoors because, simply, it's such a nice place to ball in. Try on both the modest and colossal (the latter featuring all manner of domestic and exotic percussion) takes of 'Hollywood,' an eminently hummable little ditty in which Speedy laments the passing of bigger-than-life film-stars who used to make him sick, and a very *McCartney*-ish instrumental exploration of this theme, 'Hollywood Dream'. And the delightfully-dated 'Accidents,' which here bends the mind with its late 1966 psychedelic ambiguity for nearly ten minutes and contains dazzling piano and kazoo freak-outs by Andy. And, of course, 'Something In The Air,' which you'll find as emphatic a knock-out on 600th hearing as it was on first.

Despite this critical acclaim, *Hollywood Dream* sold poorly, reaching no higher than 161 in the U.S. charts and not charting at all in the U.K. "The album's sold very badly," said Townshend. "Alright in the States."

"Obviously I felt very disappointed with the reaction to *Hollywood Dream*," Speedy told ZigZag's Andy Childs in 1975. "We didn't get a lot of airplay – we did in America but we didn't actually go there as the Thunderclaps. When I did eventually get over there I found that thousands of people really liked the Thunderclaps and recognised that album for what it was. I wish we'd gone there now because we needed that warmth – we got it in Scandinavian countries and in Scotland too funnily enough."

Childs, too, recognized the album's beauty: "*Hollywood Dream* is a brilliant album, full of great songs with poignant lyrics and beautiful melodies," he wrote.

Every track's a winner for me but my special favou-
rites are 'Wild Country', 'Accidents', 'The Reason'
and 'Something In The Air' – all of which were
released as singles. Incidentally, the b-sides of
'Something In The Air', 'The Reason' and 'Accidents'
are *not* on the album and they are 'Wilhelmina',
'Stormy Petrel', and 'I See It All' respectively...
reason enough to have them in their single form.
...Townshend also produced the whole album and
has his trademark of quality oozing out of every
groove. Honestly, it really is a fabulous LP although
sadly it's never been an outrageously fashionable
one to possess in this country. Nevertheless, next
time you're passing your local Woolworths have
a look through their record department because
mine were selling this gem off at the ridiculous
price of 72p not so long ago. A sound investment
if there ever was one.

Thunderclap Newman made a rare public appearance
to promote the release of *Hollywood Dream*, taping a piece
for Kenny Everett's television program *Ev* which appeared
on November 7th. It was not a pleasant experience. "You
can understand groups not wanting to go on telly," Speedy
told *ZigZag*. "We turned up at the studio and no-one even
spoke to us, not even Kenny Everett. A lot of people took
the piss out of Andy, which they usually do, but that doesn't
bother me – I'd rather be with Andy and Jimmy than 4
ordinary typical heavy kind of people. Anyway, it was really
depressing because it's supposed to be a zany, funny show
and there were these surly cameramen and people saying,
"Who are they?" and things like that. But you're in their
hands - you do one moody and they chuck you out."

* * *

A month before the release of *Hollywood Dream*, Speedy went back to Rome to visit his ex-wife Lydia. The weekend of September 12th and 13th saw Keen back at his old haunt the Piper Club, where bands The Recreation[68] and Ayers Rock[69] were on the bill. "We used to do two or three sets – the curtain would open and we'd play, and I remember all that I could see was the lights from the bar, which was on the other side of the stage," recalled Ayers Rock drummer Roger Felice. "And you could see this image with long hair, Speedy's image, just something I spotted when I was playing. Couple of times, the curtains open and that same image was closer to the stage. In the break, I went to get some cigarettes from the vending machine, and someone tapped me on the shoulder, and I looked around, and it was Speedy. He said, "Are you guys really from Australia?" and I said, "Yeah!" He said, "Wow – so do you know Tony Cahill?" – he was a drummer, played with the Easybeats and all that – I said, "Yeah, of course I know Tony Cahill." He said, "Do you know Dave Montgomery?", and I said "I know Dave – how do you know all these people?" He said, "Oh, through friends in London. My name's Speedy and I'm in Thunderclap Newman."

Felice took Keen backstage to meet the band. "Speedy just happened to have a joint with him, so we went with that, 'cause in Italy at that time it was very hard to get any," said Felice. "We just hung out, and we became friends. He said, "Are you guys ever going to get to London?" And I said, "I don't know," because at that time our sax player

---

68 The group 'The Recreation' had performed at the Palermo Pop Festival a few months earlier, the same festival during which Arthur Brown stripped naked onstage and was subsequently arrested, subjected to four days' confinement, and deported. *Melody Maker* reported that "the audience pelted Brown with sandals and shoes as he stripped during 'Fire,' his closing number, until he was forced to pull his underpants back on again."

69 Not to be confused with a completely unrelated Australian group of the same name which formed three years later.

was missing Australia and he wanted to go back, and the guitar player was going to Holland to get married, so that was going on in the band. And Speedy said, "Well look – if anything happened with the band, and everyone went different ways, I'd be really interested if you and Ronnie[70] would come to England and join Thunderclap Newman." And I thought wow, ok, we'll see what happens."

Within a month or so of this meeting, the members of Ayers Rock went their separate ways. "The band and I had a chat, and I said, "Let's do it," so we called it a day," Felice recalled. "I had to go back to Naples because I was doing session drumming for a studio there and I had to finish my commitments out. So when we finished our gig in Rome, the boys went on and Ronnie and I went back to Naples and I finished my recordings in the studio with this artist, and then after that I just grabbed my kit and away we went."

Felice and Peel, close friends who'd been in bands together since the early '60s, arrived in London in early November 1970. "We met up with Speedy and we went to Pete Townshend's studio in Soho – Speedy actually lived there," Felice recalled. "It was in the middle of Soho – you go in this doorway and up the stairs and they had like a tailor's shop and all these things, but when you get to the top, there's this studio. And it was really good, because after business hours, 5 o'clock or 6 o'clock, everything was shut so there's no one you could disturb, right? It was a big one room studio and it had a couple of bunks there, and all the instruments were there, and so we started playing with the band – we met Jimmy and Andy, and we started jamming, and that's how we joined Thunderclap Newman."

Asked for his initial thoughts upon meeting the group,

---

70 Ayers Rock bassist Ronnie Peel was a singer/songwriter who released several records under the adopted name 'Rockwell T. James', including 1968's single 'Love Power' and the 1977 album *A Shot of Rhythm and Blues*.

Felice said, "It was just such a weird setup. Speedy was the singer/songwriter and rhythm guitar player, long hair; Jimmy was like three inches tall with like a ten foot guitar [laughs], and Andy – well, what can you say about Andy? I mean, look – he's done no harm to me, so I can say no harm about him, but he was a very, very, very weird dude, and I mean *very* weird dude." Felice said, "there were no plans – nothing happening as far as concerts or shows." He and Peel had arrived just as the group was being dusted off and prepped for live action after 15 months of inactivity. Keen gave his new rhythm section a copy of *Hollywood Dream* and they set about learning it.

It took some time for Felice and Peel to get used to the chaos of their new record label as well. "Track Records – that was an insane entity," recalled Felice with a laugh. "Vaguely I remember, I think it was Monday or something, we'd go and pick up whatever money we had to pick up."

> One day Ronnie and I went in to Track, and all of a sudden everything went berserk, people were running around, "You've got to leave, you've got to leave!", so everyone's going out into the street, "What the hell's going on here?" We thought it might have been the building was on fire. Apparently The Who were on the road somewhere, and they couldn't get room service after a gig, and next thing Pete Townshend and Keith Moon lost it because they couldn't get room service and so they started throwing things out of the window and all that sort of stuff, and down below was a car park. So apparently a call came in sort of saying "You owe us a couple of dollars", you know. And I'm thinking 'Oh my god!'

November 13th saw the release of another Thunderclap

Newman single, only 11 weeks after the previous release – this time 'Wild Country', with 'Hollywood' as the B-side, which, confusingly, was the same track as the album's 'Hollywood #1'. This was the group's third single release in the past six months. The 'Wild Country' single was Track's first in a series of cut-price singles, about 2 shillings cheaper than the standard price. "Effective and hard-working – and retails for six bob only, for which many thanks," read one review. "The vocal is sometimes subdued, but there's some great guitar work and the drumming drives like the clappers. No guarantee, but could do things. CHART CHANCE."

"Very strange the sudden resurge of interest in Thunderclap, who first bemused us just a year ago and then was seemingly forgotten," read another. "Perhaps consciences were pricking at Track? Anyway, here indeed is a very good song – without the piano which was so good at first but so wearing after a while. Instead, Andy apparently takes to oboes, which makes for a very weird sound, especially when joined by Speedy Keen's guitar. Not a hit single I fear, but this could be the record to make us forget the Thunderclap gimmick and appreciate the Keen music."

Within only a week or two of Felice and Peel's arrival in London, Speedy Keen sat down with Penny Valentine of *Sounds* to discuss the state of his band and his plans. The reconstituted Thunderclap Newman had just begun what Valentine described as "a kind of make it or break it rehearsal and is hoping desperately that things will work out well enough to get the group not only back before audiences but take them on the road with The Who in their next tour of America."

"…I know we have all the elements of being a really fantastic stage act if we could keep going for say another year and really establish ourselves," Keen said. "There's so much to work from - we need to give Andy his head and let him wander on about his bird calls and ornithology things when we stroll on stage and then just drift into numbers. We need to establish that great personality thing we've got within the group... I just want us to get it all right on stage, get the right simplified direction going with nice uncomplicated material. Not a bunch of musicians playing for musicians but something that's new and that keeps an audience really happy. I'm not into being a great guitar player or anything – I just want Thunderclap to get back on stage."

On the same date as the *Sounds* piece – November 21st, 1970 – an ad appeared in *Melody Maker*'s MUSICIANS WANTED section: "WANTED (for top group) VERSATILE MUSICIANS TO PLAY ANY COMBINATION OF THE FOLLOWING INSTRUMENTS Saxophones – Oboe / Cor Anglais – Flute and Piano." Interestingly, the ad instructed those interested to "Phone Jack McCulloch between 10 am / 6pm." By this time, Jack had joined Andwella, along with new bassist Dave Struthers, formerly of McCullochs, Struthers and Paterson. Andwella were signed to Reflection Records and due to release an album, *People's People*, on January 29th.

Although he was no longer a member of Thunderclap Newman, Jack McCulloch always seemed to be on the periphery, keeping a watchful eye on his younger sibling. "Jack was close by because the record company that put out the Andwella album were only up the road from Track," recalled Track's Dana Wiffen. "Jack always got the best out of Jimmy, kept him in line 'cause he was very young," said Wiffen. "While Jack was around, being his older brother, he was very good at looking after him and keeping him from going too far, you know. I think later on when he joined Wings and Stone the Crows and that, Jack wasn't around to look after him and I think that's one of the reasons why he went off the rails and why we lost him so early." Roger Felice met Jack McCulloch a few months later when Jack drove his brother to La Valbonne nightclub on Kingly Street, Soho, where Thunderclap Newman performed the instrumental 'Hollywood Dream' for the film *Not Tonight, Darling*, released in September 1971.

The music press soon reported more plans for Thunderclap Newman, with the headline THUNDERCLAP INCREASES FROM TRIO TO 8:

> Two young Australians known simply as Roger and Ronnie have joined Thunderclap Newman, which is in the process of expanding from a trio to an eight-piece unit… After months of discussions about Thunderclap's future, Roger (drums) and Ronnie (bass) have been brought into the line-up. Regular drummer Speedy Keene now switches to congos and tablas, and will concentrate more on vocals. To complete the expansion, three musicians who play a variety of instruments – including sax, trumpet, oboe and flute – are being sought. British club and ballroom dates by Newman are expected to commence in January or February. The group will probably accompany the Who to America in March to appear on selected dates during a six-week tour. The enlarged group plans to record a new LP and single soon.

There's no evidence that additional musicians were ever added to the five-piece lineup of Thunderclap Newman. Keen's planned switch to percussion never materialized either; he sang and played mostly acoustic guitar during the group's 1971 gigs. Additionally, any plans The Who may have had to tour America in March were soon scrapped, as Pete Townshend's new, ambitious *Lifehouse* project began to emerge. Townshend announced his ideas, and the first concrete plans for developing them, at a press conference at the Young Vic theatre near London's Waterloo station on January 13th, 1971. "We are intending to produce a fiction, or a play or an opera and create a completely different kind of performance in rock," Townshend said. "We are writing a story and we aim to perform it on the first day we start work in this theatre. Tied in with the whole idea is the use of quadrophonic sound and pre-recorded tapes. About 400 people will be involved with us and we aim to play music which represents them." Three workshop performances were announced: February 15th and 22nd, and March 1st, all at the Young Vic. A film was also being discussed, pending the outcome of the workshops.

The *Lifehouse* concept was heady stuff, and would prove endlessly frustrating for Townshend, as most listeners ended up confused when he tried to explain the plot to them. The storyline was based around a central theme which Pete explained in *Melody Maker*. "Here's the idea – there's a note, a musical note, that builds the basis of existence somehow," he wrote in the September edition of his column, *The Pete Townshend Page*:

> This note pervades everything, it's an extremely wide note, more of a hiss than a note as we normally know them. The hiss of the air, of activity, of the wind and of the breathing of someone near. You can always hear it.
>
> Andy Newman told me once how people cannot bear to spend too much time in anechoic

chambers because of the horror of complete silence[71]. Anechoic chambers are not only completely silent but all sound that is produced within them is sort of swallowed up by absolutely non reflective walls and ceilings. You shout but you hardly hear yourself!

At midnight when you lay in bed, gently falling into sleep, it gets louder not quieter. It doesn't seem to come through the ears and the air, but it is made up of elements that are. Finally, when it reaches deafening proportions you are asleep, drowned in sound... The key to this unexciting adventure that I'm leading you on is that everybody hears it. Moreover I think everybody hears the same note or noise. It's an amazing thing to think of any common ground between all men that isn't directly a reflection of spiritual awareness... It's a note, it's notes, it's music - the most beautiful there is to hear.

Newman's influence on the project didn't stop there. The *New York Times* reported that Andy had been cast as the main character, Bobby, in a film of *Lifehouse*. When I relayed this information to Newman in 2009, he was quite taken aback. "Well I never heard that!," he exclaimed. "I'm just amazed – I'm amazed! You're telling me things I've never heard before! Oh dear. Well... I may have been cast, but I was not notified!" It was ultimately revealed that the *New York Times* report was inaccurate, but there was

---

71 "I know that if you are actually working in an anechoic chamber testing audio equipment, it does get very, very eerie because your ears get used to reverberation and you lose all sense of direction, because you're not getting the reverberation coming back," Newman told me. "And it can sort of unbalance people a little bit, I mean, if you get used to it I suppose it's all right. But certainly a lot of people do find it disorientating when they first do it. And you can't tell which direction the sound is coming from, because your ears triangulate on the sound using the sound bouncing off the objects; the sound is not bouncing off anywhere, it's just coming from the source, sometimes you have a difficulty sort of pinpointing it."

an element of underlying truth which was actually more impressive than the 'Andy cast as Bobby' story – Andy was actually the *basis* of Bobby, the central figure of the *Lifehouse* story. Townshend explains today: "Bobby was based on Andy, but would have been played by an actor."

Meanwhile, Thunderclap Newman rehearsals and plans kicked up a notch. The January 23rd edition of *Melody Maker* included an ad: THUNDERCLAP NEWMAN NOW AVAILABLE FOR BOOKINGS – CONTACT TRACK INTERNATIONAL. The group moved from Speedy's Soho apartment to a proper rehearsal space, and had promotional photos taken.[72] A short tour of Scotland was announced, to begin in late January.

Ideally, this activity would have taken place under the watchful eye of Pete Townshend, but his attention was fixed mainly on *Lifehouse*. "In actual fact, Pete Townshend was our manager," said Roger Felice, while adding that Pete wasn't around much. "But he wasn't a manager, man. He was a guitar player with a famous rock & roll band, you know? So you can't blame Pete." Felice recalled one occasion when Townshend listened in on rehearsals during this period and dispensed some advice that has remained with him throughout his career:

> Just before the Scottish tour, we're rehearsing and Pete was actually sitting outside with the door ajar, listening to the band, and then he came in and we all made small talk and laughed and all that, and the one thing that he did say that's always stuck

---

72 Dana Wiffen remembers being tasked at one point with having the band sign promotional photos. "I'm constantly being sent to knock on the door and get Speedy ready, wake him up for an interview," Wiffen recalled. "He partied late at night and then was never around during the day... I've got a pile of photos in the loft of the five of them, all signed by four of them but not by Speedy... because he never turned up to sign them."

in my head – he said, "When you're doing a show, work it like a clock – the clock's on twelve and you open up open up with your best shot, open up big – bang! And then as the clock goes down to three you slow it down, and then halfway through you're doing like a ballad or like some of your slower songs, and then you start building it up again, until you get back to twelve… so in other words it's a motion, and you take the people with you, so you come on big, and you take the people down, down, down, and then up, up, up, and you leave them on an up." And I thought, wow, that makes sense!

Thunderclap Newman's tour of Scotland began at Paisley Technical College, just west of Glasgow, on Friday, January 22nd, 1971. It was the group's first live performance in nearly 18 months. The tour was a short affair, just five college dates – Paisley, Dundee, Strathclyde, Heriott-Watt (Edinburgh)[73], Aberdeen – and ending with a homecoming gig for Jimmy at Glasgow's Electric Garden on the 31st.

Andy Newman described the group's typical set during this period to Paul Salley: "I believe in the repertoire was 'Lady Madonna'; Speedy liked that one," said Newman. "One by the Allman Brothers Band called 'Statesboro Blues' which the Australian guys introduced. There was also a Tiny Tim number called 'We Love It' which was a rendition of a song from the 1920s."[74] Newman's 'Water Music', complete with bird calls, remained in the set. Plus, of course, the group performed a selection of songs from the *Hollywood Dream* album, including the singles 'Something

73 The performance at Heriott-Watt was a fundraiser for the Ibrox Park Disaster Fund, raising money for families of victims of a crush among the crowd at a Celtic-Rangers football game on January 2nd which resulted in 66 fatalities and more than 200 injured.
74 With its 1920s arrangement and kazoo solo, 'We Love It' would have been a perfect Andy Newman showcase.

In The Air', 'The Reason', and 'Wild Country'.

Andy's old friend Rick Seaman saw this new iteration of Thunderclap Newman. "[Felice] didn't play the drums anything like Speedy did," he recalled. "When Speedy played the drums it all kind of seemed to spill out of him, and Roger was much tighter in his drums, so it changed the sound of the band. …Speedy played the drums like he looked – sort of scruffy," he chuckled. Also by this time, Keen was a more proficient singer and guitarist. "All the time Speedy was trying to practice," said Jim Avery. "He learned to play the guitar eventually, and he was learning to be able to perform with the guitar and actually sing – project his voice. So by the time they released the single 'The Reason', he could actually perform. It wasn't a fantastic performance, but it did the job."

Roger Felice remembers a rather tense situation that Andy was able to defuse in his own peculiar way during the tour of Scotland. "This basically pins Andy to exactly where his head's at," Felice said with a laugh.

> When we were doing our Scottish tour, we're driving to the gig, and I'm sitting in the back, and we're rolling joints and smoking, and the car was like half full of smoke, and Andy was sitting in the middle. And a police car pulls us over. And I thought *Jeeesus*. What do you do? They're going to smell it, you know? So I'm trying to hide all this stuff, and Andy says, "I'll take care of this, I'll…" and we said "Andy…" We were in deep shit, man, you know?! And Andy sort of wobbles out of the car and goes towards the policemen. And we can barely hear what he was saying, but we're in deep shit, full stop, you know? We're in the car with dope in the car; if they went to that car, we were gone. And I don't know what the law in England was at the time and

I have no idea what Andy was talking about, but he was saying things like, "I know the law, and you've got to take down all this information – I work for the government," and he pulled his wallet out, and he had about a hundred thousand bloody cards in there, right?

Andy proceeded to review his personal information with the officers in excruciating detail. "After a while the coppers are saying, "Look, okay, okay, we'll…","" Felice recalled. Newman, of course, had no problem confronting authority figures; he'd told off a policeman outside Bulstrode Secondary Modern back in his pre-teen years, and could be bullishly obstinate, as he had been when holding out for a retirement plan in the process of joining Thunderclap Newman. As Newman continued to browbeat the exhausted officers, the rest of the band in the car saw the opportunity to escape. "We're saying "Andy, Andy, stop – just get back in the car," said Felice. "And they're saying, "Mate, you can go," and he's, "No, no, no, no, you've got to write this down." And he had about a hundred more cards to go! And the coppers are saying, "Please leave us alone! We're sorry we pulled you over," you know?" Eventually, his bandmates persuaded Newman to get back in the car and they quickly departed. "And so that was Andy – he was so straight, it was like that policeman had to write all that information down, which would have taken a month. He wore them down, and they're saying, "Just go!"That's Andy."

During the Scottish tour, Andy Newman appeared in the ANY QUESTIONS section of *Melody Maker*, responding to the question from reader P.J. Filby in Eastbourne: "Can you tell me how to get hold of a genuine wobbleboard for serious use in a band?" While not actually answering the question, his response was perfectly Newman-esque. One wonders if he had to actually look any of this information up beforehand, or if it already resided in his fascinating brain:

> The wobbleboard is a relative of the thundersheet, which is a sheet of metal usually about 5ft x 3ft and approximately 1/32 of an inch thick, preferably made of slightly tempered steel. The thundersheet is used as a theatrical and orchestral percussion instrument to obtain such effects as thunder. The wobbleboard has the same principle, but is made either of hardboard doped with paint, or an artist's canvas which has been painted on so much that it has become very stiff, which was the method used by Rolf Harris on his hit record, 'Tie Me Kangaroo Down, Sport.' You hold the wobbleboard longways with both hands horizontally and proceed to wobble it by slight compression of the hands, so that the board is activated in a wave form, vibrating from one curvature to another and causing the sound. - THUNDERCLAP NEWMAN.

A few days after the conclusion of their brief Scottish tour, Thunderclap Newman flew to Holland for a one-off gig supporting Leon Russell on February 5th at Kasteel Groeneveld, an 18th century castle in Baarn, Netherlands. The performance was part of a live television program before an audience, called *Piknik*. A recording of several tracks from this performance survives and reveals young Jimmy's dominance in a live setting, with both 'Look Around' and 'The Reason' both featuring extended, blazing guitar solos. McCulloch rips into another extended solo during a twelve-minute rendition of 'Wild Country', with the added intrigue of a ninety-second solo on Bengali flute by Newman, who also plays cor anglais and saxophone during the song.

"I remember we were very loose at the time," Speedy told Wim Noordhoek of VPRO (Dutch Radio) a few years later. "But I remember it was an incredible gig, fantastic." Noordhoek said, "One thing I remember is that after the show, Jimmy sat on the lap of Andy Newman and cried his heart out," to which Speedy responded, "that's right, yeah." When asked about this, Roger Felice commented: "Apparently Jimmy wasn't happy with his guitar playing or something – I don't know."

But it wasn't as bad as… Jimmy sitting on Andy's knee crying his eyes out. He was obviously upset about something, and it only lasted for a couple of seconds. And I think at the time nobody really said anything because we weren't too sure what the story was, and it only lasted for a little while, and that was it, we were back to getting ready to go to the nightclub. But – never did any band member go to another band member and say, "Oh, you sang bad," or "You played bad." If it would have been a really big thing, we would have said, mate – are you alright, or what? But – if he was pissed off, or he had the shits, I don't know. And that was it and he got over it, and we had a drink and went nightclubbing.

A week after their date in Holland, Thunderclap Newman kicked off a series of fourteen dates in England over the next two months – too loose a collection to be called a tour, but a significant number of gigs for this historically road-averse outfit. The first show took place at Queen Mary College, Bethnal Green, east London on Friday, February 12th with support from Bread, Love and Dreams.

Perhaps unsurprisingly, given their fundamental differences, some friction emerged between band members during this period. Andy noted a "rather interesting contradiction" to Paul Salley in 2010: He liked Speedy's musical inclinations but found his personality difficult; conversely, he got along well with Jimmy but couldn't grow to appreciate the young Scot's favored genre of blues rock. "I had some difficulties working with Speedy because he tended to be something of an irritable character and yet I got on very well with Jimmy because Jimmy was very sort of workmanlike and straight to the point with his music," Newman said. "It was just the fact that Speedy's music, I could latch onto very easily but Jimmy's music, which was heavy rock, sort of a cross between Eric Clapton and Jimi Hendrix, I had a job to fathom."

Newman may have exacerbated Keen's irritability, as Roger Felice explained: "Everybody in the band got on really well, except for Speedy and Andy," he said.

> I've got nothing but great things to say about all of them – I loved Jimmy, I loved Speedy …and there's not one bad word that I could say about Andy, he was not a bad person. But he had a thing about Speedy. Him and Speedy just did not get on, not on Speedy's side – on *Andy's* side, you know? And he'd pull little numbers, like he knew that Speedy would be nightclubbing all night, and he wouldn't get home 'til like 5, 6, 7 in the morning and then crash, you know. So he'd pick up the phone and he'd dial Speedy's number and just put the phone down and let it ring. And poor old Speedy would stumble out of bed and he'd pick up the phone and there'd be nothing there. Andy used to do that to him all the time and it used to really get on his goat.

On February 22nd, the group performed in London at the Young Vic as part of The Who's *Lifehouse* workshops which had begun the previous week. Jeff Stein, who went on to direct the brilliant Who-sponsored documentary film *The Kids Are Alright*, was present that night. "Keith and I actually ended up on stage jamming a bit with Thunderclap Newman," Stein said in 2003. "Of course, I was just on tambourine and Keith was on maracas or something. It was surreal but at least I got to hang out with Keith and, you know, see a Thunderclap Newman gig. I don't know how many people can make that claim."

After gigs in Wimbledon (Hobbits Garden, Feb. 26th) and Manchester (New Century Hall, 27th), Newman and co. returned to the Young Vic for a second performance on March 1st. When asked why Thunderclap Newman were included in this series of *Lifehouse* workshop performances, Townshend says today, "[Andy] was invited because his aura was so important." Roger Felice recalled both Townshend and Moon joining in with the band onstage. "Pete got up and played a bit, and Keith wanted to get up and play," Felice said. "And Keith was a maniac, 'cause when he's in that environment, he's a maniac, and when he's not, he's a cool dude, so he got up and he got on the drum set and he played a song or two until he put his foot through the bass drum. So he had a big laugh and walked off, and we couldn't go on until the roadies quickly came along and changed the drum skin, and away we went. ... But it was a great night, a good vibe and it was a lot of fun."

The group performed at Rebecca's in Birmingham on March 3rd, followed by a Saturday night gig on March 6th at Brighton Polytech supported by the Third Ear Band. There are few fan reports available regarding Thunderclap's live shows, but Michael McNamara, a Canadian living in Brighton at the time, provided some details as to this performance. "It was not in a theatre, and there was no stage," McNamara recalled.

It was in a large hall, like a cafeteria, at the University of Sussex... The band was set up at one end of the room; tables had been pushed out of the way and there was some very crude spotlighting. Harsh and hard, like bare incandescent spots on stands. They were on the same level as the audience.

The audience was mostly standing and watching or dancing. The crowd was not a big one. The opening act, Third Ear Band, had done a noisy aimless set, so the mood was as I recall, low. I do remember being able to get right up close, and was fascinated with the longer pieces like 'Hollywood Dream' and 'Accidents'.

In a room full of freaks, Newman and the rest of the band were an anomaly. Newman had a very beat up piano, and a kazoo rigged up in the end of a sort of cardboard cone that was attached to the piano, so he could play the kazoo and the piano at the same time. I actually said hello to Keen and Jimmy after the show, and shook Jimmy's hand. I remember because he was a tiny guy (I'm six feet).

Further performances took place at Sheffield University on the 12th, and at Nelson Imperial Ballroom (Lancashire) on the 14th.

Around mid-March, there appears to have been some friction within Thunderclap Newman which resulted in a temporary change to the lineup. Andy later recalled "a rather ironic situation towards the end which was that Speedy became dissatisfied with Roger's drumming, and wanted to swap him with another drummer. But he forgot to get rid of the old drummer and they both turned up at the gig and we had two drummers playing in the band. It worked out rather well."

While nobody else can corroborate this story of

duplicate drummers, it's certain that Roger Felice was replaced for a time during spring, 1971. Around late March, Thunderclap Newman had a new drummer: Jimmy McCulloch's friend Chris Hunt. Hunt had been drummer for a group called The Good Time Losers, who had performed with McCulloch's old band One In A Million at the Wimbledon Palais in the summer of 1967. "I knew Jimmy from the early days," said Hunt. "I was in another band in London, and I got friendly with them. We carried on a friendship for a while and about two years later we started jamming together with Mott The Hoople – 'cause I'd worked with Ian Hunter in another band called Pendulum, and somehow Jimmy came back in the picture then, and we were sort of hanging out together doing little jams and things like that." McCulloch had called Hunt and asked him to play with Thunderclap Newman.

After minimal preparation ("I think we only had one or two rehearsals," said Hunt), Thunderclap Newman returned to the stage, Hunt's debut likely taking place on March 24th at the 'Erith College Rag' at the Black Prince in Bexley, southeast London. Further appearances in the London area took place at the end of the month: The Resurrection, Hermitage Ballroom, Hitchin on the 27th with supporting acts Flying Fortress and Pluto, and the following night at Southall Farx, the Northcote Arms, Southall.

Hunt quickly realized that this was Keen's band. "I think Jimmy musically was obviously the best one out of everybody, but I guess Speedy saw it as his band, his baby," said Hunt. "It was his band and you do things the way he wanted to do them, you know. It was pretty smooth for me, I just did what they wanted me to do, and played the drums and it was fine, and we all got on well. I got on alright with Speedy – he didn't say a lot to me; he thought I was a bit straight."

On April 6th, again remaining in London, Thunderclap Newman performed at the Resurrection Club at the Salisbury in Barnet with support from Blind, and on the 10th they appeared at the Potters Bar Youth Centre (also known as the Potters Bar Farx) with Gnome Sweet Gnome and Pluto.

During his brief stint with the band, Hunt typically hung out with McCulloch. "He was my mate, 'cause I'd known him by then for five years," Hunt recalled. "We shared the same desires for a drink and a puff. I never saw Jimmy do anything more than have a drink and a joint, and of course Andy was as straight as anything."

In late April, the group embarked on a short Scandinavian tour, supporting, of all bands, Deep Purple. It was while waiting for the flight to Sweden that Hunt realized that Keen's drug use went a little beyond that of his bandmates. "When we went to Scandinavia, we were at Heathrow airport in the bar and Speedy went and got a magazine," Hunt recalled.

And I said, "What are you reading; can I have a look?" And he mumbled and was a bit cagey about it. And he went off to the toilet and I was sitting there with my beer and I thought I'm going to have a look at his magazine. So I picked it up and between every page was a pill – he'd stashed all his pills in there 'cause he was going to go through customs and he rolled up this magazine, put it under his arm and of course it was all full of pills.

The Scandinavian tour was a short affair: Six dates over six nights, all at large venues. The first two performances on April 21st and 22nd took place at Stockholm's Konserthus, followed by a gig on the 23rd at K.B. Hallen in Copenhagen, capacity 4,500. Life on the road during Thunderclap

Newman's Scandinavian tour was quite an experience for their new drummer, who found himself sharing a hotel room with Andy. "I mean, I loved the guy," said Hunt, "but at about 2 o'clock in the morning he'd be talking about the workings of the internal combustion engine and I'm thinking, 'For God's sake, Andy, I'm trying to get some sleep now!' Smashing bloke, but totally eccentric."

Hunt's experience playing onstage with the band – particularly Andy, whose timing was known to wander – was relatively good. Perhaps his style of drumming helped keep Newman on track. "There were no monitors and such, so we couldn't hear each other that well," Hunt recalled. "His rhythm playing was fine; he was in time and everything. It was a very strange little band, wasn't it, to say the least. Eccentric character for sure, a one-off indeed. Lovely bloke though. He used to call himself the Professor of Syncopation – that sort of jerky time signature."

Two dates in Denmark followed – Aarhus on the 24th and Aalborg on the 25th – before the final performance, in Oslo's 5,600-capacity Njardhallen, the largest venue Thunderclap Newman would ever play. "It was a big, enclosed sports pavilion; a huge place," Andy Newman recalled.

When Thunderclap Newman returned to the U.K., their future appeared uncertain. The status of Felice and Hunt was in question, and although there were a handful of live dates booked, a preoccupied Townshend and an increasingly dysfunctional Track Records left the group without direction. Nobody appeared to be paying attention to the needs of the group, or formulating any strategy.

"When the band returned from Scandinavia, Speedy came straight to my apartment to see me," recalled Roger Felice. "We just got smashed and had a ball – the tour was never discussed." Meanwhile, Chris Hunt was left wondering what the future held. "We came back and I was sort of half expecting to get a call saying we're going to do some more shows," he said. But instead, he said, "I got a call from John Field at Track who said, "It's all fallen apart mate – it's finished." So that was that."

Personality conflicts within the band, which had always been bubbling below the surface, had become more pronounced, particularly between McCulloch and Keen. This tension between Jimmy and Speedy was palpable during Chris Hunt's short tenure with the group and appears to have been the final blow in driving the band apart. "The only thing that I really do remember is that Speedy and Jimmy just didn't get on," Hunt said when asked what he remembered about Speedy. "That was always there, an undercurrent. They'd argue about silly things. Speedy would say things like, "That was a bit weird tonight, what you played," and Jimmy would say, "Well, you told me to play it" – it would be silly things. Snip, snip, snip – sniping at each other."

After listening to the live recordings of the group's performance in the Netherlands in February, one wonders if frustration on the part of Jimmy – wanting greater latitude for soloing; and Speedy – tiring of McCulloch's onstage dominance; were at the core of the dispute, something Andy helped corroborate in a 2011 interview with *Mojo*. "There had been a slight disquiet between Jimmy and Speedy," Newman said. "They fell out irrevocably. Jimmy was a soloist rather than an accompanist, and solos only featured occasionally. They drifted apart. ...I felt a bit sad," he added. "We could have gone on a bit further if there hadn't have been differences between the boys, and the record label had been more supportive."

"...Speedy Keen and Jimmy McCulloch had gradually, over the years, diverged in their sort of approach to music, and they weren't getting on very well," Andy told Australian radio host John Broughton in 2010. "Eventually in the middle of one of our last tours, although I wasn't around at the time, off stage they had a bit of a row, and they weren't willing to work with one another again. And with them gone, I presume they regarded that the band was no more, so they decided that was it, end of band. And I was left on my own."

It's possible that there was one more Thunderclap Newman performance, with Roger Felice back on the drum stool. The May 22nd edition of *Melody Maker* advertised a gig at the Wake Arms in Epping that very same night and proclaimed that "Thunderclap and his merry lads are back on the road playing occasional gigs mixing rock and roll and the zany piano playing of Mr. Newman."

"To the very best of my recollection, I am sure we did at least one more show after Scandinavia, because I can remember Speedy coming over to my apartment and going through all the details with me," Felice recalled. "I can't remember where the gig was, but we definitely did a gig after Scandinavia… Oslo wasn't the last gig."

CHAPTER 9
SPLASHDOWN

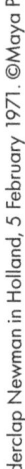

"We were the best worst band. We died but we died in style: Andy in his policeman's helmet, handing out paper hats and balloons and worshipping Bix Beiderbecke; beautiful Jimmy, playing his beautiful guitar up in heaven; and me, scarface rock & roller just trying to get across some honesty."

– Speedy Keen, *Rolling Stone*, 1973

Sometime around the middle of 1971, the band known as Thunderclap Newman ceased to exist. The arc of the original band was complete. Nik Cohn put it perfectly in *Rolling Stone* a few years later: "Out of the jumble of elements and oddities, against all logic, Thunderclap Newman created one of the finest, most truly bizarre albums of the era, *Hollywood Dream*; made Number One with their first single, 'Something in the Air'; were immediately pushed out on the road, with ornate fanfares; failed to sell another record; finally fell apart, and disbanded. From nowhere to everywhere and back to nowhere again in less than a year." It was actually two years, but still…

The end was gradual, and without fanfare. As recently as April, Pete Townshend had mentioned the prospect of a second Thunderclap Newman album in his column in *Melody Maker*, apparently perceiving enough stability within the group to be thinking ahead. A few months earlier, the weekly had reported that the group "will probably be visiting the States later in the year with the Who."

It is tantalizing to think what could have transpired had Thunderclap Newman's live work continued to improve, and had they enjoyed the exposure afforded by touring in support of The Who. The American group Lynyrd Skynyrd's career took off when they supported The Who on a U.S. tour two years later. The Steve Gibbons band enjoyed similar exposure in 1976, supporting The Who during a tour of the U.K. "When you think about it, there were these bands around The Who, like the Steve Gibbons band," Richard Barnes observed. "You could be on a huge fucking tour of Europe or America or something; it does so much good. And that could have happened with Thunderclap Newman, especially if people knew that Pete Townshend was involved and produced it and all that. So they could have had that sort of thing; it's just kind of tragic that they didn't really develop into a much more successful band."

"I think had they gone, it could have been the making of the band," said Dana Wiffen.

But it wasn't to be. While much improved during this last run, the group's live act still lacked structure and cohesion. This resulted in the friction and frustration that ultimately drove the band apart. "We played Speedy's songs from the album; that was basically the bulk of the show: 'Something In The Air', 'Accidents', 'The Reason', and so forth," said Roger Felice. "Speedy used to love Neil Young, so we threw in 'Cinnamon Girl', and I put in 'The Shape I'm In' by The Band, but it was mainly Thunderclap Newman, and it was hard for me, because I wanted to make it sound like the record, right? And I think that was one of the main problems because I don't know if that really worked in well."

Getting in the way of this, Felice explained, was the rest of the band lacking defined roles, particularly Jimmy and Andy. "Everybody was in different heads," said Felice.

Jimmy was a *great* player, but he really wanted to let loose – he really wanted to be like Jimmy Page or Eric Clapton or someone. Then you've got Andy, who much of the time was switched off, because he did not understand anything we were doing – he had his piano and his whistles and his saxophone and his – I don't know what... and sometimes he'd smoke a pipe onstage, [laughs] I'm serious! He didn't have a *clue* what was going on onstage. And that's why most of his solos, the band's not playing. Most of the time he wasn't even on, so you could be playing something like 'Cinnamon Girl' or 'The Shape I'm In', and the band's playing, and all of a sudden you'd hear a whistle and a bit of saxophone going, or a cigar being lit, or... you know. It was really frustrating.

"...In hindsight," Felice continued, "Thunderclap Newman could have been like AC/DC, for example."[75]

If you do your homework on AC/DC, it's in parts, so you've got the lead singer, you've got Angus, then you've got the three who stand at the back – they never move, they don't run around, like Ronnie Wood of the Rolling Stones – when they've got to do backup vocals, they walk up to the micro-phone, do their backup vocals, and walk straight back. When the singer's finished his singing and the guitar solo, the singer steps back and the stage belongs to Angus. And Angus plays his guitar and runs around, does the Chuck Berry and then the singer comes back up – so it's a regimented thing. You'll never see them running around.

Now when you look at Thunderclap Newman, it's the same arrangement. ...In hindsight, if we'd have sat down and said look, let's do this: Ronnie and I are the rhythm section. We'll just play, we're a done deal, we've been together for years; we know each other. We could have said look, Andy, you sit

75 Speaking of AC/DC: "I was supposed to join AC/DC," said Felice. "I was going to join them as they were getting to their peak, and I didn't join them because my wife and I had a baby. So [laughs] – I knocked back joining AC/DC."

there, and like we'd try and clue Andy in to some of the things, say try and not play a saxophone there and try and get rid of some of those whistles and you know, put your yoyo away and hide your pipe [laughs] – oh, it was crazy mate!

...If we'd have done that, the band could have really made it, because Ronnie and I, we were a rhythm section, we could have worked with Jimmy and Andy and Speedy, so it could have been cut up as in AC/DC – it could have been a regimented band where we each know what we've got to do in the song. So Jimmy can get his balls off and go mad on guitar, we do some songs that he wants to actually play and show his guitarmanship, and we'd follow him and maybe turn Andy off for a minute, right? And even at times when the band would be playing, Speedy would stop playing rhythm, and it'd just be the three of you, a trio, it'd just be Ronnie, myself and Jimmy, just going for it, you know? So in hindsight, if we'd have done that, the band could have been... but as it was, it was just a mangled mess, it was just each man for himself.

* * *

After Thunderclap Newman's return to the U.K. following their tour of Scandinavia, Speedy Keen shut himself away in his apartment and wrote. "I don't know if he was writing songs because he was a songwriter, or if he was writing songs for another album," said Felice. Several of the songs Keen wrote during this period were later released as solo material. Similarly, Andy Newman continued work on his own solo album.

Later in 1971, when Keen asked Jimmy McCulloch,

Roger Felice and Jim Avery[76] to record with him, there were questions as to whether this was for Thunderclap Newman, or for some planned solo work. "Speedy came to me and said, "Look, The Who have got studio time but they can't use it... would you do some sessions with me?"," Felice recalled. "And I said, "Yeah, sure." And he also asked Jimmy. I wasn't quite sure did he mean do some sessions with him, or do sessions with Thunderclap. And I think, again, poor old Speedy, bless his soul, some of the times he'd be a bit out of it, you know? He'd be like – he'd miss a bus, or miss an appointment, or go to the wrong... you know. So when we were there, and there was like Speedy and Jimmy and myself and ...I think it was Jim Avery, I'm thinking oh, well this is probably a Thunderclap thing, you know? But Andy wasn't there, which I totally understand – I think Andy is the sort of guy that you would put on after everything else was recorded."

After a handful of sessions, around late 1971 Felice decided to return home to Australia. "I was sitting at home one day having a smoke and I'm looking out and I can see all these chimneys and antennas and whatever and it's cold, and I thought, 'what the hell am I doing?'," he said. "And we weren't rolling in dough. So I just picked the phone up and got a ticket and went and saw Jimmy and Speedy and got on a plane and came home. But it was still Thunderclap Newman – I thought I was just leaving Thunderclap Newman." The band still hadn't officially broken up. "No one ever said, "let's break up," or there was never an announcement, it's just that – things just drifted," said Felice.

Keen and Newman would both later express their regrets regarding the demise of the group. "I think we could have done a lot better if there would have been a

76 By this time, Ronnie Peel had returned to Australia.

motivation on the part of the record company, although I don't necessarily blame them," Newman said in 2010. "I think the main problem was that Speedy didn't realize the potential he had for writing songs, and he was always comparing himself with other great pop luminaries and feeling a little inferior, and not realizing that he had some potential and that the unit we had could actually produce some nice productions with the help of Pete Townshend. But that unfortunately was as far as it went, and it's always been my regret that we didn't make two or three more albums and maybe progressed things in a more diverse manner, but that's the way history goes."

Keen, too, wished that the group would have focused on studio recordings. "If we'd have made albums, it would have been perfect for us because we had that balance; we had to compensate, to be compatible with each other," he said in 1975. "Because Andy would only play boogie, he would play nothing else, so I had to write the songs in such a way that I could get my song across but also leave a space for him in the song, which contributed as well, it wasn't just us and him, us and him."

It was a delicate balance, one which was lost during live performances. "Really, the road show killed it," Speedy told the *NME*'s Charles Shaar Murray in 1975. "It was very difficult playing live. I was the bleedin' drummer for a start, and I was up front trying to play guitar. Basically, you're talking about a lorry driver who was thrust into it because he'd had a number one... At least a guitar was something I could hold onto, and it was a better image than drums... I dunno. Also, you have to have some kind of unity in a band, and we were all opposites. It was really frustrating for Jimmy, cause he was really shit hot."

* * *

1971 also marked the beginning of the end of the relationship between Pete Townshend and his mentor, Kit Lambert, and the start of the gradual decline of Track Records. In addition to emerging creative differences, there were significant concerns over Lambert and Stamp's financial management of the label. "We had thought that we would be partners or shareholders: This never happened," Townshend recalled in his memoir, referring to the roles of the members of The Who within the company. "Jimi Hendrix was their biggest signing by far, but I'd brought them two No. 1 artists in Arthur Brown and Thunderclap Newman, and had received no royalties."

"It's unfortunate that Kit and Chris weren't able to concentrate only on Track," Townshend said in 1971, "but really had The Who at their most difficult state which was before *Tommy*, during *Tommy* and at the time two years after *Tommy* which proved to be just like a huge hump in the Who's career, which was just where we needed management most crucially and it caused everybody to go through incredible traumatic experiences and Track just got lost along the way because of it."

"Track Records really took Kit and Chris's attention away from The Who," Richard Barnes observed. "And so did heroin – I forgot that little point – they both got into heroin. Normally it's the managers trying to save the band members from taking drugs; with these two it was the other way round. I mean, I must admit that Kit and Chris were absolutely fucking brilliant managers. Brilliant. And then it got to the point where they were holding back the band, in my opinion."

Townshend drifted away from the distracted and increasingly addled Lambert. "We just generally moved apart," he told the *NME* in July 1971. "We think completely differently now."

These distractions meant that Lambert and Stamp's

attention certainly wasn't with Thunderclap Newman, either. "I got angry about Kit," Newman told Kit Lambert biographer Andrew Motion, "because if one had someone who was supposed to be a manager you feel fed up with having to wait six months for an answer to anything, then hang around the office for three days to get it."

"I later realized that the problem with Kit Lambert was that he was just like his opposite number in Liverpool, Brian Epstein," Andy told Mark Blake. "He was a one-group manager. I have always suspected Kit Lambert wanted us to have a big crash and sell no records so he could turn round and say 'You're finished'. We had the hit, but they still didn't follow it up. They were dedicated to The Who, and our career was put on the back burner."

"I think it would have sustained had Kit Lambert taken over the production and management of the band properly," Townshend said in 1983, "but also it was really a lack of follow-through in the band. Speedy Keen was the drummer and writer, and I was very much his mentor, in the same way that Kit Lambert was my mentor. Once we'd finished the album, which was meant to be a very light-hearted homespun affair, the Who went out on a massive American tour, and when we got back, it was all finished. They'd tried to put out three singles from the album, but the album really wasn't singles material. They would have done better to wait, and they also made the mistake of trying to do live appearances, which were a disaster."

By 1975, The Who had left Track and had taken legal action against the label for financial mismanagement. At the same time, Track's roster of artists had dwindled significantly. "When I left, I think it was about '75, The Who had gone," Dana Wiffen recalled. "And then not long after I left I think they moved to Carnaby Street, as like a punk label." Track's attempt to reinvent themselves involved hiring Jim Avery as artistic liaison. Avery had founded the proto-punk band Third World War in the early '70s before returning to the Track fold as a studio musician. "Track had me back as artistic liaison 'cause they were thinking of signing up Siouxsie and the Banshees and stuff like that," said Avery, "and they brought me in because they knew I was into – a bit like the early Who sounds, the really adventurous, exciting stuff. Not the laid back, groovy stuff that happened with the hippies. They sent me round to all these clubs, to see who was who, etc., but it all went kaput in the end anyway."

Track's decline was similar to that of its predecessor on the forefront of the U.K. indie scene, Immediate Records. Immediate had counted The Nice, The Small Faces, P.P. Arnold, Amen Corner and Humble Pie among their roster of artists, while Track boasted Jimi Hendrix, The Who, John's Children, Arthur Brown and Thunderclap Newman. Both labels left a legacy of daring and innovation; both also faltered under a cloud of reckless spending, debt and drug addiction. Immediate had folded in 1970.[77]

"[Track] carried the free spirit in which rock and roll bands had initially formed into a part of their lives which had previously been subservient to established commercial conglomerates," wrote Andrew Motion in *The Lamberts*. "It was a revolution in the means of production, brought about by a revolution in taste, and set a precedent which other bands – often preferring to keep their music thoroughly in their own control – have subsequently turned into standard practice."

Track had a few more notable releases into the '70s, including The Heartbreakers' *L.A.M.F.* (1977) and Golden Earring's 'Radar Love' single (1973), which was a

---

77 One of the items seized by the liquidator during insolvency proceedings was Immediate co-founder Tony Calder's high-end Mercedes 600, which ended up being bought by Pete Townshend.

worldwide hit. The label's final release was '50s throwback Shakin' Stevens eponymous album on April 7th, 1978. It failed to reach the charts. The label's last chart entry had been their final release by The Who: The LP *Odds & Sods*, in October 1974, which reached number 10 in the U.K.

PART THREE

CHAPTER 10

JIMMY

Jimmy McCulloch onstage with Wings, Cardiff, 11 September 1975. ©Barry Plummer

"I am a bit weird. Immaturity, I suppose. I've had a lot of experience in music, but the experience of life – knowing how to treat people, when to say something, when not to and when you've put your foot in it – I'm still a bit green that way. Sometimes there is a Jekyll and Hyde within me. Sometimes I really blow it and get on people's nerves."

- Jimmy McCulloch

"Jimmy was an excellent guitar player; he was an absolutely fantastic guitar player... A wonder."

- Jim Avery

By August 1971, Jimmy McCulloch was itching to get back on the road. He'd received some offers to play with other groups, but "nothing that knocked me out," he said. "After Thunderclap Newman fell through, I thought I'd get my own band together to keep working," he told Chris Welch in October. "I just put an ad in the *MM* for a drummer and got two hundred phone calls," he said, without explaining why his brother wasn't used. "It was just non-stop," he continued. "But I could suss most of them out over the phone. I ended up with Nigel Baker (drums), Robbie Paterson (rhythm guitar and vocals) and Barry Smith on bass." The group, operating as Bent Frame, quickly gained the attention of Chas Chandler, who was looking to manage them.

McCulloch had known Paterson for years, since the earlier, pre-Thunderclap version of Bent Frame. "Robbie was lead vocalist, my brother Jack played drums and we had an organist," Jimmy told Pamela Holman in December.

But that fell through, and I joined Thunderclap Newman and Robbie reformed Bent Frame. In between times we were trying to get other bands off the ground, but there were always barriers put up, and we couldn't actually do anything. But now that I've split from Thunderclap Newman I have a chance to do what I've wanted to do for a long time – working on my own material playing what I've wanted to play. It was very restricting for me in Thunderclap. I was always being told what to do, so I could never be fully creative. It was very hard for me. All that kept me going at that time was writing with Robbie. …Only now am I beginning to get out of myself and doing with Robbie everything we've learnt in the last few years.

This iteration of Bent Frame had been rehearsing for about three weeks when McCulloch received a phone call from John Mayall, who was set to begin a short tour of Germany and the U.K. Mayall had just released *Memories*, an album with Ventures guitarist Gerry McGee and former Canned Heat bassist Larry Taylor. McGee had backed out of the tour at the last minute, leaving Mayall scrambling for a guitarist. Already in Germany and with the first gig in only three days, he called Chas Chandler, who recommended McCulloch. "I caught him rehearsing with his new group, Bent Frame, and he willingly agreed to postpone the official launch so that he could play on this tour with me," said Mayall.

"I got that call to join John on the Thursday, and I was on stage with them in Germany on the Sunday," McCulloch told Jeffery Pike of *Guitar* magazine in 1975, adding that it was "the first time I really felt on the spot." McCulloch's debut with Mayall took place around mid-September 1971. "…The only rehearsal we had was on the Sunday afternoon," McCulloch continued. "There I was on stage in front of an audience, and John would turn to me and say, 'Take a solo now!' The material was easy enough, twelve-bar blues mostly, but that experience of having to react to an audience and build up a number, that taught me a lot."

After eight gigs in Germany, Mayall, McCulloch and company (bassist Larry Taylor and drummer Keef Hartley) returned to the U.K. for eleven dates which stretched from September 23ʳᵈ to October 5ᵗʰ. The tour's opening act was Eggs Over Easy, the band who backed Steve Ellis on his 1971 single 'Have You Seen My Baby' with McCulloch on guitar. "The best night of the tour was in Glasgow, my home town," Jimmy said. "Great reception! It was really nice to work with good musicians and Larry Taylor is an incredible bass player." He later recalled that the tour "was good for me, got me back into working onstage again, which is what I love most."

It's a testament to his phenomenal abilities that McCulloch, at this point just 18 years old, assumed the role of lead guitar in John Mayall's band, a position previously filled by the likes of Peter Green and Eric Clapton. "This young veteran …has at last been brought to the attention of serious concert audiences through his just completed tour with John Mayall," Chris Welch wrote in *Melody Maker*. "Once again "the Mayall school," has found a promising pupil and conferred on him an honours degree in rock. At first audiences tended to smile when they saw the tiny chap, young enough to be Mayall's son, taking such an aggressive stance behind his guitar. After a few bars of hard-hitting, inventive guitar, the smiles and jaws, dropped."

"Playing with John has helped me find my own direction," McCulloch told Welch. "I didn't have much confidence as a player with Thunderclap. It was a very freaky band, and I was in a rut. I wasn't established as a guitar player."

In early October, after the conclusion of the Mayall tour, Jimmy returned his attention to Bent Frame, with the same lineup as before, except Jack McCulloch briefly assumed the role of drummer in place of Nigel Baker. "I've wanted to get my own band going for some time but things like that don't happen easily," Jimmy said in January. "This band's only been together a short time but I think it's going to be a good 'un." The group received interest from a handful of record labels but "we really want to get playing first and get the sound of the band before we go into the studio," he told Chris Welch. "It'll be rhythm and rock and a bit of blues." McCulloch was still getting used to being taken seriously as a musician. ""I suppose people think I'm a novelty," says Jimmy, hardening his jaw, eyes narrowing," wrote Welch. ""A little guy who plays guitar. Far out. But it doesn't worry me. We're going to enjoy ourselves and get it on!""

McCulloch was eager to get Bent Frame on the road. After a few weeks of rehearsal, their live debut took place at The Roundhouse, North London, on Sunday, October 31st, with either Jack McCulloch or Ed Leich on drums in place of Nigel Baker. Jack explained the rotating personnel to Paul Salley: "Bent Frame was a workshop name more than anything else – something that gave us continuity. Whoever saw the band play live would see at least a couple of the original line-up's members in whichever version of the band it was." In keeping with the constant change that often seemed to accompany McCulloch's projects, the name, too, would soon be jettisoned.

"Jimmy felt the need to apologize frequently to the rather surprised crowd, explaining that as the band hadn't been together too long, they were having to improvise a bit," reported Mark Williams in the programme for the group's performance at the Rainbow the following January. "Well that was alright. McCulloch really *is* the original teenage whizz kid – the silver surfer of the fretboard. This 18 year old plays his axe so fast you can see sparks fly from his fingers. The art of coherent improvisation is a rare quality, but he's got it and that night at the Roundhouse he made an otherwise amiable and slightly disinterested audience stand up and cheer. In a word, he cooks."

After the Roundhouse gig, Bent Frame resumed rehearsals at a studio in Putney, during which Jimmy's £350 Gibson guitar was stolen. "Keith Richard somehow got to hear about it and sent me a selection of axes to try out," said Jimmy. "Thanks to him I've got a really beautiful 1948 Les Paul. I guess he must just dig my playing." Primarily focused on rehearsing and songwriting in preparation for recording an album, the group sprinkled in a few live dates in November and December, playing Loughborough College on November 13th, and Manchester New Century Hall on the 20th. By this time, they were being referred to in the press as the Jimmy McCulloch Band, and Ed Leich had assumed drumming duties. "Jimmy's band were refreshing to say the least," the *NME* reported of the Manchester gig. "Perhaps their main problem is that too many people think you have to be at least 25 to play the guitar well. But Jimmy's style is far more mature than most of our "established" guitarists, and yet he's only 18. The group played a selection of their own compositions, including 'Run And Hide,' [sic – the title was 'Run And Ride'] 'Time Don't Wait,' "Keep It Tight," "Sellophane' and 'All The Love I've Got.'The music was good but too far-out for the audience."

The Jimmy McCulloch Band performed at Sussex University, Brighton on December 3rd, and Portsmouth Polytechnic on the 8th. Immediately following the group's appearance at Preston Public Hall on the 21st, Barry Smith and Ed Leich departed "due to differences in musical policy," according to the *NME*. "Second guitarist Rob Paterson has temporarily switched to bass, and McCulloch is using stand-in drummers to honor existing commitments. Permanent replacements are now being sought by the band, which appears at London Speakeasy tomorrow (Christmas Eve)."

A car accident on New Years Eve proved to be a near-miss for McCulloch, who drove his Mini into a field on the way home from a party hosted by Humble Pie drummer Jerry Shirley. "He got off with a cut forehead," reported *Disc and Music Echo*'s Caroline Boucher. "The luck was that he'd missed going head on into an oak tree and certain death by six inches."

By the time the Jimmy McCulloch Band appeared at the Rainbow Theatre on January 29th 1972, the first of two consecutive nights in support of Mountain, bassist Mick Hawksworth and drummer Tony Fernandez were on board. The band played eight more U.K. dates with Mountain, including a stop at Glasgow's Strathclyde University. The final date was at Sheffield University on February 11th. The group then returned their focus to songwriting and preparing for a short European tour, after which they hoped to record an album. Then, in the summer, "if everything goes to plan," Jimmy told Mark Williams, "we're going on a six week tour of the States with the Stones." McCulloch's band had been rehearsing at the Stones' space on Bermondsey Street, London; on the Mountain tour, Jimmy played a Les Paul he'd borrowed from Mick Taylor. And Marshall Chess, president of Rolling Stones Records, "has been insistent on signing Jimmy's band since hearing the first few tapes," *Disc and Music Echo* reported in January.

All of these plans were soon derailed, however, when Jimmy experienced two successive health setbacks. First, he was bitten by a dog, requiring stitches in his hand. Then, within just a few days, he suffered a collapsed lung, a complication from the asthma he'd suffered from since childhood. "We had a couple of tours and then… I had to go into hospital," Jimmy said. "Fortunately it wasn't too bad, but the band had dispersed when I came out two weeks later!"

And so the Jimmy McCulloch Band fell apart with no

album and no tour with the Rolling Stones. While Jimmy's hospitalization was the final cause of the band's disintegration, it appears that other matters were bubbling beneath the surface. "He just kind of went off the radar," Mick Hawksworth told Paul Salley. "I think maybe the clash of characters might have had something to do with it, as he was more than a bit fiery and wasn't averse to picking a fight, although never with us. ...On the day, Jimmy could be as nice as you like, but he did have another side." This also helps to explain the constant shuffling of personnel during the band's short existence.

The sudden dashing of his plans must have been a significant blow to McCulloch, but there's no evidence that he lamented the loss of his band and their lofty prospects, at least in public. He simply did what he was best at and got back to work. McCulloch continued working with Speedy Keen on sessions for Keen's solo album, and around April, he guested on two tracks – 'I Feel Better' and 'Apron Strings' – on John Entwistle's solo album *Whistle Rymes*, the sessions taking place at Island Studios, west London.

Meanwhile, in early May 1972, the Glaswegian blues rock group Stone The Crows suffered an horrific tragedy when founding member and guitarist Les Harvey died onstage from electrocution at the Top Rank Suite in Swansea. Stone The Crows' keyboardist was Jimmy's old friend from the Pathfinders, Ronnie Leahy. When the group decided to forge ahead and at least honor their future commitments, Jimmy's name came up as a possible candidate to take over guitar duties. "Because Leslie Harvey was such a fabulous player, after he died we tried Peter Green," Leahy recalled. After short stints with Green and Steve Howe of Yes, the group turned to McCulloch. "Thunderclap Newman had broken up," said Leahy, "so Jimmy was on the loose, and Stone The Crows were – well most of us were Scottish – and we knew Jimmy from Glasgow and we liked his playing, so we thought this could be a possibility. Let's talk to Jimmy." After a session or two to "make sure we all fit in character-wise as well as playing-wise," said Leahy, "it all worked out fine. Jimmy just fitted in perfectly."

Another of Leahy's friends was Richard Stanley, the filmmaker who had sat in on some Thunderclap Newman rehearsals back in 1969/70. Stanley joined Leahy, McCulloch and the rest of Stone The Crows on a trip to the Mediterranean. "They'd done some rehearsals with Jimmy and then someone decided that we would go away to Gozo, an island off Malta," Stanley recalled. "They rented a big house, and the whole band was going to be there – Maggie and Stevie [Thompson, bassist], and Ronnie and his wife Joan, and Joan's sister and Jimmy, and the idea was to just have a few weeks together in the sun in our own house and kind of resolve these problems, because everybody was, of course, very disturbed by Les's death. So it was a chill-out session. And I got to know Jimmy much better."

Shortly after their return from Gozo, the new lineup of Stone The Crows played their first gig: June 23, 1972, in front of a packed crowd at Birmingham University. "This is a funky rock and roll band on stage, but it sure isn't Stone the Crows playing at their best," *Melody Maker* reported.

> You can't expect them to be dynamite on their first gig. Little Jimmy McCulloch fights to get his breaks and stops on time, and tries to find the right feel for his solos. Big Maggie funky chickens her way over to him, glowering in his face. She looks as hard as a Glasgow fisherwoman. ...It isn't really until the ever-glowing Percy Mayfield tune, 'Danger Zone', that the Crows started to play like a great rock and roll band: a band with charisma and one hell of a lot of power.
>
> ...Closing with the inevitable 'Mr. Wizard,' one

of the couple of remaining numbers from their old set with Leslie Harvey, Jimmy McCulloch comes completely into his own, laying down raunchy rock chords on top of one another with an amazing amount of energy and power for such a little fellow.

The following night, the band performed to another packed house, this time at St. Mary's College, Twickenham. "It was a completely different band from the Crows that played in Birmingham," read *Melody Maker*'s report. "They were more relaxed in the knowledge that the night before had worked out, although they were not that sure of how Jimmy was going to fit in in front of an audience."

… 'I've Been Six Days On The Road And I Got To See My Baby Tonight' rocks and boogies as Maggie dances across the stage threatening Jimmy. Jimmy, so unlike the night before, responds and threatens back. They pull faces at one another, tugging muscles into smiles. Just good ole Glasgow bother. His playing too, is on a different level. He's not just a good rock and roll guitarist, but a steaming power house of guitar blues, putting over the notes with a relaxed air full of poignant soul and gut bucket depths. His playing is different to the late Les Harvey, but carries the same power, so that it becomes easy to see why they never bothered to audition any other guitar players after they had heard him. … You just have to listen to his intro to Sonny Terry's 'Penicillin Blues,' to catch the difference in Jimmy and Leslie's playing. Jimmy is freer, using feedback and longheld high notes, with a lot of pent up violence, where Leslie was more of a rocker, using his guitar, for a sweeter flowing style.

After two power outages in the sweltering heat, the band ended their set in triumphant fashion. "'Is everybody ready to rock and roll,' asked Maggie when the band came back on stage," *Melody Maker* continued. "'Going Down' followed, featuring Jimmy's finest guitar solo with the band so far. Left hand reaching down the neck for those long high notes he loves to play. In time, with this band he will be reaching superstar status as a guitarist."

McCulloch had arrived. He was now a fully-fledged member of a serious, respected blues-rock outfit, and at just nineteen years of age. "Stone The Crows was possibly the first band to play really good – *really good* – blues music, sort of blues/rock mixed, you know," said Leahy, "and we were actually one of the best live bands in Britain at that time, and one of the most highly paid live bands – that was our speciality," a point reinforced by *Melody Maker*'s reporting that fans "tried climbing through windows and busting down exit doors" for a chance to be able to see the group perform live in Birmingham. "And Maggie was the most fantastic singer, so he was put into a band that were exceptionally professional and great, really good players," Leahy went on. "I'm not saying it because I was in Stone The Crows, but we were actually, you know. Jimmy was slightly inexperienced then but Stone The Crows really brought him up, raised his standards in many ways. He'd been in Thunderclap Newman before that and they were a little bit different, they were a little more commercial where we did serious music, and I think that really brought him up to a much higher standard than he'd been in before. But he was still young." Jimmy agreed. "Musically the Crows did a lot of good for me, because they were such a tight unit, and the rhythm section was incredible," he told *Record Mirror*. "They were an advanced band and it took me a while to get used to it."

Musically, McCulloch was well-suited to the role he

occupied with Stone The Crows – he enjoyed a freedom he'd previously never experienced onstage. "He could play anything he wanted," said Leahy. "It was a very free band, playing-wise. We really knitted together as a band. You'd only need to look at one of the guys and you'd know what to play, and it was the right thing and it would fit in with what you were doing. Jimmy was like that as well. I could watch him on the other side of the stage and give him a look, and we'd lock on to some rhythm or some figure. He made it quite effortless, really."

McCulloch, eight years younger than Maggie Bell and seven years younger than Leahy, wasn't in an easy position. His predecessor, Les Harvey, was not only an exceptional guitarist, but a founder and leader within the band, which must have complicated the situation for the new arrival as he worked to fit in. "I never spoke to Jimmy about that, but his playing did all the talking, really," said Leahy. "Playing-wise, he fitted in, and he had a steep hill to climb to get to be as good as Leslie was, and he did it. He had a different style, but he did it in his own way and I've got to admire him for that. He was a lovely, very melodic player." Leahy also recalled that Jimmy and Maggie "got on very well together," which must have helped enormously with his assimilation into the group.[78]

McCulloch's relationship with the other band members was good, too. "We were friends," Leahy recalled. "Not close, deep friends, but very good friends. Some of the guys in the band, we went on holiday during the summer together, and Jimmy came on holiday a couple of times with us. And we got on… as strangely as band members can be, you know… But yeah we were good friends then."

---

78 Maggie Bell, incidentally, performed the role of Tommy's mother on the 1972 album *Tommy*, featuring the London Symphony Orchestra and the English Chamber Choir. Other soloists included Pete Townshend, Steve Winwood, Richie Havens, Roger Daltrey, John Entwistle, Rod Stewart, Ringo Starr and Richard Harris.

And, notably, none of the fiery and difficult behavior that would mar McCulloch's later years – and which had been noted during the Jimmy McCulloch Band period – was evident during his time with Stone The Crows. "Nope, not one bit," said Leahy when asked if Jimmy had exhibited any such behavior during the Stone The Crows years.

Stone The Crows played a scattering of live dates over the next few months – Newcastle, Harrow, Dunstable, Crystal Palace and a festival in Belgium – while also completing work on an album which had been started with Les Harvey. McCulloch played on two of the album's seven tracks, 'Good Time Girl', and a tribute to Les Harvey, 'Sunset Cowboy'. The album, *Ontinuous Performance*, was released in September, and the band took to the road again, promoting the new record with a fourteen-date U.K. tour stretching from mid-September to mid-October. The first date took place in McCulloch and the band's hometown of Glasgow.

During his time with Stone The Crows, Jimmy also appeared on two albums by John Tennent and David Morrison, a duo that had supported the Crows on tour: *Tennent/Morrison* and *Keep It Clean*, the latter with Tennent and Morrison performing as 'Joe Soap'. The Crows also played on Scottish singer/songwriter Brian Friel's album *Brian Joseph Friel*, McCulloch credited as 'The Phantom' apparently for "contractual reasons", although his real name was listed in the credits for the two Tennent/Morrison albums. The musicians from Stone The Crows also appeared on fellow Scot (and Lulu's brother) Billy Lawrie's *Ship Imagination*, with Jimmy credited as 'Jimmy McAnonymous'. Jimmy and Maggie Bell also reportedly guested on a version of 'Maggie Mae' for Liverpudlian writer/singer Jimmy Stevens' eponymous second album at IBC studios, but the album was never released.

On April 28 1973, Stone The Crows performed at the

Rose d'Or Festival in Montreux, Switzerland. A couple of days later, Maggie Bell left the band. "The fire had gone out of us," Bell later commented. "There was no energy anymore. When Les died we lost something, and the band couldn't ever be the same again. Jimmy wasn't a writer, so we would have faced a problem in the future anyway. To be honest, we were all shattered by the loss of Les and I felt I couldn't carry on with this band."

"It was getting very strong but then Maggie left," a disappointed Jimmy told *Music Scene*. "[After Montreux] we were told she was going. It was the first I'd heard of it. The band was building all the time, but it never got the chance to hit its full potential."

In the days after Maggie Bell's departure, Jimmy participated in a few rehearsal sessions and the group began initial efforts to find a new singer, but ultimately nothing came of it. "Everybody seemed to be hanging around waiting for somebody else to do something," Jimmy told the *NME*. "I felt we could spend months like that, and eventually we decided to all go our separate ways. I suppose it showed the band wasn't strong enough to last without Maggie."

Jimmy's departure was precipitated by an offer to join all-Glaswegian group Blue, featuring ex-Marmalade singer/guitarist Hugh Nicholson, and the former White Trash rhythm section of bassist Ian MacMillan and drummer Timmy Donald. "I didn't really know anything about them," he told the *NME*'s James Johnson. "I think we have a lot in common. I had some other offers but this seemed the most interesting. I mean, I could have gone on playing blues till the cows came home. But this is a chance to get some constructive songs together and progress generally, not just as a guitar player. I think that Blue is more of a progression for me than the Crows was." He was looking forward to exploring the songs he'd written in the Bent

Frame / Jimmy McCulloch Band days. "I've got lots of material to contribute to the group," he told *Record Mirror*. "Things that I've written prior to joining."

Blue had existed as a trio for only a few months before McCulloch joined, but had already completed an album, *Blue*, set to be released on RSO, Robert Stigwood's new label, in July. "We felt we needed to expand the line-up to fill out the songs – especially on stage," Hugh Nicholson told the *NME*. "We needed another definite energy source." After rehearsals in St. Tropez, France, Blue's live debut took place at the Zoom Club, Frankfurt, on July 1, 1973, the first of three consecutive nights at the venue. Further touring was planned in the U.K. and U.S. "We want to be really good before we play Britain," Nicholson told *Sounds* in June. "It's going to be a really strong act on stage," McCulloch added. "When we do rock, it's really solid and heavy."

The group re-recorded the single 'Little Jody' in July, wishing to reflect the new four-piece lineup. 'Little Jody' was released later that month. Blue made three appearances on BBC Radio 1 in June and August, and played additional live dates on the continent in July, including Frankfurt's Summer Rock festival on the 22nd, with The Faces. "Jimmy McCulloch's my fave rave at the moment," Rod Stewart told the *NME*. "I always thought he was a great guitar player but didn't realize how great till he started to jam with us backstage at Frankfurt. When Woody and Jimmy play together… it's bleedin' incredible."

Blue struggled to make an impact. 'Little Jody' failed to reach the charts, and *Record Mirror*'s review of Joe Soap's *Keep It Clean* (featuring Jimmy on guitar) proclaimed the latter as "much more appealing, if less flashy, than Blue's." By early September, before any U.K. dates took place, Jimmy left the group, just three months after joining. "That was just like a thing because I was broke and they sent me a copy of their album," he dismissively told *Circus*.

"I was quite glad to leave Blue," McCulloch said later. "They were a good group and all professionals but they didn't have enough balls. They were good on record... but just never got through to me playing live," he said. "... They'd be walking on in Levi's and standing like statues, and I'd be in my white suit leaping around. There was no action on stage. I tend to bomb around a bit. We just didn't click." Interestingly, McCulloch had said the opposite about his previous band, telling the *NME* that "Stone the Crows were always very popular at concerts but the band was a bit of a flop record-wise, on sales. Personally, I think it was because of production. We never got the sound we had on stage - or anything like it. To me all the albums lacked balls."

After his departure from Blue, Jimmy put together a band with ex-Cactus singer Pete French. The group rehearsed and began writing material but fell apart after French couldn't get out of his former band's contract. After a brief stint rehearsing with a group put together by ex-Grease Band pianist Chris Stainton, McCulloch focused his attention on recording a solo album. "I have had a lot of experience in the last few years playing with the best musicians around, and I think the time is now right to work out a few ideas of my own," he told *Record & Radio Mirror* in December. The album, to be released by RSO (the same label Blue was signed to), was to consist of songs written by McCulloch and feature "guest musicians to be announced later". However, a meeting with Paul McCartney soon derailed these plans.

Jimmy McCulloch and Paul McCartney met for the first time at Kingsway Recorders, London, in early November 1973. McCartney was there mixing the Wings album *Band On The Run* and part of the crew was Ian Horne, a friend and neighbor of McCulloch's. "I listened, liked what I heard and thought little more about it," Jimmy told *Record Mirror*. "Then a week later, I had a phone call from the manager – would I like to go to Paris with Paul, Linda and Denny and cut some tracks? Sure thing. I was delighted, it was unbelievable. We all piled into this Mercedes truck and hit the road for Paris. We were there for three days, cut four tracks and came back."[79] Not long after the recordings in Paris, which were for Linda's solo project Suzi and the Red Stripes, things escalated quickly. "I didn't hear anything more for a couple of weeks until the phone rang again," Jimmy recalled. "Would I like to go to Strawberry Studios, Stockport and play on Mike McGear's album?" McGear, McCartney's younger brother, was recording his second solo album, with Paul co-writing and producing. It was during these sessions in Stockport that McCartney asked McCulloch to join Wings.

"I was doing a guitar track and Paul said it sounded really good and wanted to dub a harmony track on top of it," Jimmy told *Circus* in 1975. "And then he said, "By the way, do you fancy joining the band?" Just out of the blue. I said, "Yeah, ha ha, all right, I'll have a go." ...I've been there ever since, and I've no way of leaving yet." In his authorized biography of McCartney, author Philip Norman notes that McCulloch "warned his new chief he could be subject to mood swings, but was taken on nonetheless."

By this time, Jimmy's friend Martin Woodley was living near Grantown-on-Spey, Scotland, not far from where he'd attended military school. Jimmy occasionally paid a visit. "It was right off the River Spey," Woodley recalled, "so we'd walk down to the river and watch the goshawks come down and catch the salmon and eat part of the head and leave the rest, and we'd chase them off and

---

79 Two of these tracks, 'Wide Prairie' and 'I Got Up', were released as part of a post-humous Linda McCartney compilation, 1998's *Wide Prairie*.

we'd go back with the rest of the salmon." McCulloch told Woodley that the McCartney offer wasn't the only one he received during this period; he had also been asked to join David Bowie's group. He later told his cousin, Margaret Chambers, that he "went with Paul because he was the biggest star on the planet then," she recalled. McCulloch's partnership with McCartney and Wings wasn't formally announced until about nine months later, in November 1974, because of McCulloch's contract with the Robert Stigwood Organization. "I hope within the next couple of weeks to be free," Jimmy said in early December.

In the summer of 1974, Paul McCartney and Wings spent six weeks in Nashville, recording at Sound Shop Recording Studio and staying on a nearby farm, a trip coordinated in part by music publisher Buddy Killen, whose copyright attorney was Lee Eastman, Linda McCartney's father. "I bled the band in by taking them to Nashville, which for me is the music capital of the world," McCartney told *Circus* the following year.

"The first song they recorded was 'Junior's Farm', a hoedown rocker inspired by the McCartneys' rustic lifestyle on the Mull of Kintyre in Argyll," Ken McNab wrote in his book *The Beatles In Scotland*. "Initially the song was played at a bluesy mid-tempo canter, but when Jimmy worked out a lead guitar part the song took off like a rocket. The time-change infused the song with a charge of energy and jolted it in an entirely new direction. McCartney was delighted, and suddenly 'Junior's Farm' was promoted from album filler to hit single. It was a good start for Jimmy."

The good start was eclipsed in mid-July when a drunk and disruptive McCulloch arrived at the studio one evening: "[Me and] Buddy Killen were in the studio, just him and me, and we heard Jimmy hit the front door," engineer Ernie Winfrey told Nashville journalist Steve Morley. "He came in, staggering down the hall. Didn't say anything, just sat down on the couch in the front, so we couldn't see him 'cause this console was elevated and the couch was down low. The next thing I know, there was a Coke bottle in the air, headed toward the window glass… the glass inside was angled so it bounced off without breaking anything. Of course, Buddy was steaming. He stormed around there and grabbed Jimmy by the arm, and said 'Get out!'"

Later that evening, McCulloch was arrested for reckless driving and was detained at the local police station. "He was drunk and had everything in his system," Winfrey recalled. "He'd borrowed somebody's little yellow Volkswagen. Buddy got a call at three or four o'clock in the morning. They said, "You need to come down and talk to the judge about your fellow from England." And the guy told him, "The only reason I'm not putting your ass in jail is because of Buddy Killen [a friend of the judge]. I'd better not see you in this courtroom again, or you will be." …Jimmy was such a talented guitar player, there's no doubt about that, but he was just kind of arrogant. I kept wondering why Paul and Linda didn't get fed up with him and fire him, but he was good at what he did."

Drummer Geoff Britton later stated that this behavior nearly got McCulloch thrown out of the band. "Paul came to me with Linda and said he was going to replace them, keep me, go back to England and reform the band," Britton said the following month. "And I said to him, "Well, I think that's a mistake. Every band has its members that are a little bit extreme, but if you're sensible we can cover for that, think ahead and make sure those things don't get out of hand or get publicized." In my opinion, when we were up in that garage rehearsing, we had something. We had a bottom end, we had a groove, and we had energy. We shouldn't throw that away." Within days of McCulloch's arrest, and due at least in part to concern about legal exposure because of it[80], Wings' stay in Nashville came to an early end. The group departed on July 18, 1974.

And so began a back and forth between McCulloch the brilliant musician and McCulloch the troubled, conflicted young man. Happiness seemed fleeting; he shone when engaged in the studio and onstage, but otherwise appeared restless and dissatisfied. McCulloch's expectation was that the Nashville stay would see him offered a secure contract as a paid member of Wings, but this didn't happen. As a result, shortly after Wings returned home from Nashville, McCulloch called McCartney and submitted his resignation, intending to join the James Gang, who'd recently lost their guitarist Tommy Bolin and were in London auditioning replacements. "Jimmy said that while he had been an official member of Wings, the band had yet to actually perform a concert and he was growing impatient," James Gang drummer Jim Fox told Paul Salley.

He told us that he would be happy to join our band. …We began immediate plans to get Jimmy to the States and get this going. Of course, he had to tell Paul that he was leaving. He called us a few days later to say that he had resigned and that Paul had taken it well. We bought airline tickets for him and the plan was underway. A couple of days before his scheduled departure to Cleveland, Ohio, Jimmy phoned to say that Linda had called him and given him a powerful pitch to stay with Wings. She promised they would begin recording very soon and touring soon after that. She even gave him a weekly draw, which was something he had

---

80 McCartney may have been particularly sensitive to legal exposure during this period due to his own legal issues related to marijuana use and cultivation over the previous two years.

not had at that point. So, Jimmy told us that he was forced to back out of our plan.

In August, Wings began rehearsing at Abbey Road studios. Director David Litchfield recorded the activity for his film *One Hand Clapping*, capturing an enthusiastic McCulloch who commented, "It's the best music I've ever put down in my life, no doubt about that. I want to produce a monster album with Paul and the band and be proud of it. That's what I want: To be appreciated on record." Jimmy and co. recorded three tracks at Abbey Road: 'Love In Song', 'Rock Show' and 'Medicine Jar', the latter being particularly noteworthy since it was sung by Jimmy, who also wrote the melody. The song's lyrics were written by Colin Allen, drummer for Stone The Crows.

But the Abbey Road sessions brought fresh opportunities to be led astray, as well. "There was a lot of hanging around, which I think for somebody like Jimmy was dangerous because he got into drinking and he got into drugs," Litchfield said. "It's challenging not to."

> …Paul used to ask us to come into the studio every day at 9:30 in the morning, but he'd never turn up until one or two o'clock… So by the time he turned up, everybody was pissed… including me. What else are you gonna do?
>
> …Two Italian girls used to turn up every day with little presents of drugs. …I think that was really where it started.
>
> …The moment a session finished, he was off and went to the hotel or wherever he was staying, and crashed before going out later that night to the clubs. Sometimes he'd play, sometimes he'd just hang out there, but that was what he was about.

Litchfield observed that because of the age, personality and even cultural differences, McCulloch was essentially on an island in Wings. "I don't think Jimmy and Denny [Laine] were that close, which made it tricky for Jimmy," he said.

He was part of a band, but didn't really feel part of the band. It was a group of individuals that weren't close. There was tension…

After we finished the film, they did a concert in London, and many families turned up. Interestingly, Linda's family was WASP in the way they dressed and looked. …and then Jimmy's family arrived with bottles of beer and sandwiches. You just thought this was not going to work. They were culturally too far apart. It was sad for Jimmy, I think, because his family was so proud of him. They were just going crazy and so was Jimmy. I think the person most sympathetic towards Jimmy was Linda. She felt like he needed mothering.

Which is notable, because it was reported that Jimmy would snipe at Linda when the mood struck him.

The 'Junior's Farm' single was released on October 25th, 1974. The following month, Wings appeared on *Top Of The Pops* performing the new single, which was a hit, reaching number 16 in the U.K. and number 3 in the U.S. When Jimmy sat for an interview with *Guitar* magazine's Jeffery Pike at the end of the year, he expressed a level of comfort regarding his role in the group. "Wings wasn't a *band* before," he said. "It was Paul with session musicians. Now it feels like a band, and I'm able to say my own things and voice an opinion. I can say, Listen, why don't we do this? If it works, we do it. It's everybody being able to speak up and contribute, even though Paul is so dominant."

McCulloch told Pike that the new album was "about half completed. I'm very pleased that I'm singing more than ever before," he said. "This is something I've always wanted to do. It was a question of getting over the confidence thing: If you do sing out of tune, nobody's going to freak out. I'm really getting that together. Guitar wise? It was like a duck to water. It's never a worked-out guitar part, you just get the feeling of when you should play and when you should lay back and let the vocals take it, when you should pick your things and play a little lead. Apart from the chord structure of the songs, everything else is ad lib: you put in your own interpretation of a lead figure, according to how you feel that passage should go. There's plenty of freedom."

In mid-January 1975, Paul McCartney and Wings – sans Jimmy McCulloch – gathered at Allen Toussaint's Sea-Saint Recording Studios in New Orleans to record tracks for the planned album. Jimmy's arrival was delayed, presumably due to visa issues stemming from the reckless driving incident in Nashville the previous July. "The charge put McCulloch's visa status in jeopardy and nearly led to the cancellation of the Wings Over America tour," reported the *Nashville Scene*, indicating that the repercussions of this charge lasted a few years. Geoff Britton later commented that 'Medicine Jar' "helped lift Jimmy's work permit ban to getting into America. It was used to give an example that he was writing a song, so it helped him."

Jimmy flew to the sessions with his newly purchased Zemaitis 12 string guitar sitting next to him on the plane. He'd played a hired Zemaitis on the track 'Love In Song' at Abbey Road the previous year and was sufficiently impressed with its sound that he bought one. "It's a very wide guitar and it's got a really big sound," he told *Sounds*. "I used it on the *Venus & Mars* tracks in America. When I took it over, I strapped it into the seat on the plane. No way was it going into the hold!"

By the time McCulloch arrived in New Orleans, Geoff Britton was on the way out. "I actually arrived over there a week after everyone else in the band and when I got there, Geoff just hadn't worked out," Jimmy told *Record Mirror*'s Eamonn Percival in May. *Melody Maker* reported that Britton "hated McCulloch's guts," although what Britton actually said was that Jimmy "could be a nasty little bit of work."

"I never hated his guts," Britton told Paul Salley. "Jimmy was two people at the time. …When he had a drink, he had very short patience for anybody, sometimes he was a little bit hard on Linda and upset her because at that time, musically, she was exploring her learning curve and potential. On a rough day, he could be a bit short and cruel. He was young and not quite experienced enough to deal with some of those situations, but he'd have learned to be better. …Jimmy, Denny, all the other members liked to drink, do coke and all that stuff. Now I am entirely at the other end of that scale," said Britton, a teetotaler and vegetarian who was also a black belt in karate.

New recruit Joe English was brought in on drums. "When Joe flew in, everything was upside down," said McCulloch. "It was like a new band but we eventually settled down and had a ball. We just did the album and had a gas."

In late February, Wings relocated to Los Angeles, completing and mixing the album at Wally Heider Studios in Hollywood. The *Venus and Mars* album was released on May 27, 1975. A planned photo shoot in Palm Springs for the interior of the album cover had been canceled after Jimmy "had spun out of control and smashed up the interior of the Winnebago RV, forcing me to drive Paul and Linda back to Los Angeles in my car, and cancel the session," photographer Aubrey Powell recalled. "Paul was amazingly forgiving, but it made me wary as to how

Jimmy could go off on a tangent." The album was a hit, reaching the top of the charts in the U.S. and the U.K. "McCulloch and English have added new vitality to Wings as is proved by the new album," Eamonn Percival wrote in *Record Mirror*.

That summer, with the *Venus and Mars* album released, the live work that Jimmy craved finally approached. It had been nearly two years since he'd performed live, the last time having been with Blue in late summer, 1973. Wings began rehearsals in an old cinema in remote Rye, East Sussex, only a mile or two from McCartney's farm in Peasmarsh. Jimmy's friend Martin Woodley, who happened to live in Rye at the time, attended some of the rehearsals and hung out with Jimmy and his bandmate Denny Laine. One afternoon on Laine's boat off Rye Harbour, McCulloch asked Woodley to be his minder during the upcoming tour. "He said, "Hey, I want you to be my personal guy; I want you to make sure that I get on and off the planes, and get to where I should be going, and this, that and the other," Woodley recalled. "Just be his right hand man." Woodley, trying to make his own way as a musician, declined the offer. "I was like, yeah, I'd love to, but I'm trying to get my own thing together here, and if I'm going to do it, I want to do it myself," he said.

McCulloch's request of Woodley indicates a level of self-awareness and reflection that Jimmy rarely revealed in public, a knowledge that having someone to help keep him organized and perhaps hold him accountable would be beneficial. "I've always been the baby in the groups I've played with," he told *Record Mirror* in 1977. "I don't think about it often. But sometimes after I've said something, I'll think about it and then realize they've got 10 years on me, what did I open my mouth for? I've still got a lot to learn." One wonders if the presence of a minder would have altered McCulloch's trajectory in the months ahead.

It's a question Woodley continues to wrestle with all these years later.

After a month or so in Rye, Wings rehearsals moved to a bigger stage at Elstree Studios, Hertfordshire, with Jack McCulloch sitting in at times when Joe English was unavailable. Rehearsals concluded in early September, commemorated with a preview performance at Elstree's Stage 5 where guests included Queen, Ringo Starr, Elton John and Harry Nilsson.

The U.K. portion of a massive, highly anticipated tour known as 'Wings Over The World' began with a date in Southampton on September 9th, 1975. *Record Mirror*'s Peter Harvey caught up with a restless Jimmy at the Capitol Theatre in Cardiff on September 11th. "There are twenty minutes to go before Wings go on stage for their third gig of this current tour, and Jimmy doesn't know whether to sit down, stand up, eat a cheese cracker or go to the toilet," Harvey wrote of McCulloch. "He does all four in a matter of minutes, then slips into a neat new jerkin for the stage and decides he likes it. For him more than any other the other group members, the business of playing with Wings is a monumental step."

"…I knew I would learn a lot from playing with Wings," Jimmy said. "…We're into complementing each other, y'know really listening and feeling who's playing what. … It's getting simpler." After the gig, Harvey added, "…the time comes for Jimmy to go back to his hotel and watch the film *Blazing Saddles*."[81]

The thirteen-date U.K. portion of 'Wings Over The World' ended with three dates in Scotland in late September. "One of the shows was at the Glasgow Apollo and it was marvellous," Jimmy's mother Lily told Ken McNab.

---

81 Martin Woodley remembers McCulloch particularly enjoying comedy: *Monty Python's Flying Circus* and *The Two Ronnies* were favorites.

"You just felt there was so much following for Jimmy because the fans knew he was the lad from just down the road. It was probably my proudest moment."

When Jimmy was back home, he'd visit family and enjoy a little normalcy. "I like to go back to Scotland," he told *Record Mirror* in 1977. "Get back to reality. There's a lot that's unreal about the music business." McCulloch would visit his grandmother in Drumry, Clydebank, where he'd lived as a toddler. "He liked a drink and he liked a bath, but Nana would never let him have a bath at hers because she wouldn't put the immerser on," his cousin, Margaret Chambers, told the *Daily Mail*. "So he'd come to ours for a bath. It's funny to think he'd had a number one and was in Wings – but his gran wouldn't allow him a bath."

A two week, nine date Australian leg commenced in November during which Jimmy met with his old friend and former Thunderclap Newman bandmate, drummer Roger Felice. "That's the last time I saw Jimmy," said Felice.

In January and February 1976, Wings finished recording what would become the album *Wings At The Speed Of Sound* at Abbey Road studios. Jimmy again contributed a composition – 'Wino Junko', and as with his previous effort, 'Medicine Jar', the music was by Jimmy and the lyrics by Colin Allen. Again, McCulloch took lead vocals on the song, part of a slightly more democratic approach on this album, which also featured songs with lead vocals by Denny Laine and Joe English.

In late March, when *Wings At The Speed Of Sound* was released, the group undertook a short tour of Europe, beginning with two dates in Copenhagen on the 20th and 21st. Old friend Ronnie Leahy, on the road playing with Alvin Lee at the time, met with McCulloch there. "We just talked about old times and had a good laugh, and he seemed OK," Leahy recalled. "But shortly after that I heard stories that he was starting to get a bit bolshie and basically drunk, you know – too much alcohol, which was alright in some places but… he was small and he couldn't take it. It gradually started to slip away from him, I think." McCulloch's drug use didn't appear to grow beyond cocaine, marijuana and alcohol; it was just that the volume was increasing. "All the years I knew him, I saw him do some lines, and I saw him smoke some weed and that was it," Martin Woodley said. "I mean, he liked his alcohol," he said, adding that Jimmy particularly liked McEwan's beer. Whiskey was another favorite.

After Wings played in Paris on March 26th, Jimmy broke a finger on his left hand, causing the start of the U.S. leg of 'Wings Over The World' to be delayed by nearly a month. The official story was that a slip on a wet bathroom floor caused the injury, but McCartney's authorized biography reported that the broken digit was the result of "a boozy scuffle" with David Cassidy. McCulloch's hand was in a cast for three weeks. "If Jimmy had been drinking, he had kind of a hot temper," said his friend Gil Woodley, who also worked for David Cassidy for a time and noted he had a similar disposition. McCulloch was "a nice, nice guy most of the time but he had a streak in him," she said. Her brother Martin observed, "if somebody pissed him off, he wasn't one for backing down… a guy would be looking down at him and next thing you know, Jimmy's just kneed him in the nuts or something." Woodley recalled McCulloch getting into a "shoving match" at a party in London around 1976. "I seem to remember somebody coming up and saying something to him, and next thing I know it's like, "Ok, come on, come on. Time to leave"."

The U.S. leg of the tour, which comprised 31 dates in 21 cities, finally commenced in Fort Worth, Texas, on May 3rd 1976. Known as 'Wings Over America', this segment resulted in some tension between McCulloch and McCartney. "There were one or two little hiccups because Jimmy was… his own man, shall we say?," McCartney commented in the 2001 documentary *Wingspan*. The May 22nd gig at Boston Garden resulted in fireworks between the pair when Jimmy opted not to return to the stage for the encore. "It was like, what?," said McCartney. "I've never had anybody decide that ever before. So I sort of just ran off and grabbed him and said, 'You're coming back on!' He responded well to that bit of direction. He came on and he played a blinder."

"Jimmy was a strange little fella," Tony Dorsey, of Wings' brass section, told journalist Steve Morley. "He was troubled, and I just got the kind of feeling he didn't really like me that much. I just stayed out of his way but then he would over-drink and get crazy, and some of the things he would do would piss me off. My feeling was like, hey, I'm going to knock him out but if I'd have done that, Paul would have had to fire me. But Jimmy's playing, man: When he was playing, he was *playing*. He and Joe English, they were the fire in the band; they made the band sound real. Some of those licks he was playing… boy, he'd remind me of Duane Allman. He was firin' it up."

Photographer Aubrey Powell told Paul Salley that McCulloch was a "complex soul. …As a brilliant and dedicated musician, I never felt that he was comfortable in his own skin. He wanted people to like him and take notice, especially girls, but when surrounded by sophisticated and experienced folk like Paul, Linda, and Denny Laine, he seemed very unsure of himself."

This was hardly surprising as he was still so young and success had come early and suddenly. Consequently, he set himself on a perilous course, often resorting to drinking and becoming unpredictable in his moods. Jimmy excelled as a musician, otherwise Paul would never have had him in Wings, but he was frustrated with the complete musical control that Paul had over the band and often expressed it. Hear him live, playing 'Medicine Jar', and that gives you an idea of how he could rock when given his own head.

One night in Detroit, Jimmy played the solo for about three minutes, completely ignoring Paul's wish to conclude the song. Paul never wanted it to veer too far from the recording. They finally finished and went offstage. Paul ran into Jimmy's dressing room and ultimately lost his temper, threatening to fire Jimmy, who was devastated and burst into tears. Ten minutes later, they went back on for the encore. Jimmy never did that again. He wanted to rebel, but couldn't express himself in the right way, by discussion or negotiation.

McCulloch, now with a few dozen Wings shows under his belt, was becoming increasingly frustrated with McCartney's complete control of the live show. He wanted to let loose but did not have the freedom to do so onstage. "Everything with Wings had to be the same as it is on the record," Martin Woodley observed. "You listen to the record and you watch the live stuff – it's note for note. And you couldn't deviate from that." Jimmy excelled at this, but it clearly was not what he wanted.

The studio was another matter. "In Wings there's plenty of freedom to play your own way, a lot of free expression," Jimmy told *Record Mirror* in August, referring to studio work. "We experiment with lots of things," he said, before adding: "Actually I find being in the studio bloody boring, and I'm always relieved when it's over. My forte is being on the road. I get much more of a buzz out of that." But the limits imposed on his road work led to growing frustration.

McCartney appears to have given McCulloch quite a

bit of latitude, but his patience was wearing thin. "Jimmy was a great player, but he had an attitude," he said later. "This is rock'n'roll – people do have attitudes; you can't expect everyone to be choirboys." But the young guitarist – despite all of his experience at this point, he was still only 23 years old – was becoming more problematic. "We really tried to encourage him," McCartney said. "Linda particularly – "Jimmy, you've got to keep it together. Twenty years from now, it's going to be different, and you want to look back at this period and love it, be proud of it.""

Jimmy, meanwhile, was becoming more self-assured in the presence of the former Beatle. "I'm not in awe of the bloke," he said in August. "Sure he's a genius, but to me he's just a bloke who plays great bass and sings. He's a person, right?""

The 'Wings Over America' tour wrapped up with three consecutive nights at the Forum in Los Angeles. "It was my first American tour and I was well chuffed," Jimmy told *Record Mirror* the following year. "In Seattle we played to 70,000 people indoors. It was like a football crowd."

With the months of July and August off, Jimmy was able to spend time in the new residence he'd purchased earlier that year: A large two-bedroom flat on the second floor of Lampard House on Maida Avenue which faced the canal in Maida Vale, London. The flat included a studio, a bar/snooker room, and a touch of home: A set of bagpipes mounted above the fireplace. The building offered an underground parking garage, although he often parked his blue Rolls Royce Silver Cloud, another recent purchase, on the street. Martin Woodley sometimes stayed at this flat, and rode with Jimmy in the Rolls. "I remember when he bought the Rolls Royce, and he was so thrilled because it had electric seats and it would lift him all the way up to where he could actually look over the dashboard," Woodley recalled. McCulloch, now enjoying steady and sizeable paychecks

from touring with Wings, had buttons made with THIS ONE'S ON ME, which he sometimes wore onstage. He gave one to Woodley. "I used to pay for a lot of stuff," Woodley explained. "He said, "It's on me from now on"."

In September 1976, Wings returned to the road, performing a handful of shows in Europe, before three final sold out shows at Wembley's Empire Pool on consecutive nights in late October to complete the world tour. In all, the group had performed 65 times over thirteen months, to audiences of over two million. "The band were acclaimed the world over as a supergroup," *Record Mirror* reported. "In most parts of the world, Wings are now selling more records than the Beatles ever did."

"Most of the music presented here illustrates admirably that McCartney and Wings are in fact a world class performing band," the *NME* opined of the triple live album *Wings Over America* set which was released in December. "…Jimmy McCulloch and Denny Laine on guitars ravage the numbers with fierce chords and, when they are offered the opportunity, blues-orientated solos that are torn and shredded round the edges."

During the two month break after the 'Wings Over America' tour, Jimmy again directed his attention to forming his own band, this time with his brother on drums and old friend Dave Clarke on bass. The group, named Jimmy McCulloch and White Line (typically referred to as simply White Line), ostensibly aligned with road markings and with staying in one's lane as opposed to any drug-related reference, signed with EMI[82]. "It's been strange since we

---

82 White Line found themselves labelmates with the Sex Pistols, who signed with EMI in October 1976. "One day the two bands had found themselves in the same pub near the company's Manchester Square headquarters," McCartney biographer Philip Norman wrote. "Jimmy shouted at the Pistols that they were crap and, in the altercation that followed, physically attacked one of them, whose name he took pride in not knowing."

finished the tour," Jimmy said in November. "With everyone else on holiday I didn't have anything to do and was getting really bored sitting around. I went to stay with Dave for a couple of weeks. We wrote a few songs and it all came together from there."

McCulloch told the press that things were good with Wings, and that White Line was just a side project. "Wings are pretty close, I've been with them now for three years and they've gone by so fast it proves how good it is," he said. "…There is a lot of freedom within Wings itself," he went on, qualifying that statement by adding: "Everyone is working on their own projects as well as the band's. It's more fun that way." With a long run of live gigs and several stints in the studio, plus steady and sizeable paychecks, Jimmy was largely enjoying his day job. "Oh, I'll stay until it finishes," he said in August. "Wings is really, really tightening up and it would be a shame if anyone left right now. We're really beginning to get to know each other musically. If Wings are still around in five, even 10 years, then I'll be there."

White Line performed a handful of low-key pub gigs in London and released a single, 'Call My Name', on November 5th. Despite a catchy song ("I played Paul a copy of the single to see what he thought and he said, "You might well have a hit there"," said Jimmy) and heavy promotional activity, the single failed to reach the charts, and received little airplay. "Jimmy gave me the single of 'Call My Name' and I never heard it on the radio," said Martin Woodley.

With the short-lived weekly *National Rockstar* running the headline 'White Line: Not To Be Sniffed At', the band's name had become a contentious subject and McCulloch believed they were targeted by censors, resulting in the single being pulled from airplay. McCulloch was asked for comment the following June when the Sex

Pistols' 'God Save The Queen' single had been pulled. "If the BBC didn't play the record I made, I'm not surprised they're not playing the Pistols' record," he said. White Line re-released their single in late January, flipping the A and B sides, with the McCulloch/Colin Allen track 'Too Many Miles' now as A side, but it still failed to reach an audience.

Solo work continued to be a needed outlet for McCulloch. "Paul knows what he wants," Jimmy said in April 1977. "99 per cent of the time, he's great. Sometimes I go to the studio and all I want to do is blow, play away, but nine times out of ten he'll have something lined up for me. That's why in my spare time I like doing my own thing – blowing. I've always been in blowing bands before and Wings isn't one. It's a great experience to work with Paul. I've learnt so much about studios from him. He's a very hard worker. It's very much Paul McCartney's Wings. He's got a definite policy and is completely in control. Don't get me wrong. I'm not moaning. Wings has priority over anything else I do and I like it that way."

Creative freedom was important to McCulloch, who had been writing songs and trying to find an outlet for them since the beginning of his career and, save for a couple of Thunderclap Newman tracks and the few Wings compositions that he wrote, he hadn't been able to do so. It wasn't because of a lack of material – he told *Record Mirror* in November that White Line had "three albums' worth of material." While he repeatedly said in the press that White Line was just a side project – "just a bunch of mates playing for fun" – the failure of 'Call My Name' must have stung.

1977 proved problematic for the young guitarist, who longed to perform live. Linda McCartney's pregnancy meant that Wings activity this year would be particularly light. The group held recording sessions in February and March at Abbey Road, but then momentum waned. "Touring with Wings is out of the question this year because of

Linda's pregnancy," Jimmy said in April. "Just now I'm working with a couple of bands with a view to producing. We're preparing demos, but I don't want to say any more at present." Around this time, McCulloch produced several tracks by his friend and former bandmate Robbie Paterson's latest group, The Khyber Trifles[83], and occasionally sat in with them onstage. "I might knock a band together and get on the road," he said. "Yes, I do prefer being on the road to being in the studio."

Jimmy guested on a few albums by other artists in late 1976 and early 1977, playing on Roy Harper's *Bullinamingvase* and Roger Daltrey's *One Of The Boys*. On the Daltrey album, McCulloch played on the tracks 'Say It Ain't So Joe' and 'Giddy', the latter written by Paul McCartney. Jimmy appeared in the video for 'Say It Ain't So Joe,' recorded in July at Shepperton Studios along with Daltrey, and a rhythm section consisting of The Who's John Entwistle and a scantily clad Keith Moon, who for some reason chose to perform in only his underwear.

In May, Wings resumed recording, moving the sessions to a studio housed on a charter yacht named *Fair Carol*, anchored in the Virgin Islands. "Paul and Linda McCartney hired another yacht to serve as a floating home for themselves and their three daughters, while a third charter housed Wings Joe English, Jimmy McCulloch and [Denny] Laine," Paul Gambaccini reported in *Sounds*. "… The yachts anchored for days at a time in a bay or harbour off one of the three U.S. Virgin Islands, St. Croix, St. John and St. Thomas."

"This album has given me more of a chance to play than any other," Jimmy told Gambaccini, again a reflection of the freedom he was allowed in the studio. "There's one bluesy song Paul wrote in particular with a lot of

83 These tracks have gone unreleased.

288

spaces I've been able to fill in," he said. But McCulloch still hadn't found contentment or satisfaction. "Jimmy was a true prodigy but could not make the transition to adulthood," Gambaccini, who spent time with the group during this period, opined in 2013. "At one point in the evening, Jimmy uttered a terrible howl that seemed to come from the depths of his soul. I wish I could have helped him enjoy the happiness he deserved, but none of us could."

Wings spent a month recording on the *Fair Carol*. Afterwards, Jimmy traveled to Los Angeles to contribute guitar work on singer/musician (and Dean Martin's son) Ricci Martin's album *Beached*, which was produced by the Beach Boys' Carl Wilson.

In the summer of 1977, Chris Thomas was tasked with producing the music featured in the Wings documentary film *Rockshow*, which was finally released in 1980. "It was a bit of a mad thing that happened – they edited the film together from five different Wings gigs," Thomas recalled. "And then they asked me to sort out the sound, and I said, "Well I can't, because when you do this edit, the tempo changes," because they didn't play to clicks and things like that." To rectify this, Thomas worked with the individual band members, overdubbing and re-recording. "I spent way over six months and we re-recorded virtually everything for it, although it was supposed to be live, and so that's where I got to know Jimmy pretty well. ...And somehow, he was the only one where hardly anything had to be rerecorded. It was really consistent when we did the edits between these different performances, whereas Denny might have been playing a different guitar or something, so when an edit happened, you could really hear a different sound, and the level jumped up, and you couldn't really fix it, the best way was just to play the whole bloody thing through again. Jimmy had very, very little work to do. Same with Paul, really."

On July 30th, Thomas and McCulloch saw the Beach Boys perform at the CBS Convention at Grosvenor House, London. "Columbia Records used to have these conventions which were quite extraordinary events, 'cause there was this sort of clause for Columbia artists where you would have to play at the convention," Thomas recalled. "I went with Jimmy to see the Beach Boys on the Saturday night, on the last night, and it was with Brian Wilson, he was actually playing in the band. ...and it was the first time I think that they did a thing where you could hear all the overdubs being played live, so it was like an orchestra, about fifteen people, and it was absolutely sensational. I mean, it really was incredible. In fact, Jimmy taped it; I went back to his place later on that morning and we were listening to it."

During the short time that they worked together, Thomas picked up on McCulloch's frustration with his role in Wings. "The only time I knew him was during that time in Wings, but basically he had already made up his mind that he was leaving because he was very frustrated musically," said Thomas. "Effectively, a lot of the time he had to play what he was told to play. I mean, it was obviously Paul's baby."

In August, when Wings gathered for recording work in a converted barn studio in Campbeltown, on the remote Kintyre peninsula in Scotland, McCulloch's frustration boiled over. He argued with engineer Geoff Emerick and reportedly threw eggs from Linda McCartney's hens at the living room wall in their quarters, upsetting the heavily pregnant Linda (her son James was born on September 12th). McCartney biographer Norman wrote that McCulloch's actions "reduced Linda to tears and a furious Paul ordered him off the premises."

In early September, McCulloch's tenure with Wings was officially terminated. "I was rung up one morning by

Steve Marriott," McCartney recalled in 2001. "He said, "Me and Jimmy have been up all night and he's decided he wants to join me and leave the group." So I was a little bit… you know, put out, but I said to him, "Good luck guys; I'll see you, Jim.""Wings soon announced McCulloch's departure, and the JIMMY QUITS WINGS reports began to surface in the media. "He's a good lad, Jimmy, a good guitar player, but sometimes he's a bit hard to live with," McCartney told the *NME*. "It's pretty well known in the biz and we just decided it would be better if we didn't bother anymore. It got a bit fraught up in Scotland. He's with the Small Faces now, but he's done a lot of nice guitar on the new album, and on the boat he was incredibly together. He's really into playing heavy rock."

"I enjoyed playing with Wings and learned a lot," Jimmy told *Record Mirror*. "But I feel it's time for a change. The Small Faces are all old friends of mine." McCulloch's first gig with the Small Faces came within days of the announcement, on September 13th at the Birmingham Hippodrome, kicking off a 12-date U.K. tour. Jimmy's former band Blue, who'd had a top twenty single the previous year on Elton John's Rocket label, was the support act. A U.S. tour was set for October.

Record Mirror reviewed the band's performance the following night, at the Manchester Apollo: "…the new pint-sized recruit, Jimmy McCulloch, fills in on lead, seemingly reluctant to step on Marriott's fretboard, but it's definitely needed," wrote John Shearlaw.

…The band is tight and precise. When McCulloch steps forward they're easily able to move into extended guitar blues rock. …It's steaming rock, it's good, it would knock spots off… and so on. Yet it's belated, somehow out of place and perhaps a bit sad – the professionals can't be the kids and no matter how good the songs, the delivery, whatever, the urgency isn't there. The response is real but there's something missing, almost as if you're an original Teddy Boy brought back from a motor-bike grave to see Chuck Berry at the Hammer-smith Odeon – appreciation and regret just one more time.

The Small Faces' U.K. tour ended with four consec-utive dates at the Hammersmith Odeon in late Septem-ber, the last of which, on September 27th, would prove to be Jimmy's final date with the band. The U.S. tour never materialized. By the end of the year, Jimmy had left the group. "I joined the Small Faces because I was excited by the idea of being a fifth of a team again," he told the *Daily Express*. "Unfortunately there just wasn't the work or the money for which I'd hoped." The group released an album in 1978, *78 In The Shade*, which featured McCulloch's lead guitar work on two tracks: 'Thinkin' About Love' and 'You Ain't Seen Nothin' Yet'.

McCulloch was back to being without a band. In March 1978, Wings released *London Town*, the album Jimmy and the band had recorded in the Virgin Islands, and the last Wings LP to include him. The cover photo featured Paul and Linda McCartney, and Denny Laine, but no Jimmy.

That spring, Jimmy played with Kenney Jones (the Small Faces had broken up that year), Thin Lizzy guitarist Brian Robertson and former Rainbow bassist Jimmy Bain. A band, Wild Horses, emerged, but without McCulloch or Jones. That summer, Jimmy attended an event hosted by Pete Townshend, demonstrating a new ARP Avatar guitar synthesizer. Townshend made it an alcohol-free event in order to keep things manageable among those who liked to drink, including Jimmy. 1978 also saw McCulloch perform live with Tim Hinkley's 'Hinkley's Heroes' around the U.K., including a performance with Maggie Bell at the Music Machine, a venue in Camden Town. McCulloch also happened upon Andy Newman at the Speakeasy one night. "He gave me a lift home in his Rolls Royce and I'm afraid that was the last time I saw him," Newman recalled.

Later that year, Jimmy bumped into his old friend Ronnie Leahy in Los Angeles. "I was playing with Donovan and Yes on a big world tour," Leahy recalled, "and I finished that tour and Jimmy was in Los Angeles, and we got together with a couple of different guys: Miller Anderson, Charlie Tumahai, Colin Allen, and we formed a band called The Dukes." By December, The Dukes had signed with Warner Bros, and began recording an album at Rockfield Studios in Wales the following month.

Things were looking up for The Dukes, but all was not well with Jimmy. "By this time Jimmy was starting to get out of hand; that's all I can say," said Leahy. "I don't want to say anything bad about him, but career-wise, he wasn't doing himself any favors." Leahy had a unique perspective, having worked with McCulloch back in 1972/73 with Stone The Crows, and now being his bandmate again some six years later. "He was out of control then," said Leahy of McCulloch's days with The Dukes. "He was disappearing for days on end – even in the studio. It got very difficult to work with him; we made the album basically without him. He'd come in and do some things towards the end of it but… he wasn't in control. That was the problem and it showed no sign of getting any better. Even after the album was finished, it just… yeah… forget it."

"When he did manage to overdub his guitar… it was so worth the wait," Miller Anderson told Paul Salley. "We were in the middle of recording 'Try To Help' when Jimmy burst through the studio doors and shouted in a pretty aggressive way, "I want to do 'Heartbreaker'!" He seemed pretty straight. We all said, "Great! Let's do it." The equipment was quickly reset, and Jimmy launched into the song like a man possessed. It was recorded double-quick, and by the end of the recording sessions, we were so glad to have Jimmy down on the album and sounding great."

The Dukes' eponymous debut album was mixed and completed at RAK studios in late summer, 1979. The group planned to tour in the autumn and began auditioning drummers at their rehearsal studio in King's Cross. "I got a call out of the blue from his brother Jack," Jimmy's friend and former Thunderclap Newman bandmate Chris Hunt recalled. "I hadn't seen [Jimmy] for about 7 or 8 years. So I went up there and we played a few numbers, left it at that, and I went out to go home, and the last thing I remember is Jimmy coming out in the street and he said, "Oh, sorry, I didn't say goodbye," and because I lived in Worthing, on the south coast, he said, "Thanks for coming all the way up to London. I'll let you know." And I said, "OK Jimmy, no problem mate, we'll speak soon.""

On August 18th, Jimmy and Jack attended The Who's concert at Wembley Stadium and met with Pete Townshend backstage. Around this time, The Dukes added drummer Nick Trevisick and began planning a fall tour and rehearsing at Atlanta Studios, Camden Town. Ronnie Leahy, concerned about his friend and bandmate, visited McCulloch's flat in early September. "We played some music and had a few drinks and a chit chat about this, that and the next thing," Leahy recalled, "and he seemed alright then. He was not quite sober, but he seemed okay and I thought, 'That's not too bad actually'."

The Dukes' album was released on September 20th. Jimmy rehearsed with the band on Monday, September 24th. Concerned about his health, he'd made a habit of bicycling from his flat in Maida Vale to a friend's rehearsal space in Islington where he'd stow his bike during rehearsals. Friends and bandmates became puzzled when McCulloch's bike was still there the following afternoon, and grew increasingly concerned when he missed the following two days of rehearsals. On Thursday September 27th, Jack forced his way into Jimmy's flat and found his younger brother lifeless on the living room floor.

A post-mortem suggested the young guitarist had died 48 hours before being found, but any determination on cause of death was adjourned pending further testing. "The police were satisfied that no-one else was involved in his death, and further tests will be carried out before the cause of death is finally established," *Melody Maker* reported.

Jimmy McCulloch was just 26 years old. The Dukes' official live debut had been set to take place at Dingwall's the following day. Jimmy's funeral took place at the City of London Crematorium in Wanstead on Thursday, October 4th, 1979. His ashes were scattered near his grandparents' resting place in Scotland at Dalnottar cemetery, near Clydebank.

In early November, the inquest into the circumstances of Jimmy's death became a little murkier when Jack insisted that his brother didn't use hard drugs and said "he was sure someone was in the Maida Vale flat before he died," *Melody Maker* reported.

Ultimately, the report read, "The coroner recorded an open verdict after a post-mortem showed alcohol and cannabis in McCulloch's body and that he died of morphine poisoning." This verdict proved puzzling, given both the limited access and availability of prescription morphine as well as the lack of any evidence or history of McCulloch using more potent and dangerous drugs. One possible explanation could lie with Jimmy's use of the hypnotic sedative Doriden in the weeks prior to his death. McCulloch reportedly visited his doctor twice within two weeks of his death – on September 12th and 17th – and on both occasions was prescribed an unknown dosage and quantity of Doriden to manage his reported insomnia. Taken by itself, Doriden was habit-forming (a major reason why it was discontinued), and was a popular recreational drug in the 1970s, especially when taken in combination with readily available over the counter codeine products. This combination of Doriden and codeine produced a synergistic drug effect which enabled greater amounts of codeine to be metabolized into morphine in the body, causing a euphoria similar to that associated with intravenous heroin use and reportedly contributing to an increased number of accidental overdose hospitalizations and deaths. Adding alcohol to this already dangerous cocktail would only further increase the risk of accidental overdose. An overdose from this combination of drugs could appear identical to morphine poisoning on a toxicology report; perhaps this manifested itself as the 'morphine poisoning' responsible for his death.

This is, of course, conjecture. It's clear that McCulloch died from an overdose; it's not precisely clear what he took. "He was always a little dangerous," Paul McCartney said in *Wingspan*. "As an older guy I did try and warn him a couple of times, like what's going to happen when you're 30. You've got your whole life ahead of you. But he liked partying too much and was getting into too many things. In the end he was just too dangerous for his own good."

"I think his body wasn't strong enough or tough enough – he wasn't big enough – to do what he was doing to it," said Ronnie Leahy. "I've worked with Jack Bruce, and he could take astronomical amounts of everything and he kept on doing it and nothing happened to him. He was strong enough to handle it. Eric Clapton as well, people like that. They were strong enough to sort of keep on going. But Jimmy wasn't physically strong enough, and that's what finished him off."

McCulloch's young age and lack of close relationships in the music business made his a particularly difficult path. "I feel a bit of experience to withstand the hard knocks on the road and in the studio," said Ronnie Leahy.

> It's pretty tough; I mean, when I played in the band Nazareth they had put out like 20 albums and they had really had the hard knocks, but they had experience and they stood by each other, 'cause lots of things happened. And that's how they got through it and they're still playing, they're one of the longest-lived bands, and they've got a great attitude to each other, they help each other, you know... but Jimmy was too young, and didn't have very close musician friends that I knew about that would maybe help him, you know. There might have been people that were in the same state of mind that he was... it's a lot of who you mix with as well, you know.

"I think he felt very lonely for a long time, not having his own band, not having close musician friends around, not having a steady girlfriend," said Martin Woodley. "He was kind of lonely. He hadn't found himself. He really hadn't."

"I always found him very charming, and a nice little chap, and very talented, obviously," said Chris Welch.

> Everybody wanted him to be in their band, you know; he somehow seemed to end up in very important groups. It was a lot of responsibility on his shoulders and I'm not sure whether he had a real mentor. I know he had his brother Jack, and the band leaders themselves really liked to look after him, but sadly he did start to drink and he

was only a little guy, and if you're starting to drink heavily, that's not going to be good for your health or your wellbeing or your peace of mind. And who knows what was going on inside his head. Maybe he was suffering from nerves and didn't know who to trust maybe, or – I mean, *I* found the music business hard work and I was in my mid 20s into my 30s, going on the road with bands. I've seen rock musicians freaking out having breakdowns just accompanying a band on a long tour of America for example and come back a different person. So to impose all that burden on a young boy that age I think was tragic.

CHAPTER 11

SPEEDY

Speedy Keen promotional photo, circa 1972

"When it was finished, all that was left was a Lincoln Continental, a gift from Pete Townshend; it was enough," Nik Cohn observed. "That car was probably the biggest up of my life, better than having a kid, better than getting hit records, better than anything," said Speedy, a sentiment he'd surely revise a decade later when he reconnected with his daughter, Trish. "I'd dreamed of cars all my life and Cadillacs were the ultimate," he told Cohn. "So now I was skint but at least I was skint in a Lincoln. After everything I'd passed through, all the years and bummers, it was the perfect symbol. A symbol of what? A symbol of survival."

Jim Avery remembered riding in this car, and when I relayed to him the story of Speedy's time in Italy, it all made sense. "When Speedy got Pete Townshend's Lincoln Continental, this flash American car, we used to drive about in it, and he'd say, "In Italy you could drive like this…," and he'd drive on the right or left, you know – take the corners, paying no attention to the law, or what's coming the other way," he said. "And at the time I remember thinking, 'what does he know about Italian driving?' He had never told me about his Italian adventure."

While Keen had a long-held affinity for cars and motorcycles, he didn't necessarily take very good care of them. He adored the Lincoln, but it was soon rendered undriveable, as Speedy later explained to his friend Emma Hughes. "He loved it because you pressed a button and the roof went back," Hughes recalled. "He said, "I had this girl in the car and I was being an arsehole, showing off, we're doing 70, and being an idiot I pressed the button and of course it just gets ripped off, and I had to drive it to the garage with it sort of trailing behind." And this is where it's either him being disorganized or people taking him for a ride – he said they didn't even cover it and it filled with rain, so he just abandoned the car at the garage."

Another car of his met a similar fate. "He said that they were driving round London and effectively wedged it in an alleyway," Hughes recalled, adding that Keen and co. were "dodging the Old Bill because they had drugs on board."

Someone in the car was convinced that they'd be able to get through the alley, and then once they'd scraped *both* sides of the car they thought they might as well keep going – but just wedged the car, couldn't go forwards, tried to go back... but were completely stuck, gearbox screaming, and had to give up and climb out and trudge off into the London night feeling very sorry for themselves. Speedy said they never even went back for the car, just left it wedged there, all sort of scratched and ruined and broken.

"I always felt that that's the kind of thing that sums up his life for me," Hughes continued. "Something nice that he deserved, something would go wrong due to something impetuous or an accident, and then nobody would ever properly sort it out for him and he wasn't organized enough to do it, so then it would just fall apart. Which is the metaphor for everything really."

* * *

After the breakup of Thunderclap Newman, Speedy Keen needed time to process and recalibrate. His emotions and self-esteem were in pieces. "When you've got the Earth man, that's when you lose control of yourself," Speedy told Vivien Goldman in 1976. "That's why I had to go to Wardour Street, because overnight everyone said to me, "You are a fucking incredible songwriter," and I said, "I'm Johnny Keen from fucking Ealing," I couldn't write another 'Something In The Air'. I've never attempted to do that, but I hope that if I keep going I'll always be in that standard."

Speedy retreated to Townshend's top floor flat on the corner of Wardour and Brewer streets. "It was just a room with an organ in the corner and tape machines, a sink and a cupboard," Keen said. "There was a toilet downstairs, no bath." He told Goldman that he'd take the five minute walk to Piccadilly Circus and "talk to the drunks, buy a cup of soup for the meths drinkers down the 'Dilly, listen to their crazy rap which I can understand perfectly (slurs) 'life for me is a bottle of methylated spirits,' then I'd go back and try to write a few songs."

Keen lived there rent free, "which really did me a favour because I was completely skint," he said later. "It was above [boxing promoter] Harry Levine's, and I used to have to pass all these heavies on the stairs every day. But I literally locked myself away for a long time – about 1 year – and hardly saw anybody, and I thought 'Well either I'm going to leave it all and go back to driving a lorry, or I'm going to get down and do it, and do it on my own'."

While he acknowledged that he was "very grateful to Pete, because he gave me a box to climb in, go crazy, and get some identity out of it," Keen was determined to navigate this period of self-discovery and creativity without Townshend's guidance. "Before I met Pete I knew nothing," Speedy told Keith Altham. "It was listening to his early demos for the Who that really blew my mind and spurred me on. You need someone like that to get your beginnings from, but you also have to move away and do something of your own. It's like leaving your parents."

"Speedy and I have parted company for about a year," Pete said in December 1971. "And at the end of that year I hope Speedy's going to have enough songs to do a solo album. Because I think Speedy's a genius, I really do."

"That was a very difficult situation," Speedy said in 1975. "You see Pete is a very productive person and any contact I have with him ends up being productive in some way. But I read all the reports in the papers – *Rolling Stone* said: 'Speedy Keen is Pete Townshend in a blonde wig' and in the States they didn't believe I existed until I went there – a lot of people were really surprised. And although that didn't worry me I felt that musically I had to get my end together. That's why I did *Previous Convictions* on my own…"

Keen's approach was somewhat aided by the fact that the pair had already had a falling out. "I lent him money, gave him my Lincoln Continental and he started to see a woman called Anya Butler who had worked as a P.A. for Chris and Kit," Townshend recalled. "Anya and I had a brief fling when I was 19, she was 30. She had already had a fling with Jimmy Page, and she didn't like my pretty girlfriend Karen. We argued, and it affected my friendship with Speedy. Later we all reconciled I'm happy to say."

Keen's world mainly consisted of the area immediately around the flat: The Marquee club, The Ship pub, and Piccadilly Circus. And the flat itself. "Wardour Street was like a cube that had no relation to a home," he told Goldman. "You could play flat out guitar all day because the windows were double-glazed. I used to stand at the window playing the guitar with two Marshalls flat out, looking at all the people milling down below. I was very much into learning how to construct songs, that's what I was doing basically, learning every chord shape, everything…"

Keen processed a series of emotions during this self-imposed solitude, including profound sadness, revealing the tender, sensitive side belied in many of his song lyrics which appeared at odds with his upbeat, talkative, and often funny demeanor. "I had a year out of it, getting drunk, saying "I really am a right creep, I wonder why I hate myself, but equally it's a form of self-analyzation, although it hurts," he said. "I'm a sad person. I've cried my eyes out in stereo many times. I've sat there and told myself exactly what I was, I must be crazy, I'm out of my box, throw this man out the window."

Sequestered in the Wardour Street flat, Keen wrote and wrote in 1971 and 1972. He rehearsed some of this material with old friends Roger Felice, Jim Avery and Jimmy McCulloch in between their commitments with other bands. "I got to the point where I'd written a load of stuff and went back to Track and asked them to give me some studio time," Keen said in 1975. "I remember thinking that I had to do an album even if it was dire, just to prove to myself that I could do something."

Recording sessions for Keen's first solo album, cheekily titled *Previous Convictions*, took place at IBC, Island and Olympic studios. Not all of the musicians who participated in the sessions are credited on the finished album, presumably because their contributions went unused. "Speedy said, "I'm in the studio, can you come and play," but I couldn't because I was doing some other work so he had to get another bass player first," recalled Jim Avery, who by this point had written and recorded two albums with Third World War. "Eventually we got together and we brought in a drummer called Gordon Barton who did a solo LP with John Entwistle, and Michael Mertz on guitar, who had a very striking sound, I thought." Barton was not credited on the finished album but Australian drummer Dave Montgomery, of Python Lee Jackson, was. Keen also brought in "a brilliant young keyboard player" named Dave McDougall, a former bandmate of Jack McCulloch in Andwella.

The recording of *Previous Convictions* appears to have been mostly complete by late summer 1972, at which point Speedy began to emerge from his self-imposed exile and reconnected with Townshend. He later said that "there were times when I felt like calling Pete and saying 'Help!' but I was determined to prove to him as a friend that I could do it. I wanted to take it to him and have him give me a really honest opinion on it. And it was important to me that it didn't have his influence. I think he felt really bad about it at the time because he thought I didn't want to know him any more, but really and truly I needed it for my confidence which was battered to pieces by then. But it did me good and I got to the stage where I could face Pete again because he was such a heavy dude and I was bashing away getting nowhere. I took him the masters after I'd finished it and he really liked it." Townshend was thanked in the album's credits for "beginning the beginning." Keen traveled with The Who as Townshend's guest during the group's European tour in August and September 1972.

Meanwhile, on August 25th, Track released Speedy's first solo single, 'Old Fashioned Girl', which *Rolling Stone*'s Bud Scoppa called "the most accessible Keen song ever and possibly the most commercial." The single marked Keen's first production credit. "He was good at those sort of things," said Jim Avery, adding sardonically, "If you're smoking a lot of dope and you're sitting down, it's the sort of thing you *would* get into, the balancing of the sounds." Keen also produced a pair of songs for the group Valentine during this period. The single 'Time' and its B-side, 'Leader of the Band' was released by Track on November 24th, 1972.

Speedy also sat in on a session with Pete Townshend at Olympic Studios in October, where Townshend was producing John Otway and Willie Barrett. The duo recorded the song 'Misty Mountain' with Townshend playing bass and Keen on drums. This version of the song appears to have gone unreleased.

In late January 1973, Track released a second single by Keen, 'Let Us In,' with B-side 'Aries Lady'. The full album was released in June. "*Previous Convictions* has taken me over a year to complete, but I've put myself into it heart and soul," he told the *NME*. Keen had not only written ten of the twelve songs but contributed vocals, guitar, drums and piano, production and arrangement as well. He even designed the album cover. "That was really just stubborn confidence," he said. "I just had to do it all myself just to prove to myself that I could. If it wasn't any good it didn't really matter; I just had to do it."

"Pete Townshend says John Keen's first solo album makes him jealous," Nik Cohn wrote in *Rolling Stone* the following month. "Terence Stamp has ordered a hundred copies to be handed out among his friends like so many candies; and I remember Jimi Hendrix, a few months before he died, telling me that he'd been knocked sideways by some of Keen's early demos. "Finger-lickin', motherfuckin' good," Hendrix said."

The critical reception for *Previous Convictions* was similarly positive. "Like *Hollywood Dream*, *Previous Convictions* is an essential album," *ZigZag*'s Andy Childs wrote. "Speedy Keen's gift for writing truly memorable songs is convincingly confirmed, and it's no better illustrated than in the opening track, 'Old Fashioned Girl'... I must admit that I do find the strings a little intrusive at times, but not even Wild Man Fischer conducting the Portsmouth Sinfonia could ruin those beautiful songs."

"Among this man's past record is a period spent – short term though – with Thunderclap Newman," stated *Record Mirror*. "It was undoubtedly Speedy who contributed much to that line up, and carries through a lot of the feeling they created on this album. And, well, I liked them a lot, and there's a definite promise of good things here. …There's a lot of musical strength, and this is a fine first collection. There's soaring strings, some great guitar, both electric and acoustic, and Mr. Keen's own very distinctive vocalizing."

"…my colleague Roy Carr thinks [*Previous Convictions*] is the greatest thing since sliced bread," Keith Altham wrote in the *NME*. "The outstanding feature of the album for me is in fact its honesty. It is a real labour of love and if the lyrics don't always come through you can listen to the truth in the music. The fact that two of the most outstanding tracks 'Old Fashioned Girl' and 'Let Us In' were turned down by the BBC 'quality control board' is an indictment of their judgement."

"In *Previous Convictions*, Speedy is more battered than before, but he's still conjuring neverlands," wrote *Rolling Stone*'s Bud Scoppa.

> Andy Newman's silent-movie piano is here replaced by conventional but perfectly apt pop orchestrations woven through a simple rock & roll rhythm section. And the wishing and hoping this time take more conventional forms: The love song, in its various modes, dominates.
>
> …Romantic love is Speedy's solution to an intolerable world that won't leave him alone. The naiveté of his viewpoint and earnestness with which he expresses it through that eroded voice give his songs a beauty that goes way beyond the literal ideas they communicate.

Despite these positive reviews, the album's public reception was disappointing. "It did well in America but in England it hardly got any exposure at all… For some reason Radio One wouldn't play it," Speedy said in 1975, lending credence to Keith Altham's comment regarding the BBC's 'quality control board'. Keen also cited his unhappiness with the adornments added to his original, spare arrangements. "I took the finished album to Track and they said it needed strings, so they put strings on it and that did me in," he said. "I'd really worked on it and it was sparse and it wasn't multi-recorded, it was very straight so that I could perform it on the road. But Track put a 50-piece orchestra or something on it and so it killed that idea. I no longer had an album I could play live. Actually the strings are really beautifully done by a guy called Ian Green,[84] but if it needed any I only wanted three or four – maybe a viola and three violins."

"The *Previous Convicts* I took to Track and the one that came out were two completely different records," Keen explained to Vivien Goldman.

> ...If you can listen to the album without strings, that's what it is. Unfortunately in doing so I also created a lot of gaps, which they tried to fill in to make it more alive. I've got the original masters at home, before Track put on the strings. ...I'd mixed it with a guy called Keith Harwood at Olympia... Keith and I worked on quality, the position of the guitars. I'd worked at it for two years in Wardour Street, so I knew what I wanted to do. To me it was very understated, wooden, acoustic. Apart from 'Forever After' which needed strings, they really shouldn't have been there. Take 'Positively Fourth Street', which was really nasty without strings – it's lost all that.

84 Green had arranged the strings on 'Something In The Air' along with those on another 1969 number one hit, Peter Sarstedt's 'Where Do You Go To (My Lovely)'. Green's wife, the American singer Rosetta Hightower, was a backing singer on *Previous Convictions*.

The January 19th, 1974 edition of *Record Mirror* announced The Who's seven-date tour of France planned for the following month, promoting their new *Quadrophenia* album. Interestingly, the article stated, "Speedy Keen will support some of the gigs." Eyewitness accounts and media reports from The Who's February 1974 French tour reveal that a Dutch band, Alquin, supported The Who alone. Speedy wasn't there. This wasn't the first mention of Speedy Keen performing in support of The Who: An earlier *Record Mirror* piece, from June 1973, reported that Speedy was "being lined up to tour with The Who in September," to promote his just-released *Previous Convictions* album. The article also revealed that Keen's "next LP will reunite him with his band, Speedy and the Cadets."[85]

After the release of *Previous Convictions* in June 1973, plans were indeed in place for Speedy to perform live to promote the album. A band was formed around the remnants of Jim Avery's old group, Third World War, who had recently broken up. The group's guitarist John Knightsbridge, who had met Speedy a few years earlier[86], remembers Keen calling him on the phone one day shortly after the breakup. "He started talking about what he wanted to do, and believe it or not, I did my audition over the phone," Knightsbridge recalled. "I had an AC30 sitting in the living room, so I just got my guitar and he said, "Just play me something," and I played him the 'Honky Tonk Women' riff, and that obviously impressed him enough that

---

85 I found no other mention of 'Speedy and the Cadets' during research for this book, so it's unclear as to how this would have constituted a reunion.

86 Knightsbridge had met Keen at the Marquee club in 1971: "I thought he was some crazed hippie," he said. "I thought he was either stoned out of his mind or crazy, I didn't know which. There were lots of ads on TV for Pepsi at the time… he was just wandering round, pointing at people saying, "You're a Pepsi!" And I said, "Bloody hell, he's out of his brain!""

he wanted to have me meet him at the office and talk about what we could do in the way of putting a band together."

The Speedy Keen Band soon consisted of lead guitarist Knightsbridge, drummer Steve Palmer (ELP drummer Carl's younger brother), and bassist Peter 'Mars' Cowling.[87] Keen provided vocals and rhythm guitar. The group gathered in the basement of Track Records at 70 Old Compton Street, Soho, and began rehearsals. "We got put on a retainer and we must have worked with him for at least six weeks, two months, something like that," Knightsbridge recalled. "We'd go into Track five days a week and down in the basement they had a small studio, nothing extravagant." As with the lack of productivity when Thunderclap Newman convened at the Old Corn Mill, Knightsbridge recalled that these rehearsals were just as laid back. "We would throw a few songs together and basically half the day would be spent listening to Speedy telling us jokes, and if I say to you that we did nothing but laugh most of the day, you wouldn't be surprised because Speedy was very entertaining, if nothing else," he said. "What stood out for me at that time with him was I think he was a bit bored. I think he liked the idea of having his own band, but he was very nervous about actually going out and gigging."

> He would get expenses from Mike Shaw to get a bottle of brandy, and also he had an arrangement with what he would call 'deals on wheels', so he would get a delivery of probably hash, and sit there and get stoned all day. Now as you can imagine, it's not very productive. We did laugh a hell of a lot.
>
> This went on for some weeks, and of course the band's getting a little bit restless, and then Speedy decided he had to go away somewhere for a week

---

87 Cowling later went on to join the Pat Travers Band.

— I don't know where it was, or why, 'cause that was never explained, but we still went in five days a week and just ran through the relative songs during that time.

Steve Palmer, only 17 or 18 years old at the time, remembers the sessions well. "John [Speedy] was a lovely guy… humble and maybe very slightly nervy," he said. "I loved his voice and songs. I remember Keith Moon's white Rolls Royce outside the office with a big dent in the side!" Palmer recalled Keen talking about traveling to the U.S. with Roy Wood, "and getting pulled over to be searched for drugs as Roy Wood walked into the USA untouched. He was not playing with Roy Wood but traveling with him on part of the tour. I remember John saying the Thunderclap Newman LP was a cult underground hit in America with a following. I think John hoped the band would not be Thunderclap Newman Two but his band to take out to the U.S. audience that wanted to hear more than just the LP."

Palmer and Knightsbridge don't remember any specific songs they worked on beyond the obvious 'Something In The Air,' but presumably the proposed set would have consisted of a mix of Thunderclap Newman and Speedy Keen solo songs, perhaps with a few of Speedy's beloved '50s hits thrown in. "The talk at the time was that he was going to go out and do some live gigs, maybe some festivals," Knightsbridge recalled, "but getting him to actually go and do it was the real problem." The group moved from the rough basement space under Track HQ to bigger stages, but never to a live setting in front of an audience. "We went out and did rehearsals at some fairly big rehearsal spaces," said Knightsbridge. "Speedy would hire big equipment to play through. I remember him insisting on having a Hammond organ Leslie cabinet. So it would be a proper stage with stage equipment and we'd go out and rehearse there and then go back to the small studio to just work on different songs." But with the lack of actual live work, frustration soon began to set in among the band members.

"This went on and on and on and it was the same routine every day, five days a week basically, and nothing happened," Knightsbridge recalled.

And one day the other guys in the band said to me, "Somebody's got to say something to him" – I mean we all had anyway, but somebody had to say something to him: Either he's going to do something or he's not. You can't just carry on like this week in, week out rehearsing on something with no end product in sight. So after about six or eight weeks, they nominated me to go and talk to Speedy to get his arse into gear and go out and do some gigs. Needless to say, Speedy wasn't at all amused by this 'cause he thought well it's his band and he did exactly what he liked, so the next day he phoned up the other two members of the band and said that he was going to fire me and get somebody else in and we'll carry on. But of course they weren't interested, 'cause it was their idea in the first place.

"So yeah it was basically ill-fated," Knightsbridge went on. "I think it gave him something to do and a bit of prestige but I don't think he was actually even slightly interested in going out and doing a gig of any sort, even under a different name so nobody knew, no pressure. But you couldn't get him to do that, it was like his whole life was getting out and getting either stoned or drunk and telling stories, that's basically what he did. And as much as we all liked him, you just couldn't go on doing that, day in and day out, it just wasn't on. It's sad in a way because there was obviously a lot of talent there. And he could, I'm sure, have been a good front man too. But I just couldn't see him doing it, because of the nerves." Keen's next documented live performance wouldn't take place until five years later, in 1978, and it wasn't with any variation of the Speedy Keen Band.

Instead of touring with the Speedy Keen Band in support of The Who in early 1974, Speedy visited the U.S. where he "toured the radio stations and met lots of people," he said the following year, adding, "I really wanted to meet all the people who had been pushing my stuff for years."

After *Previous Convictions* had failed to sell, Keen again isolated himself and began to write. "Unfortunately nothing happened to it in England and so I went back into obscurity," he said. Keen now found himself in a position not unlike the pre-*Tommy* Pete Townshend in 1968 – his recent efforts, despite their quality, had failed to make an impact. Like Townshend, he decided to go for broke. "I wrote a concept album whereby a guy gave twelve musical aspirations of what he felt about life," he said later. "And that was going to be the concept – the tracks linked… just a story, really, that the songs fitted around – in other words, like a *Tommy* thing."

Speedy's concept piece probably began life shortly before the release of *Previous Convictions*, as his initial notes on the project are written in a 1973 day planner, beginning in the month of April. The Monday April 16th entry, again with corrections to Keen's loose grammar and spelling, reads as follows:

The story in concept album is as follows: Alien 8 comes to earth in search of music, and what it means to earth people. Hoping to learn music to take home to his planet and then teach his friends how to play, then the thought problem would be over. Little did he know that not only did he learn music but would eventually, after reflecting on what he heard on earth, start to attempt to sort out the problems on his own planet before disaster struck, but between him arriving and eventually leaving he meets 12 people and asks their opinion on what sort of music would suit them – what would they write if they wrote a song…

Other notes, written on loose-leaf paper, began with "Write a musical with Brian Patton[88], use the ALBUM concept."

"The alien comes to earth to see music," Speedy wrote. The Alien was now known as 'S', and the twelve people had been replaced by seven musicians who represented seven styles of music: *Lover / Rocker / Disco / Reggae / Blues / Mod / Romantic*. "S. comes down in Hyde Park from another planet, looking for music," he wrote. "Meet in SOHO 7 musicians who introduce him to the kinds of music. End in blues. Take Back The Blues. Stage 'Scene One' opens with the alien landing in Hyde Park where a punk is sniffing glue. Because S. is green, the punk takes no notice of him."

The story was vague and meandering, but that was beside the point: This evolving thematic structure allowed Keen to focus, and it proved fruitful – he wrote nearly thirty songs over the next several months. Track employee Dana Wiffen remembered helping Keen record demos for this project in a small basement studio at Track's new offices on Windmill Street, off Tottenham Court Road. "I had to twiddle knobs and plug things in and that for him," Wiffen recalled. "He found it difficult to get everything going sometimes and that's when he used to get me down there and say, "Turn that, push that in," and so on. But yeah, the album sounded really good that he was recording."

88 It's not clear who Brian Patton was.

Keen envisioned a double album for the project, referred to as *Alien 8*, and around late summer 1974 he approached Track with demos. Their response was disappointing. "They said something to the effect that people weren't ready for it... 'Go home and start again,'" he said in 1975. "Track being a small company physically, there was only so much they could cope with, and I felt that I needed a real push if people were going to be made aware of what I was doing." Feeling unduly constrained and with his confidence already battered, Keen began to distance himself from Track. "Track regimented my music," he told Vivien Goldman the following year. "They were good for me, it was the best apprenticeship I could have had, they kept a very high standard. If I brought in a blow, no way would they listen to it. It was good but it got to a point where it was starting to kill me because I needed someone to say Yeah! in the kindest and loveliest way to get the best out of me."

Keen duly left the label that had launched Thunderclap Newman and had released his first solo album. It was bittersweet. "...I'd been living off the small amount that Track Records supplied, and they supplied money for a long time before they knew I was going to get anywhere," he said in 1975. "And that sort of faith you can't break – I'll always respect them and love them for that because there were some points where I couldn't even put two chords together. I used to take strings off my guitar because I couldn't play with six, so I used to take three or four off. I'm really glad now that I kept at it, but for about two years I thought I was trying to do the impossible."

He wasn't without a label for long. After conducting a late night phone interview with a Detroit radio station during which he discussed his departure from Track, Speedy received a surprise call from Island Records, the groundbreaking label whose roster of artists included Roxy

Music, Sparks, Traffic, King Crimson and new signees Bob Marley and The Wailers, whose landmark album *Catch A Fire* they had released the previous year.

Keen met with Island founder Chris Blackwell at the label's offices at 22 St. Peter's Square in London on October 23rd, 1974, bringing two reel to reel tapes of the demos of his 27-track concept album to the meeting. "I really thought, 'this is it for me,' you know?," he told Rob Mackie of *Sounds* in early 1976. "I just wanted him to give me a straight answer. I wanted him to either say, 'It's shit, and you should go and be a lorry driver and live happily ever after,' because I was at the point where I could have done that, unsure of myself and what I was doing, or else if he thinks it's good, that'll be an unbiased opinion. So I made an appointment to see him, and the first day I came in, he played two of my songs, at a very minimal level, and it was nerve wracking for me, because you always want it loud so you can at least blast out the mistakes. I just did it on two Revoxes, so it wasn't particularly refined... so he put 'em on at nilge level, and turned round and said, 'Right, whaddya want?' I said, 'Tons and tons of studio time'."

The meeting was short and sweet. "I was only there ten minutes and they said, 'OK, start tomorrow,'" Keen recalled. Finding himself entering into a multi-album deal with a thriving label that was fully behind him, Keen was overcome with joy. "After I talked to Chris and we got everything sorted out, I left," he said later. "It was like October coming on for winter, and there was this huge great pile of leaves outside. I just jumped up in the air about twelve foot and buried myself in them, when I'd got all dolled up, and it was all wet and slimy and ...all you could see was two feet dangling out the top, and I thought, 'If they've seen that, they're gonna probably fire you tomorrow.'"

Blackwell's unbiased opinion was clearly that Keen was a songwriter and not a lorry driver. "Chris rang me up specifically about Speedy, so I knew it was something close to his heart," recalled Fred Cantrell, Island's general manager at the time. "I got the feeling that it was very personal for some reason, which he didn't tell me and I didn't ask, but I knew that Speedy was very important to him." When asked to hazard a guess as to the nature of Blackwell's personal interest in Keen, he said, "Well, Chris was an A&R man above all else, like I was, and it's like falling in love, you know. You meet somebody and you hear the music and you like them – it's all over."

The next day, Keen got to work on re-recording the 27 *Alien 8* demos he'd prepared during his time with Track, and was awestruck at Island's state-of-the-art equipment. "To me it was like wonderland when I saw that 16-track," he told Vivien Goldman. "I went *aaagggg!*"

Not long after Speedy had signed with Island, he began a relationship with Deirdre Redgrave, the estranged wife of actor Corin Redgrave, Vanessa's brother. Keen and Redgrave had met at a party. "He was Island Records' golden boy, the singer in whom they were currently investing vast amounts of time and money," Redgrave recalled in her memoir, *To Be A Redgrave*. "…I liked Speedy instantly," she wrote. "He made me laugh. He looked at me so hard I thought he could see right through me. A long-nosed, long-haired funky East End kid making it good, he had a kind of no-holds-barred honesty that appealed to me. When I woke up the next morning I found that what I most remembered about the party was Speedy Keen's face. And the cockney voice with the lilt of laughter in it, and the hook nose and the penetrating eyes and the humorous curve to the crazy mouth. I hadn't thought about a man with such warmth for a long time."

Redgrave wrote that Keen "started coming around in the evening before going to the studio to record. Sometimes he would turn up very late at night, when recording session or rehearsals had finished. I began to look forward to these nocturnal visits. …We began a long, intense relationship that helped me surface from the loneliest struggle in the world, from an isolation terrifying beyond description." Keen lived with Redgrave at her flat in Coleherne Court on Old Brompton Road, Earl's Court, for a time. "Dad often mentioned their relationship," Speedy's daughter Trish recalled. "They were very close – he said she would ring every Christmas for years after they split up to see how he was doing. He thought the world of her."

In April 1975, Island released their first Speedy Keen single, 'Someone To Love', recorded at Island Studios in Hammersmith. "If the single 'Someone To Love' is any sort of indication of what we can expect of a forthcoming album, then we're in for a treat of the most sumptuous delicacy," wrote Andy Childs in his review in *ZigZag*. "It's a gorgeous song, Speedy producing and playing everything and it has the most seductively relaxing feel about it. Definitely one of the very best singles to be released this year. The flip-side, 'Fighting In The Streets' is excellent too... a convincingly aggressive rock'n'roll number. …If there is any justice to be found in the squalid, festering circus called the 'rock business' then Speedy Keen will emerge from the shadows this year and take up his position as one of this country's best songwriters. 'Someone To Love' is only the start of something much more rewarding... I'm sure of it."

Record Mirror was less complimentary: "It's got an end-of-the-day feel to it, and isn't unpleasant, but possibly not catchy enough for the charts." The single was not a commercial success. "We put a lot of work into it," Fred Cantrell recalled. "I know Chris was really on the case… It bubbled under the top fifty for about four or five weeks, and never quite broke through."

By the summer of 1975, Speedy Keen had re-recorded all of the demos he'd brought with him from Track. The sessions again took place at Island Studios, a small basement studio in Hammersmith. The core of Keen's band during the bulk of the sessions would become part of Back Street Crawler, the group formed that same year by Paul Kossoff of Free: Bassist Terry Wilson, drummer Tony Braunagel and keyboardist John 'Rabbit' Bundrick. In addition, on guitar were Butch 'Peaches' Sandford and pedal steel guitarist B.J. Cole. In addition to vocals, Keen contributed drums, guitar and keyboards.

"I've recorded those 27 tracks properly now," he said in July. "We were planning to release the double album, but considering peoples' general financial situation, it would be suicide.[89] So it will probably be two single albums now. But I've done a lot of work and I hope to be starting on a new one soon. The position I've always wanted to be in is one or two albums in front of myself. Island have been really fantastic, they look after their artists, not to the extent where they baby them, but they give you a perspective within which to work, and for someone like me that's all I need."

A second single, 'Bad Boys', with B-side 'Cold Hand Warm Gun', both Keen compositions, was released in September. "Backed by up-coming reggae-rock band Third World[90], this brilliantly evolving reggae-tempo and sound FX tale of living for the city is actually overshadowed by the instrumental flipside version," read James Hamilton's review in *Record Mirror*, "which is a pure and far more direct dub which ranks with the best of the genre. My own fave of the week."

Speedy Keen's second solo album, titled *Y'Know Wot I Mean?*, a nod to the phrase he frequently peppered his

89 The U.K. entered its first post-war recession in late 1973.
90 Jamaican reggae band Third World released their debut album on Island in 1976.

conversation with[91], was released in late 1975. The cover photo showed Keen pinching thumb and forefinger, holding up his other three fingers, perhaps indicating that this was his third effort, *Hollywood Dream* being the first (or perhaps he was just pretending to hold a joint). The record contained nine tracks, the majority of which were originally part of the *Alien 8* concept which fell to the wayside as the individual tracks were plucked from it. "I wrote 29 songs, and as I brought each one in, they'd say right, we'll have that one on the album… that one… and that one," Keen said. "The only thing I felt I didn't do was get more cohesion."

There was one cover song, Roy Orbison's 1958 release 'Almost Eighteen', with which Keen was "just trying for a straight rock'n'roll '50s sound," he told *Sounds*. "I think it was the first song Orbison ever wrote. I was just looking around for something I could identify with as being the punkish me, that signifies all the things about being 18." Plans to release this track as a single never materialized.

Keen had covered another '50s track, Eddie Cochran's 'Something Else', on his last album, *Previous Convictions*. During his radio tour of the U.S. in 1974, Keen had met a Detroit radio DJ who "had loads of old Eddie Cochran demos that people had never heard before," he said. His love of '50s music was such that he had also planned to "organize a gig at The Lyceum in London where he and a carefully chosen bunch of rockers will perform a complete set of Eddie Cochran numbers, some old standards, and some previously unheard of songs," *ZigZag* reported in July 1975. "Speedy, like his mate Townshend, is a devout Cochran fan, and has apparently come across some of his songs that the man himself never actually recorded. It is to

91 "I'd have gone stir-crazy if I'd transcribed every time Speedy said 'Y'know what I mean'," Vivien Goldman noted in her 1976 feature on Keen in *Sounds*.

be hoped that this gig (if it happens) will be the forerunner to a Speedy Keen Band taking to the road and performing his material." The gig never took place.

Also that year, Speedy contributed harmony vocals to a version of 'Something In The Air' by the Australian singer Ronnie Charles. The heavily layered and orchestrated cover was produced by Lou Reizner, with the London Symphony Orchestra and the English Chamber Choir, and was included on Charles' album *Prestidigitation*.

Meanwhile, reviews for the new album were numerous and largely positive. "It's ages since we saw the previous album from this character who keeps a very low profile," read *Record Mirror*'s review by Ray Fox-Cumming. "He specializes in love songs in the rock idiom and he's extremely good at them. There is always enough energy to prevent his work from appearing slushy and his words, which are never twee, contain some delightful lines. He doesn't go out of his way through public appearances to help you discover him, but it's well worth buying this and doing it for yourself."

"To get a major carp out of the way right up front, the arrangements – most of which are heavily biased towards a predominant acoustic guitar embroidered with limpid pedal steel – are righteously bland-o," wrote Charles Shaar Murray in the *NME*. "However, the songs are alternately (and sometimes simultaneously) sweet, deranged and unexpectedly powerful, plus Speedy's singing greeeeeyat, mon."

"It has to be said that, like *Previous Convictions*, it's not perfect," Vivien Goldman wrote in her four-star review in *Sounds*.

> There's always the feeling that Speedy is reaching out for something perfect, that he's striving to express himself absolutely, in search of the lost chord as one beat combo expressed it. But then,

that's part and parcel of his appeal, in a way.

It's encapsulated in his voice, husky, tremulous, never ringing out full and sturdy, but more atmospheric and moving than any rock'n'roll shouter. Whatever the album's slight flaws, there's sufficient material on this album to knock you sideways if you have ears to hear – Speedy has a way with a love song that penetrates the hardest defences, like on 'Crazy Love' where there's an irresistible charm that brings a smile to my face even when I'm writing a review… But don't, please, fail to check out the opening tracks on side two, 'I Promise You', and 'Someone To Love', both knee-tremblers extraordinaire; the former builds up to an exquisite surging climax, the latter is a classic. I kid you not. It was a knockout as a single, and it's a jewel now.

In case you think the album's too slushy from my description, there's a dose of chirpy paranoia on 'Nightmare', lashings of cynical socialism on the chunky 'Fighting In The Streets', and a pleasing ska tribute on 'Bad Boys'. This album is part of my continuing love affair with Speedy's music; there's something about his personality that comes over in his music that has me well and truly hooked, I can't resist Speedy's style, and as far as I can see, the more people that agree with me, the better it will be. We can't afford to ignore a musician like Speedy Keen.

Praising Keen's "fuller and more assured delivery," *Rolling Stone*'s Charley Walters wrote that "*Y'Know Wot I Mean?* reclaims much of the ground Speedy Keen laid out on *Hollywood Dream* but lost on his first solo try, *Previous Convictions*," while *Creem*'s John Morthland struck a more disappointed tone. "There's nothing on here nearly as bizarre as his songs from Thunderclap Newman, and what he does rely on is fairly routine pop romancing and posturing," Morthland wrote. "…It's a shame, too, because I'm still convinced that underneath that bland surface there lurks a genuine pop original, maybe something along the lines of an aging Jonathan Richman. Whoever it is, I hope Speedy lets him escape soon."

Dana Wiffen, too, was disappointed with what he'd heard, having been involved in the recording of these songs a few years earlier when Speedy was still with Track. "I heard the Island one and I wasn't sure if it was actually the same album, 'cause I didn't think it sounded that brilliant," he said.

Y'know Wot I Mean? didn't chart, but sold reasonably well. "I would imagine it would have sold somewhere between forty and fifty thousand in the U.K.," said Fred Cantrell. "It wasn't a great album, but it was a good album. Nobody expected it to chart; that was the feeling I got at the time." Asked whether Keen seemed disappointed with the album's reception, Cantrell replied, "He seemed very pleased with the amount of work we were all doing on his behalf, that's one of the things that I do remember; he was very grateful for everything that was done for him, which is most unusual for an artist. Everybody else wanted to know why you weren't doing more!"

There were no live gigs in support of the album, nor any apparent plans to do any. "I never heard any mention of him doing live gigs, including from him," Cantrell recalled. "If there had been any desire on Chris's part or Speedy's part to do live gigs, I would have known about it, and I would have done something about it." With no momentum toward live work, the focus quickly returned to another album. Speedy still had a host of recently re-recorded songs which hadn't been selected for inclusion on *Y'know Wot I Mean?* "I've still got 19 tracks left over that

Chris hasn't even heard yet," he said.

It's unclear what the plan was for that second album. In early 1976, Rob Mackie of *Sounds* wrote that a second album was already complete, while at the same time Speedy told him that he was "off to L.A. to do some promotion and record an album at the Record Plant."[92] Perhaps Mackie was referring to the stack of completed tracks left over from *Y'know Wot I Mean?*, and perhaps the plan was for Keen to re-record some of these at the Record Plant. Or maybe the album to be recorded at the Record Plant was to be a *third* release. "To me, the albums I'm doing now are working up to another Thunderclap Newman album," Speedy told Vivien Goldman, without explaining precisely what he meant.

It was reported that Steve Smith, who had produced albums by Jim Capaldi, Robert Palmer and Bob Marley and the Wailers, all Island releases, was set to produce Keen's work at the Record Plant. The only evidence of any recording work with Smith emerged on July 16, 1976 when the Speedy Keen single 'Your Love' was released. 'Your Love', produced by Smith, and the B-side 'Heaven', produced by Speedy, were both Keen compositions. "Insidious repetitive hymn from Speedy that carries the listener well, finishing just before it turns into a dirge," read *Record Mirror*'s review. "A clever man and a hopeful winner." The single failed to reach the charts. After 'Your Love', all went quiet. There were no further Speedy Keen releases on Island, or on any other label, for that matter.

The circumstances of Keen's departure from Island remain murky. Chris Blackwell's recent autobiography *The Islander* includes no mention of Speedy, and attempts to contact Blackwell for this book were unsuccessful. Fred

---

92 In almost the same breath, Keen complained to Mackie of his nearly unbearable foot pain. "I can't even walk most days," he said. "Bleedin' rheumatic arthritis."

Cantrell isn't sure what happened either, but was able to provide some useful context. "Chris was very, very fond of Speedy," he said. "When Chris was instrumental in signing someone, it was completely different to anything else. They'd either be completely under his wing like Bob [Marley] was, or they'd be somewhere sort of hovering around, which I think is where Speedy was."

"It was all a bit fractured," said Cantrell, adding, "when the company were all working to the same end, we were unbeatable." A prime example of this was the label breaking Bob Marley. "So when it worked, it worked big time, and sometimes some people fell through the cracks. Unfortunately, Speedy was one of them."

"So my analysis would be that the problem with Speedy is he fell outside the A&R net," Cantrell explained. "Everybody thinks that A&R is about signing bands; it's not. That's obviously a part of it, but it's a very small part of it. It's actually guiding them, almost like being their manager before they do anything. That's what I mean about Speedy falling through the net, because Chris signed him, but then didn't hand him over to anybody else – and this is conjecture; I don't know, but if he did hand him over to somebody else, they didn't do a very good job." In other words, Keen fell victim to the same circumstances that occurred with Thunderclap Newman on the occasions Pete Townshend's focus was elsewhere: Keen could provide the creative spark, but he needed consistent guidance, encouragement and structure in order to produce finished work. With Island, he didn't receive this. It didn't help that Chris Blackwell was a tax exile during Keen's tenure with Island and was therefore rarely on site. "Most of the time my dealings with him were over the phone," said Cantrell.

Cantrell still fondly remembers Speedy, and the times they spent at the pub just around the corner from Island HQ. "He was a very funny man," Cantrell recalled. "He was lovely. I mean, I met him and within ten minutes we were chatting as though we'd known each other for years. He was just so easy to talk to."

Whatever the precise reason, Speedy's departure from Island caused him considerable pain, which he would reflect on in a letter to the label several years later. He stopped writing and returned his attention to his mentor and his former label. "Speedy and I did some boat trips together on the Thames in 1976, with Billy Nicholls and Richard Barnes," Pete Townshend recalled. "I believe he may have had some time in the Merchant Navy because he knew all the jargon: "Cocoa Sir?" "We're taking water!" "The oven has exploded!" etc."[93]

"[Townshend] had a boat with a Grand Banks flying bridge," Richard Barnes recalled. "It's an American fishing boat and the flying bridge is a high bridge. When we came back, we couldn't get under Hammersmith Bridge – the tide had come up." Townshend and company had decided to take the boat out to the Isle of Sheppey, in the Thames Estuary. "Of course, it takes absolute ages to go down this winding river," said Barnes. "By the time we got there it was dark, and I remember we got lost," he recalled with a laugh.

> First of all, you get there and there's a bloody sunken warship full of bombs and it says KEEP AWAY. So you have to go round that, and we went round to Sheppey and we went and had an ice cream or something and then when we got back on, I remember Pete's got the instructions on the chart, and he said, "Look, we've got to find this flashing buoy, and aim for it," but there's an Esso or Shell petrol refinery there with about ten million

93 Perhaps Keen picked this up during his time with the Boys' Brigade.

flashing lights! So he said, "Can anyone see it?" and it's ridiculous! Somehow, I saw it, and we aimed for it and we got back. But when we got to Hammersmith Bridge, the tide had come up, and with this flying bridge, we were stuck there, we couldn't get by – so we kept going forward, to about an inch of the bridge, to see, because the tide was slowly going down and we could just about get under it, and then we'd have to back off, put the anchor down and wait a bit, and go and try again. We got back about five in the morning.

* * *

In February 1977, Speedy Keen was called upon to produce The Heartbreakers, a punk-tinged American rock group formed in 1975 by guitarist Johnny Thunders and drummer Jerry Nolan in the wake of the breakup of the New York Dolls. The Heartbreakers, part of the Sex Pistols' infamous Anarchy Tour in December 1976, had recently signed with Track Records. The Heartbreakers' signing with Track appears to have been facilitated by Chris Stamp; it's reasonable to assume that Stamp also was behind Keen taking on the role of producer.

On the face of it, this is an interesting shift to contemplate for Keen, who had often been described as a hippie, and whose songs were more on the tender, delicate side. But this was 1977, and rock was taking a harder turn, spurred on by the punk wave. "I can't say I'm really surprised, because it wasn't a great time for a regular pop or rock group, simply because of the punk thing that was starting to become big," said John Knightsbridge, the guitarist who rehearsed with the ill-fated Speedy Keen Band in 1973. "That sort of put Speedy and so many other people into a different bag altogether." In addition, the '50s-throwback rock and roll at the core of The Heartbreakers' sound was the type of music Keen had been brought up on and had always cherished.

When asked if Speedy seemed proficient at studio engineering, Knightsbridge responded, "No – but to be honest, if you're going to be a producer as such, a lot of the technical stuff doesn't actually have to be a problem of yours. I've worked with a bunch of them that basically leave most of the donkey work to the studio engineer. They just record it, people throw in ideas – the producer would obviously have some idea as it progresses as to how he wants the ultimate thing to sound, but the actual recording technique – where you put the mic, how many to use – unless you're a really experienced producer, you'd probably just leave that to the engineer."

Initial sessions for The Heartbreakers' album took place at Essex studios in February before the group moved to The Who's Ramport Studios in Battersea the following month. The group also performed twice at the Speakeasy in March, with both performances being recorded, presumably with Keen's involvement. The Heartbreakers sessions were completed at Ramport Studios in July. The resultant album, *L.A.M.F.*[94], was released on October 3 after a six month struggle to get the mix right. The mix on the finished album was widely criticized for its murkiness[95], with Keen's production named the culprit. But it was the mix, and not the production, that was at fault. The sound quality issue was rectified later when the master tapes had been retrieved and a reissue occurred in 1994. "As tapes later found from the sessions testify, The Heartbreakers played their parts brilliantly, and Keen and [co-producer

---

94 An abbreviation for *Like A Mother Fucker.*
95 Drummer Jerry Nolan resigned in protest of the album being released with a substandard mix.

Danny] Secunda did no wrong," wrote Nina Antonia in her Johnny Thunders biography *In Cold Blood*. "Therefore, the problem was either down to the cutting process or the manufacturing. Although their record company was entering its twilight, Track had a history of quality releases from Jimi Hendrix to The Who, yet none of their personnel were able to unravel the Heartbreakers' mix mess."

In the midst of the Heartbreakers activity, Speedy Keen became involved in the recording of another album by another hard-edged, seemingly incongruous band: Motorhead, who were on the verge of a breakup and had decided to perform one last gig at the Marquee, to be recorded using Ronnie Lane's mobile studio and to be produced by Speedy. Keen had probably known Motorhead frontman Ian 'Lemmy' Kilmister for years. Lemmy's band The Rockin' Vickers had opened for The Who in May 1966, back when Speedy was driving Pete to gigs. There was another connection: Lemmy was a roadie for Track artist Jimi Hendrix in the late '60s. In addition, according to former Motorhead manager Doug Smith, "I really think that Eddie and Phil knew Speedy and probably hung out with him," said Smith, referring to Motorhead guitarist 'Fast' Eddie Clarke and drummer Phil Taylor. "And because they were all speeding, they all sort of fitted together and they probably said, "Oh, Speedy, it's our last gig," and he sort of went, "Oh, I'll produce you, man – let's have another toot.""

By this time, Keen's use of amphetamine sulphate, or speed, lent another meaning to his nickname. He wasn't alone: 'Fast' Eddie Clarke's nickname ostensibly reflected his prowess on the guitar, but his use of speed also fit right in. "The band was known mostly for Lemmy's speed habit, which he enforced on everybody," Smith recalled.

Plans for recording Motorhead's April 1st, 1977 gig at the Marquee were scrapped when the venue asked for a sizeable 'facility fee' which their small independent label, Ted Carroll's Chiswick Records, was unable to provide. "The outcome of it was that the recording didn't happen, so the gig went ahead and Ted and I were there and watched the show, and he had already spoken to the band and said, "Well I'll tell you what, we'll stick you in Escape studios and you can make a single"," Smith recalled. Three weeks later, on Wednesday night, April 27th, Keen and the band drove to the studio and went straight to work, arriving there shortly after midnight. "We'd been playing these songs for a year, so we thought fuck it, we can do an album," Eddie Clarke told *Uncut* in 2017. In a few hours we had all the backing tracks down. Put the vocals down. Bit more speed, put some more guitars on. Few more beers – we were fucking steaming."

Ted Carroll arrived at Escape studios in Kent on Thursday evening, less than 24 hours after the band's arrival, to see how things were progressing. "I got there and met Eddie as he emerged from the house," Carroll wrote in the liner notes to the album's 40th anniversary release in 2017. "…He took me out to the studio where Lemmy was in a vocal booth, in the middle of laying down a lead vocal. John Burns and Speedy Keen were crouched over the mixing desk. The volume was deafening, as they had taken down the large monitor speakers, normally suspended high up in the ceiling, and placed them on two small tables in front of where they were sitting." Unsurprisingly, Speedy's daughter Trish remembers him saying his hearing was never the same after these sessions.

"After completing his vocal, Lemmy took a break to come outside for some fresh air," Carroll continued. "He told me that they had got a great sound in the studio, so had decided to go for it and straight off laid down almost a dozen backing tracks. John and Speedy were knocking out the first of a couple of dozen rough mixes of 'Motorhead' to play back to me." Keen and Burns stayed up all night mixing the single. The next morning, Clarke recalled to *Uncut*, "We go in the studio and their eyes are out on fucking stalks. They've done 45 mixes of 'Motorhead'. They'd given each mix a mark: three stars, four stars, eleven stars. They didn't know which one was which."[96] Recording of the album, titled simply *Motorhead*, was complete within three days. It was released on August 21st, 1977 on Chiswick Records.

In early 1978, an interesting, if not particularly successful, offshoot from the Heartbreakers and Motorhead sessions emerged in the form of The Muggers, a group consisting of Speedy on guitar and vocals, The Heartbreakers' Billy Rath on bass, and Motorhead's Phil Taylor and 'Fast' Eddie Clarke on drums and guitar, respectively. "The only reason this band came together in the first place was because Motorhead couldn't, at the time, do anything because they were in dispute with their manager," said rock journalist Malcolm Dome. "They were pretty much on hiatus until it was all sorted out. They couldn't record, couldn't tour, so I think it was basically Phil Taylor and Eddie Clarke saying, "Fuck it – let's do something," you know."

The group rehearsed briefly at the Rainbow Theatre around April, after which they supported Wilko Johnson's Solid Senders on a handful of dates during their U.K. tour in April and May. More than a decade later, a live recording of The Muggers performing in April 1978 at a birthday party/ball held by one Lady Alexandria Reading in Oxfordshire was discovered in Motorhead's vault and was included as bonus content in the band's 1993 collection *All The Aces*, with liner notes by Dome. 'The Muggers Tapes' consists of eight tracks – five Keen compositions

96 The single was released on June 10th, after Keen and Burns remixed it in May.

('White Lightning', 'Space Chaser', 'Would If You Could', 'Nightmare', and 'Killer, Killer'), the Eddie Cochran classics 'Something Else' and 'Summertime Blues', and Neil Young's 'Cinnamon Girl'. There are aborted starts, entire verses left unsung… it's a mess, but Keen and company sound like they're thoroughly enjoying themselves. "Oh blimey," said Jim Avery. "It must be awful, right? They're all on sulphate; they're all speeding."

* * *

The early 1980s were a period of reflection for Speedy Keen, still without a label and without a band. He was apparently without a permanent address either, living in a room at his friend Frank Andrews' farmhouse in Capel, Surrey, which also housed Ridge Farm recording studio.

Around 1983, Keen wrote a heartfelt letter to Island Records, looking back over his time with the label and explaining his current mindset. "Dear Martin," Keen wrote, addressing the letter to Island's managing director at the time, Martin Davis. "I am writing to ask a favour. …I last worked for your label in 1974 [sic] when I had a deal with Chris Blackwell, unfortunately this did not work out, I actually let him down very badly.[97] It wasn't entirely my fault, as I feel the company was going thru its own changes at the time. Anyway, it ended with me giving up being an artist and moving on to record production and involvement [in] many other things." Among these other things was an attempt by Speedy to become a field A&R representative.

---

97 "I don't think Speedy did let Chris down; it's much more likely the other way round," said Fred Cantrell. "The problem is… well it's not a problem actually, but everybody falls in love with Chris, 'cause he's that sort of guy; if he walks into a room, doesn't matter who's there or whether they know him or not, he just takes over. Very charismatic, great guy. It takes people a long time to realize that sometimes he's not Mr. Perfect."

"I did GENUINELY feel I could have made a good job of it," Keen wrote.[98] "Nevertheless, thru possible timing and circumstances it was not to be."

"The reason I am writing to you now," Keen went on, "is because I have a desperate request and I write to you in earnest of this."

> I haven't been an ARTIST for many years, and I haven't written any songs for a long time. My life has changed considerably since I moved to the country. I have changed my whole outlook on life, also what I would like from it. Now to get to the point, when I was with the label I recorded nearly 45 songs, 12 of which [sic] you used on an album, I haven't heard the others for 7 years. ...I would like to hear them again as they were part of a concept album. I have absolutely nobody interested in me or my music so I don't feel I pose a threat to the company; it would mean a lot to me if I could listen to them again.
>
> ...when I left your label I left a bad situation, which over the years has turned into a DEAD situation, which is heartbreaking for me. In other words you are sitting on tapes that are absolutely useless to you, the reason being half of them are unfinished, and the rest were written for a concept album, and are useless individually. And as I am no longer functioning as an artist now, I just feel that if I could have them, and be left alone to slowly go thru them, and see if I had even the slightest thing that I could use to start me back to doing what I really want to

---

98 Cantrell had left the company just before this period and was unaware of Speedy's overtures regarding an A&R job. "I wish he'd have told me about it," said Cantrell. "I would have given him a job straight away."

do. I don't want to get into the madness again under any circumstances, and I could only approach the tapes as a "hobby", but obviously setting out to do a concept album and nearly finishing it leaves a big hole in your creative life. And I would like to finish it. Obviously I could only do it by borrowing friends studios here and there, and I'm sure it would take me a long time.

...I must emphasize that I am not asking you for anything, other than to let me hear my tapes, I don't want to hear them in your studios, or be involved in Island Records at all, it will not cost you anything, it's just that I can't move on in my life until I have sorted this stuff out. If by some miracle in 5 months time I come up with a dynamite concept album, it would belong to you the same, all it would mean is that instead of a dead situation, with my tapes lying in your cupboard, rotting away, and producing heavy metal, which is making [me] deaf, I might just have a chance to finish something, which I started a long time ago, it might also help me get back to what I do best.

In response to this plea, Island apparently sent Keen cassettes of the remaining tracks. There's no evidence that he picked up the *Alien 8* concept again. His reflective mood did, however, lead to him beginning work on a memoir around this time. "In this book I hope to put down some of the main things I did and thought in order to understand them now," he began.

I will start the book at the beginning which was a period when my granny was alive and I think the major factor in why I turn out so different from what was expected, she started me to dream, we would sit alone in front of her old black stove and she would tell me stories of when she was a little girl and how life was then. Another favorite character in my life was my Uncle Monty, my father's brother. These will be interspersed with my own thoughts; you have to understand this if you are going to understand the book.

He wrote about traveling to Rome, playing at the Piper Club – "one of its features was thousands of spotlights on frameworks in the ceiling" – and meeting Lydia. "There was a woman who came every night and she sat in the balcony above me... To cut a long story short, we got together and had a little girl called Patricia, my daughter. I haven't seen her for 18 years, I wish I could... it's far too late now, but I would love to see her again."

The memoir, which was left unfinished, included reflections on his drug habits: "I took far too many drugs and I regret it now, I still like to smoke now and then, but I haven't taken speed for years now, it was the drug I loved the best out of them all. My ideal day ten years ago would have been to wake up, light up a joint, get in that euphoric state I was always in, a good line of speed to override the down of the joint, then spend the next hour trying to override both of these."

Keen also recorded his candid and tender observations on Thunderclap Newman and Pete Townshend. "I started working with Pete, Jimmy and Andy and remember playing Pete my demo of 'Something In The Air' and him saying he could really make something out of this, but we never thought for a moment it would be a number one," he wrote.

The thing about Townshend was I was so engulfed in the guy, I thought he was everything, I never met anyone like him and never have since. I went through incredible conflict when I was with him, he did everything so well for a start, one half of me would respect him the other miffed by the fact he was so clever and always did everything so well, the one way I could match him was I reckoned I was a better driver than he was and that would please me. I loved him like a brother and would have done anything for him and he doesn't know now but I still would.

It was a family affair, we created everything in his house, but without his guidance we virtually destroyed ourselves. I hope the man realizes he changed my life for me and I owe so much to him. Sadly after a while we split so far I just couldn't reach him, compounded by the fact that everything we did went wrong and everything he did went straight to the top or whatever. It's funny but I still think of him as my best friend. I ran into him recently at a venue, we said a few words then he disappeared, I still miss him.

It wasn't long after he'd written about his wish to see his daughter again that Speedy and Patricia Keen would reconnect. It was around the age of seven that Trish had become aware that the only father she'd known, an ex-RAF radar technician named John Smith who worked for the Port of London Authority, was actually her stepfather. "Mum calls me into the living room one day and plays a record," Trish said. "It was a 45 single; I think it may have been 'Something In The Air' or 'Let Us In', which she set to play on the 78 setting which speeded up the recording, making it sound like Pinky and Perky. At 7 years old it sounded very funny and while I'm laughing she then tells me that the singer on the record is my dad. I'm pretty confused by this new information but figure he must be a nice person as he was unknowingly already making us laugh! After that mum very rarely mentioned him, her view being that the relationship was in the past and over. So that was that."

One morning in 1984, 18-year-old Trish was reading the horoscopes section in *The Sun*. Under Trish's sign – Taurus – "It said, "Whatever you want, go for it now", "she recalled, "and I thought 'I would like to meet my father,' so I set about trying to make that happen." She asked her mother about the area where they used to live, and took the train there, knocking on doors in an effort to find anyone who might know her father's current whereabouts. "After several weeks of getting nowhere, mum said he had been very good friends with Pete Townshend," Trish said, "so I thought as a last resort I would contact The Who fan club in the vague hope that they would see my letter and pass it onto Pete and that he might still know of dad's contact details." This effort worked.

Speedy soon contacted Trish and arranged for a visit. "Feeling utterly unprepared, nervous but excited, mum and I sit waiting, and around 6pm there's a knock at the door and mum answers it," Trish recalled. "Finally dad walks in; one of the most treasured moments of my life."

Dressed casually, he looked tall but noticeably hunched over and I was surprised by this, wondering if he was okay? He later explained he had a back problem which was due to a childhood accident, from falling out of a window.

After a long overdue hug, we sat down and held hands for an hour whilst we chatted. I cannot remember what was said as it's all a bit of a blur, the whole experience felt slightly unreal, albeit very joyful. He stayed for a few hours and then shortly after we met again.

The second meeting was more relaxed. I felt a huge sense of relief and peace in my heart that if nothing else at least we had finally managed to meet and we knew what we actually both looked like?! …Dad was chatty, charismatic, great company.

Speedy told Trish that at one point he had found out where she lived via a private investigator. "He drove over to see her," his friend Emma Hughes recalled, "and he said, "I just saw you coming out of the house with your mum and this other man who's your dad", and he said, "I just sat in the car and watched and I couldn't disrupt that." And he said it broke his heart again, but at least he felt like she had family."

Speedy and Trish kept in touch, wrote letters, exchanged phone calls, and visited when they could from this point forwards. "Over the years, there were many cherished, happy memories," she said. "I had some limited knowledge of dad's musical career and dad would occasionally speak about it, however the most important focus for us was to simply spend time together as a family, especially Christmas and birthdays."

Speedy was still living in a room at Ridge Farm studios. Ever sociable, Keen would chat with Andrews' mother over cups of tea in the kitchen, or interact with the artists who came to record there. Wayne Hussey, of The Mission, remembered coming across Speedy at the farmhouse in 1986 when the group were working on their debut album, *God's Own Medicine*. "While at Ridge Farm we'd hear this euphonious guitar playing emanating from one of the bedrooms on the ground floor from the other end of the house, the area where the owners and the staff had their quarters," Hussey recalled. A conversation with the source of the music revealed the backstory, and Keen and The Mission became friends. "We had rock deity among us and we didn't even know," Hussey said.

> We were due to play the Reading Festival on Friday 22nd August… But as we hadn't played since the beginning of the month we figured we needed to play a warm-up show. …Nearby was the market town of Horsham which boasted a grotty little venue called Champagne's. We arranged to play there on the Tuesday before our Reading appearance… Word quickly spread and the place was jammed, with the crowd spilling out onto the street. It was sweaty mayhem… Anyway, on that first occasion at Champagne's, Speedy Keen had gotten up onstage and played a couple of songs with us. He and we enjoyed it so much that we insisted he come to the Reading Festival with us on the Friday and do it all again with us there too. Speedy needed little persuading.

Keen performed onstage with The Mission at the Reading Festival that year. Unfortunately, there appears to be no photographic evidence of it.

John Knightsbridge also saw Speedy at Ridge Farm studios around this time. Knightsbridge was there recording a track on the *Strange Land* album by Box Of Frogs, released in 1986.

Keen next popped up in 1989 with a re-release of 'Something In The Air' by an outfit named Thunderclap 2, featuring Speedy and producer/musician Tony Mansfield on the Trax label. A synthed-up, '80s style version of the original Thunderclap track featuring re-recorded vocals and piano, the single's B-side was an instrumental version of the same song. The single didn't reach the charts.

By the early '90s, Keen departed his lodgings at Ridge Farm and purchased an ex-hire houseboat on the Thames at Penton Hook Marina, in Chertsey. An unlikely friendship was struck up around late 1991 when Emma Hughes, a teenager who lived with her family on a barge at the marina, was out for a walk one day when it started raining. "I was stood under a tree outside his boat waiting for the rain to pass," Hughes recalled. "He came out to see why I was there – he was a little paranoid about someone just standing there, the boat was on a little pontoon on its own in the corner because it was not exactly a gin palace – always covered in tarps and basically falling apart."

Once his suspicions had been allayed, Keen wanted to know what Hughes was listening to on her Walkman. "My neighbor at the marina had got me into Marillion, and I was now listening over and over to Fish's album[99]," said Hughes. She told him about one track in particular that she liked – Fish's cover of 'Something In The Air'. "Speedy absolutely spit feathers!", she said. "He said, "What? He doesn't even do the verses in the right order!"Then he said, plaintively, "I WROTE that song!""

Keen and Hughes struck up a friendship centered around their mutual love of music. "He met my mum because she was the manager of a recording studio and he came in and did some work," she said. Hughes herself went on to work as a tape operator/admin at several recording studios. "He was a huge friend to an awkward teen," she recalled. "Whilst I lived at home I was round there at least three evenings a week eating toast with jam. I had to scrape the mould off ("Emma stop fussing, it's edible honest") and drinking gallons of tea (but not the powdered lemon stuff Speedy had). He was a safe place to hang out and be cheered up – the loveliest, loveliest guy."

99 Fish's solo album *Internal Exile*, released in October 1991.

Keen was immediately aware that such a friendship between a middle-aged recluse and a child might arouse suspicion. "He did say, "Are your parents going to be alright with you coming round?", " said Hughes. "He would have felt like he had to explain why he had this friendship with this young kid. And then my mum went over and had a cup of tea." Much later, Hughes asked her mother about this meeting. "I said, "Were you going to kind of check and see if he was alright?" and she said, "No, in a way I was going round to reassure him that I'd already been told he was fine and not to worry,"" said Hughes. "It genuinely really was entirely innocent. He was very paternalistic, in a sort of distant way, to a lot of people." Looking back, Hughes reflects that her mother's visit to his cluttered quarters would have been "really difficult for him because he didn't let anybody on the boat; well – he let me, and he had a couple of other friends, but he never tidied or anything and he was very self-conscious about it." She also mentioned that Keen "was so reclusive that he wouldn't come over to our boat for parties or anything."

Keen hid his marijuana habit from his young friend until she was a little older, "and even then, though he knew I was smoking it… he still never let me smoke it with him. So when I think about the hours I spent there drinking all of his tea, he must have been desperate," she recalled with a laugh. "When he did tell me, he said a lot of it was because he was in such constant pain from his back." Keen suffered from chronic back pain during his later years, which was another reason he kept to himself. "He'd go to an osteopath and then he'd switch to a different one, a chiropractor," said Hughes. "He was always seeing different people about trying to alleviate his back pain."

In addition to music, Keen and Hughes found that not only did they have boats in common, but a love of the local wildlife. When Hughes's mother had asked her husband about Keen, he responded, "Oh he's fine – he's the bird man." "He was known in the marina as the bird man because he fed all of the ducks and really cared about them," said Hughes, who added that every duck, swan, moorhen and coot in the marina would make their way over to his boat around 3pm every day to be fed. "He would get really upset when it was mating season, which is quite savage, and he'd spend ages going round trying to shoo the males off to give the female ducks a break. He was so kind and concerned about wildlife and the environment. He was devastated when the swan's nest was raided for eggs, and spent every subsequent night sitting a little distance from the nest to make sure no one came back for the rest of the eggs. He was there every night until they hatched. A beautiful soul."

Speedy was "talking about basically green politics decades before anyone else was," said Hughes. "He'd go off to St. Anne's park with a view out over Surrey and he was so concerned about airplanes not keeping to the right limit. He would say, "Oh they're flying too low," – and they were. And he would video them and be like, "I'm trying to gather evidence," but I don't know if it ever got submitted." At one point he was organizing a fundraising event for environmental issues featuring local artists, but it's not clear whether it ended up taking place.

Keen mostly kept to himself at the marina, in part because of the snobbery of some of the other residents, and in part due to his anxiety. "At first all of the pontoons were quite rickety but then they gradually upgraded them," Hughes recalled, "and they came out to talk to him and said we're going to need to move you so we can do a new pontoon and he was really anxious. He said, "Oh, they're trying to get me out of the marina.""

Another reason Speedy kept a low profile was his constant fear that tax collectors or other authority figures might pay him a visit. At one point, Keen apparently owed a sizeable sum in tax debt, which remained a great source of stress and anxiety even after he'd settled it. "He was hugely fearful of tax bills," Hughes recalled, "and he'd always say to me, "I'm really scared they're going to come and take everything away." Because of this, Keen was particularly difficult to track down. "I remember years and years afterwards, nobody knew where he'd gone," said Doug Smith, who'd been looking for Keen in order to pay him his producer royalties for the Motorhead album. "He'd disappeared, and Ted [Carroll] used to call me up and say, "Any idea what Speedy's address is?" And I'd ring Lemmy up and he'd say "No, I haven't seen him in years, don't know where he is.""

Pete Townshend, too, had difficulties locating Speedy. "If you're out there Speedy, I found about $150,000 that belongs to him, of misdirected money," Townshend told an interviewer during Keen's years at Penton Hook. "I think he's living on a houseboat on the Thames somewhere, so he can put the flags out. 'Cause that song's getting a lot of play in America. I think it's on some kind of new collection album, it's selling a lot of units somewhere, I don't know." Townshend had reached out to others as well. "Townshend sent me an email saying, "Where's Speedy?," Jim Avery recalled. "'Cause Speedy went missing. I spoke to Chris Stamp about this, I said, "Where is Speedy?", 'cause he'd lived on a boat for a while, and kept himself very much to himself. And he said, "Oh, he's got old, man. He's got old." And I did see him briefly. He had aged a lot; you know how some people age real quick? It's unfortunate. He seemed to be going down and down."

The sensitive and observant Keen did seem world weary at this point. "I think that the people that you meet that are very creative, part of that is because they feel everything very deeply," Emma Hughes observed, "so any pain around them that anyone else is experiencing, whether it's the ducks or the family up the road that are having a hard time, he'd really absorb it. If a bit of money had arrived, he'd be like, "Let's go out and have lunch," and he had his favorite places that he felt didn't look down on him, weren't funny about him going in, and he would chat to all the staff there, but then he would kind of take on all their problems as well, and I'd say to him, "They're fine; yes it's drama but they'll be ok, don't worry.""

Keen had set up a small recording studio in the bow of his boat and seemed to rediscover his creative spark. "He was always working on stuff, but I don't know how far it progressed," said Hughes. "He'd play me little bits – he'd say, "This is what I've been doing today," and sometimes he would go off to Capel in Surrey to his friend's recording studio there. He'd tease me that I had to function and get on with stuff in the 'real world' whilst he had done his work and earned the right to be a night owl and create and not be stuck in the 9-5. That was his life, experimenting and recording all night, then sleeping until lunchtime, early afternoon."

Speedy possessed a sizeable amount of his own tapes, the majority of which were stored in his sister's shed. "He asked after it one day and she went, "Oh, the council came and cleared the shed and it's all gone"," Emma Hughes recalled. "So anything that he had created or produced that he had, went." This included reel to reel tapes of Jimi Hendrix from the Track Records days, of which he'd told his daughter Trish, "This will be my retirement."

"He seemed genuinely happy at that point in time and had a really good life pursuing whatever interested him at that specific moment," Hughes said.

> He'd been able to connect with his daughter and adored having a grandson… that meant everything to him. …He spent his time in a daily routine that

347

kept him in contact with people who would be chatting amiably to him, from the family that ran the convenience store on the way in to Staines, to the staff at the independent little restaurant places, who knew him as 'that lovely bloke who was in that band', and treated him with kindness and respect. I remember reading that Ian McEwan said the best thing about having such success as a writer, so young, was that it gave him the financial freedom to spend so much of his time reading. And that's what Speedy had. Yes, he was always anxious about money, felt the taxman was going to reach out and take everything from him, so he should spend it as quickly as it came in, but he had his boat, and the freedom to keep his own hours, go out and about and chat to people, feed the ducks, soak up some inspiration, and make music. Not a bad way to live!

In the late '90s, Keen placed an ad in the local paper looking for an assistant. As a result, he met Fiona Calkin. A relationship blossomed and the pair had a son, Robert, in April 2001, Speedy's second child, nearly 35 years after his first. Keen telephoned friends, full of excitement about the new baby.

Not long after Robert's birth, Speedy told his friends that he was planning to have back surgery. "He was really hoping that was going to help," said Emma Hughes. However, other far more serious health matters would quickly unravel all plans.

In 2002, Speedy had a heart attack, his second in about two years. He was admitted to St. George's Hospital, London. "Due to the distance we lived apart, I didn't see how unwell dad had become," Trish Keen recalled.

I think he concealed and played down how unwell

he was feeling as he didn't like to cause worry, so it was a huge shock when I got a call to say he was in hospital. During his last visit, he stayed a week and although he didn't look a picture of health he certainly didn't seem particularly unwell, in fact, quite the opposite: He seemed to have far more get up and go than me. I always tried to encourage him to spend time, sit and relax and enjoy healthy homemade food rather than rushing about here, there and everywhere and wanting to dine at happy eaters. I suspect quite a few letters he wrote to me were penned in a happy eater restaurant or a café. Overall I think he felt responsible to try to look after everyone else and completely overdid it, tragically overlooking and disregarding his own health.

Upon hearing the news of Speedy's heart attack, Trish immediately traveled to London to be with her father. Doctors told Trish and Fiona that Speedy's chances of survival were about 90% if he had heart surgery, and 90% of not surviving if he didn't. Not surprisingly, the decision was made to proceed with the surgery. Speedy never regained consciousness. Trish sat at his bedside, holding his hand. He died in the hospital on March 12th, 2002, only 56 years old. His son was not yet a year old.

Speedy had been working on a solo album in the months before his death, and left a sizeable collection of reel to reel tapes and mini disks which had been stored on his boat and in his caravan in Sunbury, about seven miles east of the marina. Trish later spent hours listening to these recordings of unfinished fragments of songs and demos of full songs, and considers the unreleased track 'Children of the Fields' to be one of her father's best songs.

During one of their visits, Speedy gave Trish the silver bracelet which can be seen on his wrist on the covers of both of his solo albums, a gift that she cherishes today. In addition to his partner Fiona and children Trish and Robert, Speedy was survived by a grandson, Aaron, 12 years old. Trish later had two more children: Jayde, now 19, and Ryan, 17.

A final note regarding Speedy's legacy: "…As it turned out, the final vision came not from Townshend but from Keen," Bud Scoppa wrote in *Rolling Stone.* "He wrote and sang the classic single 'Something in the Air', and his voice, songs and unmistakable charm turned Thunderclap Newman's lone album, *Hollywood Dream*, into what is surely the most intimate and touching work to come out of the largely overbearingly ambitious concept-album school of rock. McCulloch's youthfully plaintive guitar and Newman's primitive, nostalgia-drenched piano were made for Speedy, whose songs ached for a soft-focused past or an impossibly harmonious future, and whose thin voice was really just a weary but never hopeless sigh. As the expression of an unyielding belief in a world that never was and never will be, *Hollywood Dream* was heartbreakingly affecting. Unflinching innocence in the face of bitter experience."

CHAPTER 12

ANDY

"I just wanted to let you know that we had the best time. He was engaging, intriguing, charming, knowledgeable... His talent was prodigious. One of those people that you can honestly say heard an orchestra as soon as he heard a riff. Those people are the ones you want to be around."

- Angie Bowie

"I once asked Andy what the hell a guinea fowl was. One hour later, he finished a 'Darwinian' type lecture – having started with amoebas and vertebrae, right through every damn creature crawling out of the sea and then learning to fly, every species in the jungle, the extinct dodo and even the turkey that descended from the dinosaurs – no winged fowl was left out – never again – close my big mouth!"

- Bob Flag

By the second half of 1971, Andy Newman was again performing in public under the name 'Thunderclap Newman', this time without Jimmy and Speedy, who had moved on to other commitments. "I tried to form another band, and each one I formed didn't really work out; we never made any sort of impact," he said later. Some of Newman's friends expressed surprise that he didn't return to the anonymity and routine of his former job. "He worked for the GPO and had quite a good position," remarked Richard Stanley. "I would think he'd have gone back to that. He always talked about it as a fun job."

On August 5th, 'Thunderclap Newman' appeared on the bill at the Winning Post pub in Twickenham with Roger Spear, Andy's friend from the Ealing Tech days who had been with the Bonzo Dog Doo-Dah Band until their breakup in 1970. In late November, the *NME* reported that both Spear and Newman were cast in "a rock'n'roll pantomime titled 'Alice in Boogieland' which is to be presented at Lincoln Theatre Royal, opening on February 14. The show may subsequently go on tour." Given the absence of any media reports, it's unlikely that this production took place, but Newman's association with Spear would continue.

The support act for Newman's performance at Croydon School of Art on December 5th was a new group named Kilburn & The High Roads, featuring vocalist Ian Dury. This was their first gig. "The gig was on the third floor and we had to carry a piano up the stairs," Kilburn & The High Roads' drummer Chris Lucas told Ian Dury biographer Richard Balls, who noted that "the stress of the group's first public performance weighed heavily on [pianist] Russell Hardy, who had never played a rock'n'roll gig before, although Thunderclap Newman made his evening by asking if he could borrow his piano."

That same month, work concluded on Andy Newman's solo album. "Andy's finished his album – it was finished today," Pete Townshend told *ZigZag*'s John Tobler in December. "I've edited it and done some mixing and stuff like that... sort of 'creative production'."

"It will be made up of multi-track recordings on all types of instruments," Newman told Chris Welch back in 1969, not long after work had begun on the project. "I play the piano, kazoo and saxophone, but for the brass I may try to find some session men. It's being produced by Rick Seaman, and when we sent some rough recordings to Pete Townshend he was delighted. Rick was on the verge of applying to London Transport for a position as a bus driver, but old Pete was so chuffed when he heard them, he said they could be put out as an LP right away. But of course we want to do something much better."

Predictably, Newman took a unique approach to the recording process. As he had done with Seaman (recall 1970's 'Stormy Petrel', recorded at an empty Hammersmith Town Hall using an ex-GPO van outfitted with a mobile recording setup), Newman drove around in his van with his friend Chris Glass looking for locations with interesting acoustics. "He was a charming fellow," said Glass, who studied science at Ealing Tech and shared a flat with Roger Spear.[100] "I remember he came to my flat once and I had this new sort of art deco swivel chair. He plopped himself down on it and it promptly collapsed. But yes – we used to go to all the funny little rehearsal rooms and put bits together on tape. I think that must have been in preparation for having his own album."

"I commissioned the album and paid for the construction of the studio in a van,"Townshend recalled, this studio referred to in the album's credits as 'Eelpie Sound'. "They then moved to Sound Techniques in Chelsea to finish it off."Townshend received an executive producer credit on the finished album, with Seaman named producer. "Pete didn't actually directly produce it,"Newman explained in 2009. "What he did was he sort of made the arrangements for it to be done, and he put Rick Seaman in charge of producing it – directing the sessions. And basically what I did – it was purely myself on my own, multitracking, but being able to multi-track on eight and sixteen-track recording machines, which were available in the studios by then."

"Andy's real talent lies with himself, not with organizing, not with playing with other musicians,"Townshend said in 1971.

> He wants a band, I suppose, because the human being is a social animal and likes to work in that way. But really, again, and it points right back to the fact that Thunderclap Newman had brilliant potential as far as recording – it's that Andy has always done what I have done, since before I even knew what tape recording was, he was into

---

100 Glass later helped design recording studios, including Eden Studios in west London. "He and Andy would sit down and talk impedance to each other," said Richard Barnes. "I wouldn't know what the hell they were going on about."

it. Multi-tracking – bird songs and locomotive recordings, you know, special effects, echoes. I've got a stack of tapes upstairs that he did as early as 1960 – which are all done just on piano, or his version of 'Rock Around The Clock' with Andy Newman's saxophone sixteen times. I think the album he's just done is good because he's done it all himself.

Recalling Seaman's previous production credit for the recording of 'Stormy Petrel' (as 'R. Cardboard', a co-credit with Townshend), I asked Newman if his friend had produced anything else. "Oh no – he'd never done any producing at all," Newman said. "He knew nothing about it – he was a coach driver! He used to drive people down on their holidays." Seaman had indeed become a tour guide, taking tourists to various sites of interest around Britain. "But," Newman pointed out, "he sold me to Pete Townshend in the student days, and Townshend turned to him and said look, you obviously know how to do this, and do it. And *Rainbow* was the result."

Seaman recalled that Townshend "met me at a party and asked me if I would make a recording of Andy. I had nothing better to do really, and made a solo album of Andy which is beautiful in its way but it's very, very strange." Seaman reiterated that he had no experience working as a producer. "I didn't really know what to do – I'm not musical, you know," he said. "Sticking me in a recording studio… I really don't know what's going on. I felt a bit embarrassed by it." When asked what his role was during the sessions, Seaman responded: "What was I doing? Probably not a lot, to be honest. It was mostly Andy, you know – Andy's expertise. He would sometimes ask me questions; whether I thought this would go with that, because we used a lot of different instruments on it. His main dream was orchestration. It was never really to materialize, but that was what he would have liked to have done, and that's what we did, to a large degree. Andy was playing all the different instruments, just multi-tracking them. He ran everything."

The move to Sound Techniques studio in Chelsea took place late in the process of recording the album. "I think they quite liked Sound Techniques because of the acoustics," said Glass. "It was semi-live; it wasn't a totally dead studio like a lot of the pop studios were." Newman took full advantage of his expansive new surroundings, despite the fact that he was recording solo. "Andy had this thing about trying to get a real stereo sound," recalled Glass, who visited the studio one day while Newman was recording. "It was just him on his own, but he had the microphones set up for recording stereo as you would normally do for a whole band, and then Andy moved his chair to different positions for each take when he played a different instrument, so that it appeared in different places in the stereo mix."

"He was technically very astute," Seaman observed. "He knew how they would record a big orchestra, and he knew a lot about microphones and recording and so on. And I don't know if he had perfect pitch or anything, but... on one track he sang three parts himself – the bass part and the tenor and the soprano or whatever, and laid them all one upon another and they were in perfect harmony."

Another example of Newman's technical abilities is demonstrated by this recollection, from Clive Smith: "Pete has this great story about Andy visiting once and being outside the house and rummaging through Pete's recycling or something and he pulled out this old two inch tape."

And he said to Pete, "Do you need this? This is good tape." And he said, "No, no, it's all used tape." So Andy takes it away and a few days later he returns and he shows Pete this device he'd just made where you pull the tape through and it passes through seven blades and it reduces the two inch tape to eight quarter inch tapes which are now usable in a quarter inch tape machine. That's the way Pete told it to me, and it was *so* Andy. The fact that he grew up inventing his life, inventing everything he did, inventing how to do things, how to play the instruments, how to record the instruments, how to overdub the instruments.

Despite the already lengthy recording process, Newman felt that the *Rainbow* album wasn't fully realized. "The problem was that we were working on the thing and we'd got about three quarters of the way through but it needed finishing off," he said. "And then I don't quite know what happened – they suddenly decided to stick the thing out as it was." Chris Glass's opinion is that it came down to both money and practicality: "I think Pete wasn't prepared to pay for full studio time," he said. "Because that was a full-size studio, and really what Andy was doing, he just needed a bedroom with a microphone."

"A selection of the numbers that we'd done were made, and I'm not entirely sure that all the ones I would've preferred to have gone on actually went on," Newman said in 2009. "And some that I probably would've thought twice about went on, but that's the way it ended up, and I don't think it sold a hell of a lot," he said with a laugh. "In fact, I remember the only critical acclaim we got was one of the music newspapers – I can't remember which one it was – said 'if only the album was as good as the sleeve'!" The album's cover photo, incidentally, was taken by Graham Hughes, who had taken the cover photo for *Hollywood Dream*.

"It was okay," said Seaman of *Rainbow*, "but it wasn't as good as the original piano and kazoo stuff from earlier."

I didn't really know what to do with Andy to be honest, because he had no rhythm in him, that's the thing. He was immersed in early jazz and he loved classical music, but there's nothing contemporaneous about it; there was no feeling for contemporary beats at all. I remember Pete at the time with enthusiasm about Dr. John and the album he made at the time[101], which was beautifully produced and maybe in the back of his mind he was thinking Andy could do something like that, but he didn't have that beat in him, that rhythm in him. In fact, in Sound Techniques, he wanted to lay down a drum track, but it was so funny that everyone was laughing at him trying to play the drums.

For his part, Townshend thought the album was brilliant. "Andy's new record is like a work of art and that's the end of it," he said. "It stands up against *The Ring* or anything Debussy did. I mean, it really is incredibly heavy stuff – fantastic stuff." In 2003, he oversaw a re-release of the album on compact disc, on his Eel Pie label.

"[Newman] absolutely floors me with his soloing on a dozen different instruments and with his arrangements," Bob Flag wrote in his memoir. Flag, despite having worked with Newman throughout the next three decades, only discovered the album when it was re-released by Eel Pie.

Rainbow is a display of his versatility – it is multi-tracked – and multi-faceted – unique in style and conception – I knew he was good, but never realized he was a genius. We didn't have even an

101 Likely a reference to Dr. John's 1968 debut release *Gris Gris*, which *Rolling Stone* referred to as "the New Orleans appropriation of California psychedelia, dressed up in Mardi Gras finery and spiced like a gut-busting gumbo."

inkling of that in Thunderflag[102] – which is partly his fault – he never pushed the sort of conceptions he had within him, for that album, nor his ideas on to what we purveyed – we just indulged in the beauty of those gems of the 1920s - and partly my fault – I never thought there was more to him than just that period of white jazz and dance music. I was also guilty of being set on injecting as much comedy as possible into our shows.

According to Flag, at one point Newman referred to the album's producer – presumably he was referring to Seaman – as "tone deaf", a label Seaman would likely not argue with. "To be fair to the 'tone deaf' producer Andy referred to," Flag continued:

All that multi tracking and getting one bloke to sound like Duke Ellington at times and Jelly Roll Morton at others must have done something to his hearing. Hardly anybody was ready for that approach in the 1970s – they hadn't yet got over the Beatles – they were still besotted by the 'unlimited talents' of Paul McCartney. And what sort of idiot reviewer wrote 'the best thing about the album is the sleeve'? There are moments of sheer genius and its re-release on CD is timely – the world may just now be ready for where *Hollywood Dream* left off and to where *Rainbow* pointed the way – an interesting fusion could still be on the cards.

In keeping with Flag's 'hardly anybody was ready for it' angle, it appears that there was some hesitation about how to approach the release and promotion of this odd,

102 More on Flag and 'Thunderflag' later in this chapter.

distinctly radio *un*-friendly album. "I think that's where good management comes in," said Richard Barnes. "There is enough eccentricity and stuff in there that he could have made quite a good career – I mean you just need the manager to put them on the right radio shows and the right TV spots. It *isn't* commercial, but there is an interest there – I mean, listen: I know people that bought and played Yoko Ono albums, so for fuck's sake, if they'll do that…" And, as Dana Wiffen pointed out, Track had released the single 'Queen Of The Alley Dogs' that same year, a recording of various dogs barking to music. "Vernon was good with that," said Wiffen. "He promoted that and got it in the charts, so if he can do that, he can do anything!"

But Pete Townshend had wanted to ensure Newman was taken seriously and not packaged and sold to the public as a novelty. Because of this, he had wanted the album released on a label other than Track. "A lot of my friends think he's a freak – but in the best sense of the word, a real individualist," *ZigZag*'s John Tobler told Townshend in December 1971, to which Townshend responded:

> He's certainly eccentric, but above that, the word 'freak' means different and he is different to other people – he's a darn sight more talented than most people and he's a musical genius. That's what I think and I'm right about a lot of other people and I think I'm right about Andy. I think he's a genius. …I'm worried that if we get a contract for this record, that the record company will decide, "It's another R.R.S. [Roger Ruskin Spear] – Hey, some of this sounds humorous – let's just dress him up in a top hat and put an ad in the paper." This is why I don't think Andy should go with Track, because Track have got a bit of a reputation for tasteless ads in the paper and they might be tempted to do that

– because this album really does what should have been done, *eventually*, by Thunderclap Newman. It brings Andy out as a musician, 'cause we never really got the time to do that on the first album. I suppose the only section where he got full rein was in that little bit in 'Accidents' where I just surprised him by saying, "Why don't you do that bit on your own and multitrack it?"

Regardless, Andy Newman's solo album *Rainbow* was released by Track on August 11th, 1972. Six of the album's ten tracks were Newman compositions (including 'Water Music', the song which had often been included in Thunderclap Newman's live set) while another, 'Appalachian Champagne', was a co-credit with guitarist and Roger Spear associate Jerry Gardiner. The remaining tracks were covers: Walter Donaldson's 1930 song 'That's What I Like About You', the Max Freedman and James E. Myers classic 'Rock Around The Clock', and J.W. Roycroft's 'After Tonight'. As he did on *Hollywood Dream*, Newman plays a dizzying assortment of instruments. The list of those used on the track 'Red Skies' is a good example: "Piano, Kazoo, 3 Bass Recorders, Glockenspiel, Oboe, Tin Whistle, C Melody and Soprano Saxophone, Tea Chest Bass, Cor Anglais, Tuned Sleigh Bells and Effects."

Rainbow received sparse attention and did not reach the charts. "There are artists who cunningly size up what will sell, what will be easy to promote, and what will be easy to understand for the listener," wrote Connor McKnight in his review of the album in *Time Out*.

There are artists who stumble on a form of music that is all those things, and flog (or sell) it to death. Finally there are artists who just play the music that they have in their fingers and in their palms and usually they're lucky if it ever reaches an audience wider than old school friends, immediate family, collected lovers of the bizarre etc. Andy Newman is without doubt one of the latter.

…His music is born of years of playing piano, kazoo, and just about every wind instrument that was ever made. He knows more about the history and origins of saxophones, clarinets, oboes and horns than anyone I have ever met. To hear him talk of his prized (I think Hungarian) wooden saxophone is to be dazzled by the love of music that only the very lucky enjoy.

…Thunderclap Newman's old album, *Holly-wood Dream*, was one of 1970's great ignoreds and if you're one of the blessed and own it, you'll recall the incredible passage in 'Accidents' where Andy really lets go. That solo was sprung on him by Townshend and forms a splendid introduction to the music on this album.

* * *

Andy Newman next surfaced in the credits of 'The Yum Yum Song', a single by the 75-year-old singer/actor Monti De Lyle, playing claves, guiro, bass recorder, and – along with Roger Spear – tenor saxophone. The single was recorded in spring 1973 and released in September, when Newman was again working with Spear, whose *Unusual* album was recorded at Olympic Studios and Pete Townshend's Eel Pie Sound (Goring) studio from August to December. Newman's fingerprints were everywhere. He borrowed a set of tuned bells from Keith Moon for the group's rendition of a fittingly odd 'Pinball Wizard' on which Andy played the piano and the siren whistle, and which was engineered by Chris Glass. Newman also played wood blocks on 'I Love To Bumpity-Bump,' and added bone-dry spoken-word vocals on 'Heartbreak Hotel', the liner notes re: the latter poking fun at Newman's sanitized delivery: "The vocal recitation in this number is by A. L. Newman who delivers his lines with true feeling, conviction, soul and just plain guts, Man."

Townshend's support of Spear was consistent with his mentorship of "outsiders" during the early years at Track. "Pete was very good to me – and to Thunderclap Newman – when we were sort of starting out," Spear recalled. "'Cause Pete had all this stuff. I did go over to Pete's place in Goring and record quite a lot of my first album, *Electric Shocks*, on his machines out there.[103] I did all my backing tracks there." Spear also recalled working at another of Townshend's studios, located by the river in Twickenham and which became known as Oceanic. "He was building a recording studio there, so while he was building it, he let me doodle around there," Spear recalled. "Thunderclap and I were going to make a video there, but I'm not sure that that happened, actually."

Newman and Spear also performed at a garden party on Townshend's Goring property in the early '70s. "Pete asked me to arrange this party," Richard Barnes recalled. "He had got this house at Goring, it was by the Thames, with a lovely great big huge lawn; he used to call it 'boring Goring' but I thought it was a great place."

We lived in Ealing and next door was Hanwell, where Speedy came from, and they used to have these brass band competitions and the winner of this competition was the Hanwell Silver Band – they didn't have brass instruments, they had silver

---

103 Newman contributed bass saxophone, kazoo and backing vocals on *Electric Shocks*, released in 1972. *Melody Maker*'s Chris Welch played drums on several tracks.

– and they were brilliant, so we booked them. There were about forty of them or something, all in their uniforms. I remember in their contract was a clause that after every three numbers or whatever, they had to stop for beer. And we had to provide a crate of beer for every three songs – it was wonderful, all written down as a contract. I thought it was brilliant. It was a great day, one of those days that seemed to go on for ages and ages. Andy played there, and so did Roger Spear. He played, not with the Bonzos but just his band and he had his robots on stage with him. We loved it. He played 'Pinball Wizard' on the trombone – really well. Pete was in hysterics; it was really funny.

Around this same time, Newman performed at another Baba-related garden party by the river in Twickenham, hosted by Mike McInnerney, Townshend's artist friend and fellow Meher Baba devotee. Newman and Spear also toured together sporadically during this period. "I did a double act with Andy for many years on the college circuit," Spear recalled. "Andy built a very heavy and complicated 'control unit' in GPO style to control all our lighting and stage pyrotechnics.[104] We used to travel around the country doing gigs in our vans with two-way radios. Andy was in his ex-GPO green van with a massive tank aerial and Army surplus wireless set no. 62 in the back. He also converted his van to gas in the petrol crisis years of '73."

Track Records office employee Dana Wiffen saw Newman and Spear at Goldsmiths College around this time. "It was like a comedy act really," Wiffen recalled in 2009.

---

104 Spear noted that he saw this 'control unit' pop up for sale on eBay recently.

They had these things with wires coming out – you'd put them on your throat and then you'd hum a certain tune and they played along to it and things like this, so it was like really sort of silly, experimental – very Bonzo Dog-ish, and Andy's plonking around in the background.

He actually stayed at my house, when I was still living with my parents, and he came in his old post office van, and he had it all done out in the back with all his instruments in there – he had a tiny little saxophone and then he had the massive great [contrabass]. He actually got them out in the road just before he left, and started playing a tune in the middle of the road and all the neighbors were looking out! My mum cooked him breakfast in the morning. He slept on the sofa and when I saw him recently, he said, "I remember that – I woke up with about six cats on me," and I said, "Hang on, we only had two cats!"

On Saturday February 15th 1975, Newman and Spear performed with Bob Kerr's Whoopee Band, an offshoot of the Bonzo Dog Doo-Dah Band, at Southampton University's Valentine's Ball. "There was quite a lot of that – Trad Jazz, as they called it," Rick Seaman recalled. "All the art school students and people like that used to go to gigs with trad jazz, and there were some big names back then or before then – The Temperance Seven, and Andy was good mates with a guy called Bob Kerr, who had a band called the Whoopee Band, you know, it was all that sort of jokey sort of traditional jazz thing." Chris Glass recalled rehearsing with Newman in Kerr's basement rehearsal room. "It had a very low ceiling," said Glass. "I remember him playing a contrabass saxophone in the basement and he had to tilt it over as it was over seven feet on its stand."

Back in early 1973, Andy had met David Bowie's wife Angie, who was interested in recording her song 'Some Of My Best Friends Are Strangers' with him. The pair met at the studio during Newman's recording sessions with Monti De Lyle. "They ran over a little bit and I was listening to them – fabulous horn section," Bowie recalled. "They got to the end of the song and they piled out, and after a while I got up and looked into the studio and there was Thunderclap, cleaning the mouthpiece on his saxophone." Newman and Bowie discussed her song over dinner at a nearby Chinese restaurant. "He said, "Are you going to sing it?", and I said yes," she recalled. "And I started singing it. And so he starts playing an imaginary sax and then with the other hand in between, he's beating it out on a piano keyboard that doesn't exist. And we finished eating and we went back to the studio and we did a take. That's how easy it was to work with Andy."

The pair recorded further Bowie compositions together over the next few years. Plans to release an album never reached fruition, and these tracks are now lost. Bowie's 2002 album *Moon Goddess* contains re-recorded versions of many of these songs. "*Moon Goddess* has 'Some Of My Best Friends Are Strangers', 'Fires Are Burning', 'Success', lots of the original stuff I did with Andy," she recalled. "They're not the same unfortunately, but they are exactly how he arranged them."

In 1975, Bowie was working with actor, fringe comedian and jazz musician Bob Flag[105] on the musical sketch comedy production 'Krisis Kabaret', which set various crisis situations to music, born in part out of the recent UK energy crisis that led to the government's mandate of

---

105 Even if his name doesn't sound familiar, you've probably seen Bob Flag's face, the image of which was used as 'Big Brother' in Michael Radford's 1984 film adaptation of George Orwell's *1984*.

a 3-day work week in 1973/4. "I was introduced to Andy by Angie Bowie," Flag recalled in his memoir. "We were visiting Track studios, where Andy happened to be installing all new sound equipment." The pair clicked instantly. "On mentioning that his famous piano solo in 'Something In The Air' was very much like those of Bix Beiderbecke, we discovered our mutual love of wonderful, virtually unknown songs from the 1920s," Flag recalled.[106] "Andy had a vast repertoire of the same, which he had dug out from his record collection of vinyl 78s and he could play them all on piano (with the verses) – wow! He was immediately recruited to join Angie and myself in 'Krisis Kabaret' – he became its musical director."

Bowie, Newman and Flag began rehearsing 'Krisis Kabaret' in the basement of the Little Theatre on St. Martin's Lane, Covent Garden. "Before we knew it we had an hour and a half show which was absolutely fabulous," said Angie Bowie. "Bob Flag was a born comedian, and Thunderclap was the straight man. Thunderclap would suddenly go *BDMBLDM* on the piano, almost like you were in a silent theatre with one of those accompanists as the titles rolled."

"I had so much fun," Bowie recalled. "Thunderclap encouraged me and helped me and was the most wonderful music director to work with onstage."

He was an absolute joy. In the middle of our show I could say, "Andy?" And the thunder would go. He also knew he had to count me in – I'm totally useless; I would start listening to the tune and how fabulous it sounded. And we'd go round again and

---

106 "Before I'd ever met Andy, I had used his no. 1 hit single, 'Something In The Air' many times in my cabaret shows," Flag recalled. "I considered it and still do, to be the best single, from the best album, of all time."

he'd go, "Angie – *now!*" He was the dearest man. He would do flourishes when I came onstage or when I walked by. He did things that were the generosity of sharing the stage with people that you don't find a lot.

I do have one funny thing I should tell you… just charming. A gal in 'Krisis Kabaret' did some fabulous belly dances, and they would always use Andy as the straight guy. Andy was so funny – he'd stand up and stroke his beard as they were gyrating around him and giving him the jingle bells on their hips on their belly dancing costumes.

After the conclusion of their month-long commitment at the Little Theatre, the ensemble performed 'Krisis Kabaret' at Webbington Spa in Somerset. "We played a week there and that was very odd; it was one of those hotels and theatres all in one thing and you feel like you're on a cruise ship, you can't escape – very bizarre," Bowie recalled. "But it was great fun, we had great shows and the fans came out so that was fabulous."

When Newman and company had begun rehearsals for 'Krisis Kabaret' in the basement of the Little Theatre, they met Ted Green, who was living there at the time. Green, who Flag referred to as "one of the U.K.'s longest serving squatters and claimants," was also a brilliant violinist and pianist (Flag compared Green's playing to that of Thelonious Monk). He and Newman shared a love of early American jazz, but they also had something else in common: "When we met, he was homeless himself," said Green. "He was actually living in his van with all his gear and all the instruments and stuff. In fact, he got broken in and he had a lot of stuff stolen from the van."

After the conclusion of 'Krisis Kabaret', Green moved out of the Little Theatre and, along with Newman, found lodgings in Swiss Cottage, north London. "It was a beautiful, big house," Green recalled. "We had the basement, more or less." Newman immediately put his skills as an electrician to use. "He used to just connect us up to free electricity," Green recalled, adding that Andy had a nice hi-fi system. "He had this very together sort of deck and separate amplifiers, but I used to ask him to turn it down," he said. Green remembers Newman being quite old fashioned and 'straight' at times. "I used to smoke dope," he said. "Andy didn't approve, although he allowed it. He said, "Not for me, but you carry on." Green also recognized Newman's more adventurous behavior when in a musical environment. "He'd disapprove of certain things, but on the other side, when you saw him in theater, he was completely free, you know."

When asked his opinion of Newman's playing style, Green responded, "Well, he wouldn't class himself as a pianist, you see. He'd play the chord with his right hand; he'd play flourishes and things with the right hand, but you'd rarely hear him play the actual melody with his right hand. Usually people play the melody right hand, and the chords left hand. He would play this strong bass, like a walking bass with his left hand, but he would play around with the rhythms, I suppose you'd call it contrapuntal, when you'd sort of double or quadruple the timing for emphasis." Green recalled that Newman "used to go around to markets and pick up all these [recordings by] obscure sort of bands. I had my mother's music from when she was in ENSA[107] – all the old Horatio Nicholls arrangements, the old show tunes, and so he was photocopying those."

---

107 Green's mother performed at Guildhall, London during the war as part of ENSA – Entertainments National Service Association, an organization that provided entertainment for the armed forces during the war.

In 1977, Newman and Green relocated to Rectory Gardens, an 'L' shaped Victorian street in Clapham whose twenty or so houses had suffered significant bomb damage during World War 2. In the '60s and '70s, a group of squatters moved in and over the next four decades renovated the homes, dug a garden and formed a community of artists, hippies and other creative types. Andy moved in to number 5, a home recently vacated by Jo Wolf, a carpenter who passed the occupational rights along to Newman. "Andy was my very best friend in the U.K.," said Wolf, who had moved to London from Germany. "He came from working for British Telecom so it was relatively easy for him to do the next step and do electrical conversion, rewiring etc. We operated a loose building cooperative doing commercial jobs and advertising in commercial magazines in London."

By this time Newman, unable to afford the costs of operating and maintaining a vehicle, had abandoned his battered ex-GPO van, and the old VW Beetle he had used during the Thunderclap Newman years sat rusting outside his brother's house until Robin eventually had it towed away. "He relied on me if he needed some transport, or he used public transport," said Wolf, who had his own ex-GPO van. When Newman walked or used public transport to get to gigs or electrical jobs, he'd transport his musical instruments or tools on a small metal-framed shopping trolley.

By the time he had moved to Rectory Gardens, Andy Newman's musical activities had dwindled to very much a part-time affair. His full-time occupation had become that of electrician, and helping with the administration of the housing cooperative he was now part of. An article in *Music Week* from the very beginning of this period, October 1977, mentions that a "Sixties rock package," planned to appear at the Roxy Theatre in Harlesden, had been canceled after the local council refused to approve the new venue. One of the acts scheduled to appear was 'Thunderclap Newman', but it's unlikely that Andy had anything to do with this, and it certainly didn't include Speedy or Jimmy. This illustrates a problem that had emerged by this time, as Bob Flag recalled: "Around that time, other outfits were surfacing, playing material from the wonderful *Hollywood Dream* album and brazenly billing themselves as 'Thunderclap Newman.' …Andy protested and tried to put a block on the practice – he had lawyers deal with it and writs were issued – but it was all to no avail." The practice caused Newman endless aggravation for the ensuing four decades.

This became yet another reason that Newman, already sour at having made practically no money from his time with Thunderclap Newman due to the woefully mismanaged finances of Track Records, turned away from the music industry. "He would do session work and meet up with some of the old friends," said his friend Colin Hill, "but he was quite disillusioned by the music industry generally, as a result of his being… well, Thunderclap Newman as an entity were pretty screwed by the management, etc., but he didn't actually quantify the amount of money; …years and years he spent trying to get legal help to recuperate some of the money that was owed to them."

"I like music, but the music business is a completely different affair to actual music and the making of it," Andy said in 2010.

> It's a very, very complex business. …Seeing a show from the front, it looks great, it looks easy, but you try and put the show on, and all the finance and money that has to be done to keep the thing going and all the personalities, and all the effort, mental and physical that has to go into it – no I don't think I missed the music business. I'm not one of these people that absolutely has to perform in front of an

audience. There are some people in this world who they've got to have the adulation of an audience otherwise they become very depressed. I'm not one of those people. ...So I think frankly, compared to what we did when the Thunderclap thing was going, I think I preferred an ordinary day job.

Newman's day job certainly kept him busy. Once, he rewired a chapel in the Forest Of Dean and while there hiked Sugar Loaf, part of the Black Mountains in nearby Monmouthshire. This was relayed to me by Andy's brother Robin, who remembers because again the family was looking for him, with no idea where he was. He installed studios, including one project with Jo Wolf working for Joe Strummer near Portobello Road for two months. Newman also rewired – and built a chandelier for – Vivienne Westwood's shop at 430 Kings Road, formerly *SEX* but probably (and disappointingly) named *World's End* by the time Newman worked there. "[Westwood] always asked after him," recalled mutual friend and Rectory Gardens resident Julian Hall.

When the pair were on construction jobs together, or during occasional visits to the pub, Newman and Jo Wolf would get into long, meandering conversations, but rarely about music. "Andy and me, we could sit together for hours and hours and we'd jump from one topic like British rail and jazz music, politics..." said Wolf. "We would talk about God and the world and would start a conversation... I compare it to – You want to drive from like London to Edinburgh, and there's a straight road, but if I was traveling with Andy he would say, "Why don't we go through Swansea and have a bit of a look there?" I used to call him a walking encyclopedia. He knew dates, names – you name it. He made mention every now and again of the music industry, but because financially he got screwed, to put it mildly, I never pushed that topic," Wolf said[108], adding that he and Newman were more likely to delve into the details of the Enigma code's impact on the outcome of World War II or some other esoteric subject.

While he stayed away from more serious musical endeavors, Newman enjoyed the lighthearted work he did with partners such as Bob Flag and Roger Spear, work that was done for the pure enjoyment of it. "Bob Flag was just unbelievably fabulous; just fantastic, and Andy's the same," Angie Bowie enthused.

> And we're not talking about druggies or alkies, we're just talking about amazing musicians who were busy doing their thing and enjoying life *thrilled* that they could be musicians. I always thought that that was a very honest and straight-forward and correct way to look at a career choice. So that even when things got desperate or things got difficult, you remember that there are just as many desperate and difficult things that may pay you more, but will give you even more heartache and harm to your body. And the joy of being an artist and being a musician, one has to count that right up there at the top 97%.

After the conclusion of 'Krisis Kabaret' in 1975, Newman and Flag continued to work together as a duo – "he on piano and me, with my 'one man band' schtick on drums, saxophone, and various horns and both of us on vocals – under the name of 'Thunderflag'," Flag recalled. From 1975 to 1982 the pair performed regularly in and around London, also engaging in U.K.-wide tours in a tiny Morris Mini-Traveller. "Straight from 'Krisis Kabaret' we

108 "He always talked very positively about Pete Townshend," Wolf pointed out.

gigged," Bob Flag recalled, "mostly in Universities, colleges, bars and clubs."

It was not successful enough to hit the 'big-time', even with Andy's fame – the material was too dated, but it was rewarding and regular enough to continue for more than seven years, for the love of it and even financially, as it allowed us both to take on other show-biz gigs. Although Andy was a 'stickler' for our mutually cherished 1920/30s repertoire (for example, we both felt that wherever possible, the verse, as well as the chorus, of any song we performed, should be included) he did not accept that I wanted to update the famous boxers named in the song 'Stepp'n Out', to ones more recent and more recognizable. He did, however, to my surprise, accept and enjoy the comedy ideas I introduced. Indeed, in 1982, we did a comedy show-reel for Pete Townshend at his Eel Pie Studios which he filmed.[109]

In 1979, Newman performed some electrical work at a pottery near his home and met Colin Hill. "We were looking for an electrician in setting up my partner's pottery – she runs a pottery and a pottery school here in London, and Andy was a neighbor," Hill recalled. "Andy's a fantastic raconteur and he's always good company, lots of stories. And he's a polymath really, an avid reader and he always had a story to tell of something or other. We sort of had a standing joke that when he was working on one of the kilns, for example, he would be telling you a story and it would go on and on and on, [laughs] and one would have to interrupt and say, "Andy, I've just got to go and

---

109 Sadly, this recording appears lost. Townshend has no recollection of it.

do something," and go off and do whatever it was that needed doing, and we would come back and he was still telling the story!"

Hill recalled Newman's ingenuity and technical abilities, pointing out that at one point he built his own record player. "He was also an avid ham radio fanatic," said Hill.

He built his own aerials and – in fact, he lived in a street that was a housing association after they'd squatted it back in the early '70s, and there were lots of difficulties with – because they were all hippies, really – people in the street were having trouble with motorcycle gangs and stuff who were coming round wanting to beat up the hippies, that sort of thing. So Andy devised an alarm system for the entire street, so there was panic buttons in every house.

Throughout his life, Newman enjoyed socializing and sharing meals with friends and neighbors, relishing the company and the conversation. "He was always welcome at my house, and he was always so gracious, would never refuse an invitation; it was always lovely to have him around for a meal," said Hill. "He had lots of people who really admired him; for example, a good friend of mine who now lives out of London, but whenever she would come to London she would bring him a roast pheasant or a rabbit stew, or something like that, and Andy used to appreciate her roadkill gifts, which they usually were," he said with a laugh.

These social visits always took place at other peoples' houses and never at Newman's. "I don't know how easy it was actually to *be* in Andy's house," said Julian Hall, who later became a neighbor of Newman's at Rectory Gardens. "For example, we never had a co-op meeting at Andy's house; we would rotate that with various other houses, and I was always told that Andy's was stacks of papers and that you were literally walking in this maze, so there wasn't really a huge amount of room to sort of sit down or anything like that." Colin Hill said he was never invited over to Andy's house for dinner. "No – never," he said. "Andy lived on sandwiches – I don't think he ever cooked."

"His living conditions were just extraordinary," said Hill, comparing Newman's lodgings to that shown in the '60s and '70s U.K. television program *Steptoe and Son*.[110]

> Andy lived in absolute squalor, basically. It was so odd. He was never embarrassed by it or anything – he just didn't even notice, I don't think – but it was a pretty squalid existence where he lived. One time I went round to see him; he wanted to get rid of the piano because it was taking up too much room and he wanted some advice. And it was an extraordinary endeavor, trying to get this piano out of his house, there was just so much junk and stuff lying about. It was winter, and we were sat around his coal fire, and either side of the fireplace there was mounds of ash and debris from the coal fire, so he would empty the fireplace and just mound this stuff up in the living room, either side of his hearth. It was pretty primitive. But you know, he always came out smelling of patchouli; he loved his patchouli – sprinkled it on the outside of his clothes, just to make sure he smelled okay.

Much of the clutter in Newman's home was an accumulation of bits and pieces of whatever interested him over the years. He had an enormous collection of old recordings,

---

110 Later remade in the U.S. as *Sanford and Son*.

one which had already taken up an entire wall of shelving at his childhood home in Hounslow, and it had grown considerably since then. This collection consisted mainly of thousands of 78 rpm records which Newman had picked up at various shops and markets. In addition, Newman had a sizeable collection of various instruments, including a whole range of saxophones, all the way up to the enormous contrabass. "I think there's only three of them in the whole country," said Colin Hill. "This enormous great thing. He'd have to carry it about on a trolley it's so big."[111]

There were also countless bottles of rum, all of which sat unopened. "He was pretty much teetotal, really," said Hill. "He had this friend who would every Christmas bring him a bottle of overproof Wray and Nephews rum. And in his kitchen there was cupboards full of the stuff – he never touched it. He drank coca cola by the gallon; that was his vice."

Newman's collection may have even included items of a more volatile nature. "Andy had worked for the GPO and was a great collector of their cast-off technology," said David Glasson. "I am told, though I have no evidence, that he had a heavy concrete bunker in his back garden where he lived, to store explosives. It was all legal, and followed all the council regulations about the minimum distance from any dwellings, and securely locked at all times, etc."

Running amongst this chaos were Newman's pets, Miss Thing and Pearl. "He had a little dog, Miss Thing," Ted Green recalled. "He used to put her in his coat when he was crossing the road and that sort of thing. And Pearl, his cat," who was brought in to help keep the mice and rats

111 Ted Green recalls himself, Newman and Bob Flag performing at the Kenneth More Theatre in east London and Newman using this massive saxophone onstage: "Bob rigged up this little trolley for his sax, so we'd go round the stage, we had like a little procession at the end of the show with us all playing, and Andy with his sax on a little trolley."

of Rectory Gardens at bay. "Oh yes, we had loads," Green recalled.

In 1980, Newman contributed a cover of comedian Sandy Powell's 1935 novelty song 'Sandy The Dentist' – here renamed 'Andy The Dentist' – to musician/composer Morgan Fisher's project *Miniatures*, a collection of fifty-one one-minute miniature songs. "Andy visited my tiny studio bedsit to record his miniature," Fisher recalled.

> He managed to lug a baritone sax up the four flights of narrow stairs, and each time I opened the door to a wheezing Andy, his miniature Yorkshire terrier ran between my legs and at lightning speed sniffed every nook and cranny in the place. My piano, fortunately, had not been tuned in months, so it sounded suitably out of tune. Ideal for the music hall song Andy chose to record. As an intro he told one of the worst jokes ever recorded, to which unfortunately I was a party.[112] Sorry about that. I should have cracked my producer's whip a little harder. But it is quintessential Andy.

In 1982, Pete Townshend's solo album *All The Best Cowboys Have Chinese Eyes* was released.[113] The album included a ninety-second track entitled 'Prelude', which, according to Townshend, was "based on one of Thunderclap's haunting themes." While Andy appreciated the compliment, he was somewhat baffled at the same time. "I was contacted by Nick Goderson, who was sort of looking after the publisher, who asked me if [Townshend] could

112 AN: "Now Mr. Fisher, before I pull your tooth out, would you like a little something for the pain?" MF: "Yes, I think I'll have gas." AN: "I'm sorry sir, we've only got electric lights."

113 This was the second of three consecutive Townshend solo albums which were all produced by Chris Thomas.

use one of the ones off the *Rainbow* album called 'Arctic Sunset'," Newman recalled in 2009. "And the idea was he would use the melody from that and put his words on top. So basically I got the sort of joint publishing on that."

"However," Andy continued, "there comes a sequel to that – and this is purely my reading of the thing; it may be Pete saw it a different way, but fairly recently, in the last year, I was asked by the band I'm working for if we could do any of the ones on the *Rainbow* album, and I thought, well, none of these are going to be suitable for in-your-face rock bands," he laughed. Still, Newman gave his bandmates copies of *Rainbow*, and they chose 'Arctic Sunset' as a track that they'd like to explore for possible inclusion in the live set. "So I managed to get a copy of Pete's 'Prelude'," he said. "I'd never actually heard it, 'cause I didn't get advance copies of the thing; all that happened was that it got released and then suddenly I got a few royalty checks come in, which was very nice. So what happened was that I thought, 'Well, let's get Pete's version and transpose that, and let's get 'Arctic Sunset' out and work out what I've done there'," said Newman.

Well there's about three themes on 'Arctic Sunset', and none of them in my opinion bear any relevance to what Pete put musically down on 'Prelude'. So I don't know why he felt that he had to include me as the composer – but don't tell him I said that! [laughs] It seems completely different to me.

However, they say that Fats Waller claimed that he copied 'Alligator Crawl' from George Gershwin's 'Someone To Watch Over Me', but if you play those two, they're completely different. And yet to his dying day, which was in 1943 on a train somewhere in Kansas, apparently in the middle of a joke, Fats Waller swore he nicked the melody from George Gershwin! But it's not the same; its not even related! Maybe he *thought* he took it. Maybe he *thought* he heard what he heard... Still, I'm not going to complain, because I got credited for the music, and I got some money out of it, so c'est la vie.

That same year, Newman appeared on two episodes of Channel 4's *The Cut Price Comedy Show* as part of Tatty Ollity, a band which consisted of regulars Roger Spear (vocals, sax) and Dave Glasson (piano, vocals) and a host of guests including Bob Flag (sax) and *Melody Maker*'s Chris Welch (drums). "Andy featured on two of the ten songs Roger Spear and I wrote for the series, playing bass sax on 'William Tell' (November 3rd, 1982) and synthesizer on 'My Friend's Outside' (December 8th, 1982)," Glasson recalled. "The shows were recorded in front of a live audience at TSW Studios, Plymouth throughout September 1982. ...Andy also played with Tatty Ollity on a number of live gigs up and down the country, and sometimes travelled with us. My abiding memory was his fondness for jelly, and he would always request a motorway stop so he could stock up on jelly and other favourite sweet treats!"

Around this time, Flag arranged a televised 'piano duel' between Andy Newman and Morgan 'Thunderclap' Jones, the Welsh pianist who shared a nickname with Andy and who also happened to be Flag's neighbor. "I ...managed to get him and Andy 'Thunderclap' Newman a spot on local TV (the 'motive' was a spoof dispute – they were supposed to be 'rivals' over the 'Thunderclap' tag – in reality it was to promote our 'Thunderflag' activities)," Flag wrote in his memoir. "The two 'Thunderclaps' had a play-off at the piano keyboard, which was a 'draw' and settled nothing." Flag and Newman continued to work together into the 1990s, intermittently performing under the 'Thunderflag' name, including appearances on jazz nights at the Sir Richard Steele pub on Haverstock Hill, north London with Dave Burman. "Both on trumpet and even more surprisingly, on piano too, he was like Bix reincarnate – wonderful," Flag said of Burman, which must have made Andy reel with delight.

* * *

In March 2002, Andy received a call from Pete Townshend's office, passing along the sad news that Speedy Keen had died. Newman attended the funeral and met Trish Keen, later attending a reception at her home. The pair would connect again in the coming year.

On July 30th, a Hungarian musician named István Etiam performed a gig at a bar in St. John's Hill in London with his friend, an American musician named David Buckley. The pair called themselves East Meets West; Etiam played guitar while Buckley sang. This gig was particularly notable because a third musician tagged along: Andy Newman.

Etiam had known Newman for nearly two decades, having met him back in 1985 during a break from a recording session in the basement of one of the houses on Rectory Gardens – a session organized, incidentally, by Jo Wolf. "There was no electricity in the house and it was freezing, so Jo said take this kettle next door and ask the guy to boil the kettle and we can have a cup of tea and talk about music," Etiam recalled. The figure that answered the door filled the door frame. It was Andy Newman. Etiam was stunned, having been a fan of Newman's work for years. "From then on, I got to know him and I saw him regularly," said Etiam, "and soon after that I decided I must get a band together – maybe we could get Thunderclap Newman together again and, you know – just play the songs. So I kept at it, but he was very reluctant to reform the band." Newman told

Etiam that Speedy had wanted to reform the band at one point as well, but still, Andy wasn't interested.

"I kept at it and I realized soon that Andy liked his food," said Etiam, "so I asked him round to my place on a regular basis, and I cooked him goulash. He loved that. So basically I think over the years, and it took me 15 years or so, roughly, to cook goulash after goulash and he got to know me; he got to trust me." Etiam's persistence and authenticity finally paid off. The trial gig in 2002 was a success. "He played his songs and we played our songs, and he loved it," Etiam recalled, and proposed assembling a full band. "We said, "Look, we'll get the musicians together and come on, let's do it." But then again he took quite a while, because Andy was a very cautious person."

The next chapter occurred in early 2005. "These chaps came back to me and said that they wanted to re-form a band which would produce the same music as the Thunderclap Newman band; could I help them," Newman recalled. "First of all they did ask me if I'd like to join it and I said I definitely didn't." Etiam and Buckley, now augmented with drummer Antonio Spano, bassist Brian Jackson, and guitarist Stefano Tirelli, asked Newman if he'd at least help them with rehearsals, to which Newman agreed. "I said I'll try and help you as best I can, so they booked a studio and they fixed up a keyboard and I went in there and we started going through all the numbers and I really got sucked back into it, so effectively I was sort of a Russian volunteer!"

"He was our musical director and seemed to come to life with all of his parts on the record," Buckley recalled, adding that Newman obtained the sheet music to all of the songs and provided clear instruction to the band members as to how to properly perform them.

Again, things moved painfully slowly. The Thunderclap

Newman Band's[114] first gig took place two years later on July 1st 2007 at Ariadne's Nectar, a west London pub across the road from the group's rehearsal space. "We got Antonio, our Italian drummer, to buy Andy a suit and fedora hat for gigs," David Buckley recalled. "He looked amazing and loved the new look. He wore his work boots on stage – he just polished them." Bob Flag attended the performance and was suitably impressed. "At long last... the Andy Thunderclap Newman Band, with Andy himself on keyboard and wind instruments, exactly as in the *Hollywood Dream* album and sounding as near as one could possibly get to that wonderful LP (for me the best LP of all time – along with Steely Dan's *Aja*) – appeared in public," Flag wrote in his memoir. "...All that dedication and rehearsal had paid off and we fans and lovers of not only Andy, but the LP itself and indeed of the guys who had brought it all back to life again, had an amazing treat. We were taken back in time."

The Thunderclap Newman Band performed sporadically from 2007 to 2009, mainly around London. In addition to the songs on *Hollywood Dream*, the group performed 'Heartbreaker' by Jimmy McCulloch's final group The Dukes, Speedy's solo single 'Someone To Love', and 'Armenia City In The Sky'. Both Trish Keen and Jack McCulloch attended performances, in addition to many who had seen the original Thunderclap Newman. One gig, at the Half Moon in Putney in March 2008, brought a little extra attention. "Andy was accosted by a woman who tried to get into the dressing room screaming, "I want to fuck Thunderclap Newman!"," David Buckley recalled. "Andy was very calm about this but really surprised! She had drunk quite a lot and was hauled off by her friends."

---

114 There was a proprietary issue with the use of the Thunderclap Newman name at the time, prompting the addition of 'Band'.

The Thunderclap Newman Band had limited success for a few years and then stalled. "We were gigging through 2007 and 2008 quite successfully," Andy said in 2010. "In 2009 we weren't doing well at all. Work wasn't coming in at all and what gigs there were, were basically losing money." The group's final gig took place at the Limelight, Crewe, on August 23 2009. In all, they performed live eleven times over a three year period. The group discussed touring in 2010 to mark the 40th anniversary of *Hollywood Dream*, but this didn't happen. They recorded some demos, including a version of Speedy Keen's 'Someone To Love' single, which had been part of their live repertoire, and a new song written by David Buckley titled 'Hollywood Revisited', but proper recordings of these songs were never made.

One Sunday in July 2009, the Thunderclap Newman Band's rehearsal was visited by a couple of guests with a link to the original group's past: Mark Brzezicki and Simon Townshend. Brzezicki, drummer for Big Country, among other bands, had worked with Pete Townshend for years. And Simon of course was Pete's younger brother, as well as a musician in his own right. The pair had visited rehearsals at the behest of Ian Grant, manager of the re-formed Track Records, who was interested in signing Thunderclap Newman as a nod to the label's past.[115]

Newman was flattered at this attention. "Mark's sort of taken an interest in what we're doing, which is quite nice, but it certainly surprised the musicians when Simon Townshend came to the studio with him," he told me a week after the visit. "It was absolutely fantastic." Brzezicki's assessment was that the group had room for improvement. "They were okay, but they weren't generating the sound

---

115 A few years earlier, Grant had begun working with Andy Newman, Jack McCulloch, Trish Keen and Pete Townshend in an effort to trace and recoup Thunderclap Newman recording royalties.

that Thunderclap Newman were kind of famous for, with the guitar style and the piano," he observed. "And in the end I said to Andy I could put a band together – I know some great musicians that would be really suited for this." With the current band's prospects looking bleak due to lack of gigs and several members contemplating moving on to other ventures, Newman had a difficult decision to make – difficult because he didn't want to hurt his current bandmates. They sensed this, and urged him to go for it if he so wished. Newman agreed to join the new group on a trial basis.

Brzezicki duly set about putting a new band together, soon arriving at a lineup of Josh Townshend (vocals, guitar), Tony Stubbings (bass), Nick Johnson (guitar), and Brzezicki himself on drums and lead vocals. "I thought about using Josh Townshend because he's my Godson – he's Simon Townshend's son," said Brzezicki. "We used Josh because he was young, and great looking, could sing, play guitar, and he was a Townshend; I wanted him for that link; he had that thread with Pete. And funny enough, he looked like a doppelganger of Jimmy McCulloch to a certain degree at times. I remember the fans thought he was reincarnated! I met Tony by playing some covers and some music we were doing with another guitarist called Nick Johnson who Tony knew before me. Me and Tony were going to do something together anyway, because we kind of hit it off musically as a rhythm section."

The prospect of Brzezicki as lead vocalist came up during a phone call with Newman. "He actually said, "Can you sing?"; I mean I didn't offer that," Brzezicki recalled, before conceding, "I've always done backing vocals in Big Country, and I've got quite a high voice." Before the conversation got any further, Newman astounded Brzezicki by demonstrating his expertise in all things telephonic. "I had a really old 1940s Bakelite telephone that I was speaking to him on," said Brzezicki. "And he said to me, "Um, Mark – are you on a P963045S telephone?", and I said, "Um, yes, it *is* that," and he said, "Oh, I thought I recognized it by the aperture sound that is producing your voice"," Brzezicki recalled with a laugh. "So it was quite a funny start."

Newman asked Brzezicki if he could sing in Speedy's register. "I said, well I can sing pretty high, and he gave me a key to sing in and I sort of went "LAAA" down the phone and he went, "Can you go an octave higher than that?", and I went "LAAA!", and he went, "Can you modulate a third octave above that?," and I went "*LAAAA*!" He said, "Marvelous, that's marvelous. I think you'll do well." So we went with me doing lead vocals, and we had Josh sing some songs."

The new band began rehearsals at Tony Stubbings' studio, initially without Newman. "I'll tell you how hard Andy hit the keys on a piano," Stubbings said. "We were told by Mark to learn certain numbers, and we did our homework, and then Andy's going to turn up on this day, and I set up a keyboard for him, and he smashes into this keyboard and one by one all the hammers break off of it! And now he's going, "This one doesn't work anymore… this one's not working," so I had to take the keyboard apart, and I took all the high hammers out and put them where the low hammers were, and I said, "You can't use that bit of keyboard for now," and he was quite happy! He said, "Oh, I won't use up there, don't worry about that." And he carried on."

Once Newman was on board, the songs took on another character. "All of a sudden it felt like we were playing Thunderclap Newman songs, where before it felt more of a covers band," said Josh Townshend. "As soon as he got his piano out and his cor anglais, all of a sudden it became the sound of Thunderclap Newman, which was really awesome, it was a big sort of like, 'Oh wow – there it is! That's was what missing!' It was really cool."

Always one to enjoy a conversation and a meal, Newman quickly grew to enjoy these rehearsals. "He was very grateful for small things," said Brzezicki. "We had the studio at Tony's, and Tony's family embraced Andy, and it was lovely to see because Andy really didn't have anyone."

"My wife used to come home and make lunch for us at one o'clock," said Stubbings. "So we used to come in to the main house at one o'clock and there'd be this feast on the table, sandwiches in foil – like a party. They all used to sit down, have lunch, then feel a bit tired and go down the studio."

"It's one of the most special bands I've ever been involved in," said Brzezicki, "because it was so unique and we had kind of a social at Tony's house. It wasn't just a rehearsal, it was a meet-up with friends and food, and a bit of rehearsing, you know. I miss it." Josh Townshend concurred: "I think most of our fondest memories being together was not just rehearsal, but it was sitting down in the kitchen, having lunch, just chatting," he said, "because he was very story orientated and he liked to speak about the old times, which was great, and we'd just sit there like schoolchildren listening to a teacher."

The reconstituted Thunderclap Newman's first gig took place on February 19th, 2010 at the Constitutional Club in Lewes, Sussex. Josh Townshend quickly noticed how particular Newman was about his instruments. "Andy always liked to set up his own stuff himself," said Townshend. "He was very protective, I think those instruments that he had were so old and they meant a lot to him, so they were his babies."

"Guess who was in the front row on the first show?," said Tony Stubbings. "The old band. And that's a bit daunting when you walk out and you've nicked their job. But yeah – they were all standing there." Another notable attendee at this first performance was the original group's former Track Records labelmate, Arthur Brown.[116]

The group's second performance took place on February 27th at the Memorial Hall, Farrington Gurney, Somerset. Shortly after these first two live performances, they re-recorded 'Something In The Air', 'I Don't Know', and 'I See It All' at Black Barn Studios in Surrey. A compact disc titled *Beyond Hollywood* was soon released on the Track label containing the three studio tracks, plus seven which were recorded at the Farrington Gurney show: 'Hollywood #2', 'When I Think', 'Accidents', 'Wild Country', 'The Old Cornmill', 'Wilhelmina', and 'Look Around'. It was Thunderclap Newman's first release since 1970. The group resumed live performances in May, and by the end of the year had performed nine gigs, all in the U.K.

Newman's new bandmates found him quirky and endearing. Mark Brzezicki fondly recalled Newman's love of swing and early jazz. "He would often be singing these classic songs from the era, like "*I'll be loving youuuuuu alwaaaaays*" – his heart was really in it; he was from a bygone era. He had something very magical about him because of that."

> When he presented himself onstage, he was quite immaculately dressed, with the hat… and there was a good rapport, 'cause we used to sit quite uniquely onstage – we were all in a line onstage, like the drums weren't at the back, he would be on stage right, side on to the audience, I would be on stage left, and then Nick and Josh and Tony would be in the middle, so we would have banter right across the stage, from myself to Andy at the end. The way we were set up made it really entertaining,

116 Mark Brzezicki had played drums in Arthur Brown's band for about seven years.

even introducing songs, you know? He was so well-spoken, it was like, "This is a piece [rolls his 'r'] wrrritten in 1968, in the key of D…"

Brzezicki noted Newman's unique timing. "He had his own tempo; it was almost orchestral," he said. "If you tried to discipline him, he would play either in front of you or behind you slightly – but that gave him his charm. It was the looseness that really worked. I think that's what Pete loved about him as well. But he was very keen to get it right – he wanted to do good; he wanted to rehearse. Dare I say he was very critical on himself. He didn't think he was that great a keyboard player, and he couldn't work out why he had the hit. There was always that going on, and all these marvelous things that have happened, and he still hasn't worked out why. He was very humble, and he would always question his own playing – is he doing it right and could we hear him okay."

As he had done with the Thunderclap Newman Band, and as he continued to do with the Rectory Gardens housing cooperative, Newman fastidiously kept his new group's accounts in order. "Even though we weren't generating any form of money, we'd have a weekly meeting to discuss the accounting," Brzezicki recalled. "It was '22p for a sandwich, the train fare…', always written in pencil, and how much we'd made to date, to the penny."

Even when the group weren't actively performing or rehearsing, such as during the holidays, Newman would visit Stubbings, relishing the company and the conversation. "There was no one around him family wise," said Stubbings. "He had a few friends up in Clapham that maybe he'd spend Christmas Day with. We'd have him over either Boxing Day or Christmas Eve. And we'd say to him, "What are you doing for Christmas Day?", and he'd say, "Well, same as usual really – if we get a turkey, I may have turkey. If not, I won't." And that's it! And then he'd talk about neutrons and electrons, and how the whole world was going to blow up in two hundred years' time!"

Stubbings recalled Newman's endlessly practical dress sense, always wearing a green military sweater and carrying an electrical screwdriver in his top pocket. "He wore the same boots every day," said Stubbings, "and I said, "Have you got any other boots?"; "No, why would I have another pair?" He turned up at my wedding – not a tie, not a shirt, he had a jumper on with holes in it – he always wore a green jumper with holes in it, and I'm standing there as the groom and all that, and he said, "Awfully sorry – no one told me it would be a dress-up do." It was a *wedding!*"

The new group's plans for 2011 included further live performances and a studio album, to be released on the Track label. "At the moment we're just gigging around but hopefully next year we will be doing festivals," Andy said at the time. "We're going to do a proper studio recorded album and we've been promised that Pete Townshend's got some unreleased stuff of the original Thunderclap Newman. [117] Also, we've got some songs which Speedy never recorded, which had never been published that we're working on that are completely fresh, so we've got brand new Speedy Keen material."

Newman had maintained contact with Trish Keen after the pair met at Speedy's funeral in 2002 and had arranged a visit to review his tape archive. "Speedy's daughter stayed at my house for a couple of days, because she'd got these loads of digital tapes," Tony Stubbings recalled, "and they didn't have any equipment to play them on, so they didn't know what was on them. They also had loads of reel to reel and they didn't have any equipment to play it on. Well, I've got all that, so they went in the studio with

---

117 Townshend isn't aware of any unreleased original Thunderclap Newman tracks.

Nick Johnson. What they wanted to do was try and find a hidden song, or a hidden *something*, and out of the two days he spent in there going through it, he couldn't find anything of any use," Stubbings said, before remembering that there was "one little bit of something" that the group did rehearse. "Most of it was garbled," he said.

After a handful of gigs in early January 2011, the momentum of the reconstituted Thunderclap Newman slowed considerably. Their next gig – at the Constitutional Club in Lewes, Sussex – didn't take place until May 13th 2011, and it would be more than a year before the group's subsequent performance. "I think that something happened with the management where they lost interest, or the momentum just… there was nothing happening," said Mark Brzezicki. "We turned up at a couple of gigs and it hadn't been advertised," Stubbings recalled. "So I was then running round the town getting leaflets printed: 'THUNDERCLAP NEWMAN ON TONIGHT' at wherever… So I don't know what happened, but at first it was like, flying high – I mean, it was really good at first."

On June 23rd 2012, the group performed at the Isle of Wight Festival, a gig arranged by Brzezicki himself. "We were having to do more organization; I mean, I rang John [Giddings, Isle of Wight promoter] myself," he said. "He's an old friend – he used to promote Big Country. And it was as simple as that – he put us on."

By this point, Newman's band members insisted that he upgrade the antique shopping trolley he was still using onstage. "He used to carry his clarinet and things in a sort of little trolley pull-bag thing, whatever it was called," said Brzezicki. Stubbings provided more clarification: "It was a supermarket trolley – you know what a lady uses to go to the supermarket? He loved them!"

And I said, "Andy, we're going to gigs now, we're

doing the Isle of Wight Festival, you can't go on stage with a trolley!" So I went out and I bought a flight case, and you know, you can get this foam that goes inside, and I made the foam out for the clarinet and I made the foam out for his little penny whistle and all that, put it all in there, and I got everything in there apart from his sax, it wouldn't go in there, and it was like a trolley, and he zipped it up and he was over the moon with it; he's never ever had anyone do that for him. "It's yours, you can have it" – you know. "Oh, that is *bloody* good of you – that is amazing. That is wonderful." And then when he was uncomfortable on his stool, I got him a chair from a garage, where they come along and buff your car, they sit on these stools, and it was adjustable. And he was over the moon with it – "This is a wonderful stool, wonderful."

"That was amazing," Josh Townshend recalled of the group's performance at the Isle of Wight festival. "It was a really thrilling show, 'cause there were so many people there and they all knew the song. It was great – it was the biggest stage we'd played together since I'd joined them. 'Something In The Air' was fantastic 'cause everyone was singing along."

The Isle of Wight gig proved to be Thunderclap Newman's last. "It was great, and I kind of regret that not a lot happened after that," said Brzezicki. "I used to say how rare this band is, and if they only knew, they would come along, but we didn't have that kind of machine to get the people to the gigs, you know. And I think now that Ian had kind of dropped off the radar slowly regarding doing things. We got to a point where we were rehearsing, but we didn't have anything to rehearse for."

Not long after the band's momentum had begun to

wane, Newman reunited with some old friends, attending Rick Seaman's 70th birthday party (after some detective work by Clive Smith, who tracked Newman down). Richard Barnes, Chris Glass, and Smith all attended. Shortly thereafter, in April 2015, Smith invited Newman to an event at his studio, Play Deep Studios in Shepherd's Bush. "He was so delighted to be there," Smith recalled. "I felt at the time that he was a little bit lonely, maybe, because he was so happy to have been invited. He really enjoyed it, and sadly that was the last time I saw him." In October, Newman paid a visit to Dana Wiffen. "He came down to Bexley and met my cousin and I," Wiffen recalled. "He'd slimmed down a bit. It was a nice sunny day and we were just sitting in the park with a coffee and we talked and talked, not realizing that there was an underlying health problem and that when he went away, thinking we'd see him again and then suddenly he's gone. I was quite upset about that. It was a shock to everyone."

Around this time, the long-standing dispute between the Rectory Gardens housing cooperative and the local council came to an end, with the residents all being rehoused. After turning down several proposed homes because the bathtubs were too small[118], Newman was eventually housed in a flat on Goldsboro Road, Vauxhall, southwest London. Although Newman had resisted moving to the very end, he quickly grew to appreciate the new lodgings. "He was pretty happy with what he got in the end," said Julian Hall. "And I wonder if that contributed… he sort of relaxed at the end…"

Newman was sufficiently content with his new surroundings that he invited friends over, something he rarely did at Rectory Gardens. István Etiam visited

---

118 "He had a beautiful bath tub [in Rectory Gardens]," Ted Green recalled. "It was one of those old Victorian tubs. The toilets and the bath were outside."

Newman at the new place. "He was very happy, he found this beautiful place with a little garden and he told me he was going to plant vegetables – he had a new lease on life," Etiam recalled. The new flat was significantly smaller though, so Newman had to downsize. "It was so small, he had to get rid of a lot of stuff," Ted Green recalled. "In fact, I managed to get a few of his bits and bobs, because he was putting it outside the house for people to pick up. He moved into a small, one-person flat."

Andy contacted his brother, Robin, to see if he could house his enormous record collection. "I saw quite a lot more of him in the last few years of his life than I ever did earlier," Robin said, "simply because of where he was living, and he wanted to store a lot of his possessions."

"That was one of the things that we spent an awful lot of time doing, in the last year before he died, was trying to find some home for his vast record collection," said Colin Hill. "We're talking wall to ceiling, all stacked in their sleeves. Tens of thousands, probably, of albums. It's all stacked up in a couple of concrete bunkers at his brother's house in Hammersmith. It took us weeks to transport it all over there."

The brothers grew closer as a result of their more frequent interactions. Robin recalled Andy telephoning to check the spelling of certain words when writing letters – 'boulevard' was an example. The pair visited Kew Gardens together in early 2016, and Robin recalls growing concerned at Andy being winded after climbing a spiral staircase there. Not long after this visit, Newman told his brother that he was experiencing dizzy spells and visited the doctor about it.

With no piano at his new flat, Andy continued to rehearse (and socialize) at Tony Stubbings' studio. He was there on Monday evening, March 28th 2016 and planned to return the following day. "He left here at 9 o'clock and

397

he said, "Can I come back tomorrow and rehearse a few things if you can let me in?," Stubbings recalled. " 'Cause everyone had a key to my house, but he would never have a key, he said no…" Newman arranged to be there at 10 o'clock the following morning, a time that allowed him to use his discounted old age pensioners pass on the train. "I saw him off on the train from here at 9 o'clock the night before, "See you later Andy", and he always waved backwards. "'Bye!" And off he went. I never saw him again."

The following morning, "10 o'clock comes and I'm still here, waiting for him," Stubbings recalled. "…So I rang him and – he wasn't in to mobile phones. We bought him a mobile phone, but he gave it back. He said, "I've no need for this." So I rang his house number, and it was the answer phone, which it always was for Andy. So about an hour later I rang it again, and a bloke answered I didn't recognize and he said, "Who are you looking for?", and I said, "Well who are you?," He said, "I am police officer whoever; now I have to ask who are you?" I said, "I'm his bass player." He said, "Well in that case I have some bad news for you; we just found him dead"."

"I had spoken with him the night before and he said he was feeling a bit dizzy,"Ted Green recalled. Green had gone to Newman's flat the following morning. "I knew there was something wrong when he didn't answer,"Green said. "I was knocking on the window and calling him. There was a woman upstairs and we called the police and they forced an entrance, and there he was in front of the telly, gone, expired. Sitting in his chair in his green shorts. What a shame."

Andy Newman was 73 years old. Robin visited the flat shortly afterwards, and remembers finding unused British Rail tickets to East Anglia lying on the floor, presumably for a planned bird watching trip. He recalled seeing a Marilyn Monroe biography on Andy's nightstand. His brother's passing was a shock. "He did tell me at one point he weighed 19 stone, but he had certainly reduced from that," Robin said.

He wasn't terribly overweight, but it might have left some permanent damage. It was a pulmonary embolism, I think they call it – a blood clot which is carried up to the lung and very often proves fatal. And you know, he was quite fond of eating and that, but I think in latter years he was certainly taking more care of his health. It might be that once the damage is done, it's done – I don't know. But I certainly didn't expect that to happen. He had been quite helpful to me in latter years, but he was never one to sort of – you know, I always thought at one point we'd be able to sit down and talk about things in the past, and of course then quite unexpectedly, suddenly, he's not there anymore, you know. That's usually the way it happens.

Andy was buried in the suit he wore onstage. A few months after a small funeral service, a larger gathering took place in September at St. Paul's Church Hall, Rectory Grove, Clapham – just down the road from Andy's old home on Rectory Gardens. "When we went in there, the church was full of people, and they weren't just musicians," Dana Wiffen recalled. The gathering included railway enthusiasts, musicians, actors, poets, friends from the housing cooperative, fellow members of the London Phonograph and Gramophone Society, even some with ties to the military. "That's when it hit me and all the other people who were gathered in one room: Andy led many lives," said István Etiam. "Everybody was stepping up to the microphone, including me, and they repeated the same mantra: I didn't know that Andy was part of this group, and that group, that had nothing to do with each other, and people didn't know each other from these various groups, you know?"

"That totally bears out what I felt from that service," said Julian Hall. "That he had all these facets to his life... all the sort of background color came through during the service, which I suppose is often the way with peoples' lives; it wasn't like you couldn't imagine him doing it. It was like, oh, right, so this is sort of the other side."

At one point during the service, a letter from Pete Townshend was read to the gathering:

Andy Newman was a true genius in my opinion, lost in time between the pop music of the 20s and the 30s and that of the 20th century. He often worked miracles to bring those two eras together. Jazz has always been an uncomfortable partner with rock music, but Andy, when invited by me, rose to the challenge, and with our band, the eponymous Thunderclap Newman, created impressionistic musical departures, almost entirely improvised, that made basic rock songs into enchanting cinematic journeys back and forth through time.

I first saw Andy when his 'method' was introduced at Ealing Art School, where I was a student – this was probably in the early summer of 1964. He asked for requests, and I think someone suggested The Beatles' 'Hard Day's Night'. His version of the song actually gave us all two insights: One was that the Beatles' song was so much better than we thought, so much more orderly and conventional in structure than it seemed. The second was that Andy made it swing, he made it lilt and laugh, even more than it did in its original form. Andy's 'method' was to bring a kind of adoration for the days of Bix

Beiderbecke and men with bow ties, cornets and banjoes, to the modern age.

Yet he didn't just play old trad jazz songs. He unearthed a plaintive poignancy and sadness from the trad jazz era that others seemed to have missed. In a sense, Andy played a version of the blues that was rooted deeply in the razzmatazz frivolity of the '20s that everyone else failed to divine. Only in New Orleans funeral music do you hear what Andy was able to do so easily. He went *so* deep.

I had been looking forward to making another record with Thunderclap Newman, but it's not possible without Andy. But I'm so glad I managed to find time in the busy schedule of the Who to work with him back in the late '60s and to have helped him reach a wider audience. As a person he was eccentric and a loner, but polite, contained and only slightly ambitious, but was always looking forward to more recording, and in our last meeting, hadn't aged at all. It was a shock to hear he'd passed away, but he was most definitely not forgotten and never will be.

After the funeral service in March, Robin Newman gave Jo Wolf a box Andy had said belonged to him. It contained two £5 notes, so old they were no longer valid – money that Wolf had left behind when he moved back to Germany. "I gave one to his brother and said, "This is in honor of the degree of honesty between Andy and myself"," said Wolf. "I'd trust him with money and down to a penny he would be honest. In a human to human relationship, he was just a straight, straight guy."

"Yeah, he was extraordinary," said Rick Seaman. "He was also a very kind and decent person, you know. He was a complete and utter one-off. And it still puzzles me why

I got to know him so well, to be honest. As I said I can't really think of whatever I had in common with him, but he had an extraordinary interest in just about everything, he was like a walking encyclopedia."

Shortly after Andy Newman's passing, his friends set up a memorial fund in his name with Future Talent, a U.K. charity which supports gifted young musicians from low-income background. To learn more about Future Talent, please visit www.futuretalent.org

EPILOGUE

We nearly had another Thunderclap Newman album.

After their final performance at the Isle of Wight festival in 2012, Thunderclap Newman continued working on plans for a new studio album. "There was definitely a little bit of meat on the bones in the embers of Speedy's writing, and we were also writing," said Mark Brzezicki. "I had some ideas, we all did as a band; we were writing some ideas and knocking out some new songs together, and they were very Thunderclap Newman. I've still got them, funnily enough, on my iPhone. And they're very choppy piano, very quirky; I was trying to keep it in the same tradition as the *Hollywood Dream* album."

Crucially, the group's original mentor and producer Pete Townshend became involved in the process. "I remember this, and again I always thought that Andy had something very special left in him," said Townshend.

"I had two meetings with Pete at his house, discussing him wanting to move forward with putting something very special together with Thunderclap Newman and doing writing as a team," said Brzezicki, "where Pete would write as well and be very involved in it. And they were going to move forward with some really crazy ideas with different vocals, you know; he wanted it to be radically different, and how unique it was from the start, he wanted to create that uniqueness again, and sadly while we were in talks, it was only weeks later Andy passed."

ACKNOWLEDGMENTS

When I interviewed Jon Astley for my book about Pete Townshend in early 2007, the interview took place in Jon's home and studio on the Embankment in Twickenham – a home which belonged to Pete Townshend many years ago. The room where I interviewed Jon was once Pete's home studio, and the very same room where most of *Hollywood Dream* was recorded.

A couple of years later, I interviewed Andy Newman for a planned update to my book. That update never happened, but I was left with the lingering memory of a wonderful 90-minute telephone conversation with Andy that took a dozen twists and turns. I've included excerpts from that conversation in this book, so there's no need to go into further detail here. Andy later sent me a letter (on "A.L. Newman" letterhead) and a C.D. copy of a BBC Radio 4 program about Pete Townshend's baroque influences called 'Baroque and Roll'.

Two books later, in the middle of the pandemic, I picked this project up and conducted a few fact-finding interviews, which led to my contacting Pete Townshend, who remains incredibly fond of Thunderclap Newman and was happy to provide input. Here we are, three years and nearly fifty interviews later. What a fascinating adventure and a joy this project has been.

I am forever grateful to Pete Townshend for his input and for his support of this project.

My sincere thanks to the interviewees: Steve Adams, Jim Avery, Richard Barnes, Angie Bowie, Vernon Brewer, Mark

Brzezicki, Arthur Brown, David Buckley, Fred Cantrell, Malcolm Dome, István Etiam, Roger Felice, Norrie Gilliland, Chris Glass, Ted Green, Julian Hall, Colin Hill, Emma-Jane Hughes, Chris Hunt, Trish Keen, John Knightsbridge, Ronnie Leahy, Peter Maggs, Romano Morandi, Chris Morphet, Andy Newman, Robin Newman, John Otway, Steve Palmer, Gil Pearson, Rick Seaman, Christopher Sidwell, Clive Smith, Doug Smith, Roger Spear, Richard Stanley, Tony Stubbings, Chris Thomas, Mike Thorne, Josh Townshend, Pete Townshend, Chris Welch, Dana Wiffen, Jo Wolf, and Martin Woodley.

A note about Jim Avery and Malcolm Dome, who both sadly passed away recently: Malcolm was gracious, kind and accommodating as I asked dozens of questions re: The Muggers. Jim was kind, insightful, thoughtful and very funny. I'm so grateful to have been able to speak with both of them.

Many thanks also to: Nina Antonia, Brian Blevins, Chris Charlesworth, Oliver Double, David Glasson, Mike Griffiths, Steve Hammonds, Trace Harrill, Roger Hayman, Amanda and Kelly Hettinger, David Hossack, Wayne Hussey, Nicola Joss, Jayde Keen, Brian Kehew, Matt Kent, Pat Lyons, Michael McNamara, James Mills, Alan Morley, Nathan Morley, 'Motorhead Mick', Andy Neill, Jonathan Oates, Michael O'Shea McGoldrick, Nick Page, Paul Salley, Mark Saunders, Valeria Sgarella, Shel Shapiro, Terry Stamp, Reggy Tan, Simon Townshend, Richie Unterberger and John Woodhouse.

Thanks to the British Library and those in Chicago, Cincinnati, Louisville and New York.

Thank you to Eddie Vedder for believing in this project.

Thanks to Chet Weise, Jack White, Ben Blackwell and the rest of the Third Man team for joining me on this adventure.

Endless thanks and love to my family.

REFERENCES

BOOKS

Antonia, Nina, In Cold Blood, Jungle Books, 2019

Balls, Richard, Sex & Drugs & Rock'n'Roll: The Life of Ian Dury, Omnibus Press, 2011

Barnes, Richard, The Who: Maximum R&B, Plexus, 1982

Black, Johnny, Jimi Hendrix: The Ultimate Experience, Carlton Books, 1999

Blake, Mark, Pretend You're In A War – The Who & The Sixties, Arum Press, 2014

Bowie, Angela (with Patrick Carr), Backstage Passes, Jove, 1994

Campbell-Lyons, Patrick, Psychedelic Days, Global Recording Artists, 2009

Flag, Bob, Drum Schtick, 2017

Grundy, Stuart, and Tobler, John, The Guitar Greats, St. Martin's Press, 1984

Grundy, Stuart, and Tobler, John, The Record Producers, St. Martin's Press, 1983

Hill, Robin E., It Ain't Rock & Roll: The biography of drummer John Kerrison, Publish Nation, 2016

Kent, Matt, and Neill, Andy, Anyway Anyhow Anywhere: the complete chronicle of The Who, Sterling Publishing Co., 2005

Marsh, Dave, Before I Get Old: The Story Of The Who, St. Martin's Press, 1983

McNab, Ken, The Beatles In Scotland, Polygon, 2012

Motion, Andrew, The Lamberts, Hogarth Press, 1987

Norman, Philip, Paul McCartney: The Life, Back Bay Books, 2016

Palmer, Tony, Born Under A Bad Sign, William Kimber & Co., 1970

Redgrave, Deirdre, <u>To Be A Redgrave</u>, Simon & Schuster, 1982

Salley, Paul, <u>Little Wing: The Jimmy McCulloch Story</u>, Lotown, 2021

Spence, Simon, <u>Immediate Records</u>, Black Dog Publishing, 2008

Townshend, Pete, <u>Who I Am</u>, Harper, 2012

ARTICLES

(unsigned), "Scene." <u>Disc & Music Echo</u>, 18 Mar 1967

(unsigned), "Track Signs Stars." <u>Disc & Music Echo</u>, 18 Mar 1967

(unsigned), "Massive U.S. Campaign to Push Hendrix." <u>New Musical Express</u>, 18 Mar 1967

(unsigned), "Spotlight." <u>Disc & Music Echo</u>, 11 Jan 1969

(unsigned), "Further Outlook: Thundery." <u>Disc & Music Echo</u>, 31 May 1969

(unsigned), "Who Charged With Assault On Police In States." <u>Melody Maker</u>, 24 May 1969

(unsigned), "Presenting Bent Frame." <u>Disc & Music Echo</u>, 31 May 1969

(unsigned), "Brian Auger on the latest sounds in BLIND DATE – Thunderclap Newman – Something In The Air." <u>Melody Maker</u>, 31 May 1969

(unsigned), "Britain's First Eight Track Studio Recorder." <u>Melody Maker</u>, 7 Jun 1969

(unsigned), "Pete Townshend Fined." <u>Melody Maker</u>, 28 Jun 1969

(unsigned), "Bent Frame." <u>ZigZag</u>, Jul 1969

(unsigned), "State Of The Pop Scene." <u>Disc & Music Echo</u>, 5 Jul 1969

(unsigned), "Newman & Who Co-Star In Big British Package For America." <u>New Musical Express</u>, 5 Jul 1969 (unsigned), "Clap of THUNDER at cop of chart." Disc & Music Echo, 12 Jul 1969

(unsigned), "Pop-opera Tommy to be filmed." Melody Maker, 12 Jul 1969

(unsigned), "THUNDERSTRUCK! Thunderclap Newman tops the pop 30." Melody Maker, 12 Jul 1969

(unsigned), "Newman Expands to Five." New Musical Express, 12 Jul 1969

(unsigned), "Thunderclap Ban." Melody Maker, 19 Jul 1969

(unsigned), "Pop Think-In: Robin Gibb." Melody Maker, 26 Jul 1969

(unsigned), "Thunderclap Newman comments on old and new sounds in BLIND DATE." Melody Maker, 26 Jul 1969

(unsigned), "Thunderclap Album." Melody Maker, 2 Aug 1969

(unsigned), "Mailbag – Thunderclap Newman and Strauss…" Melody Maker, 9 Aug 1969

(unsigned), "Thunderclap Newman Split: McCulloch and Pitman-Avery Leave." Melody Maker, 16 Aug 1969

(unsigned), "Life-Lines of Thunderclap Newman." New Musical Express, 16 Aug 1969

(unsigned), "Newman, Shack, Kinks in Hull Pop Festival." New Musical Express, 16 Aug 1969

(unsigned), "Newman: U.S. Tour Off Till Spring, Two Members Quit." New Musical Express, 16 Aug 1969

(unsigned), "Nice Replace Thunderclap." Melody Maker, 23 Aug 1969

(unsigned), "Bent Frame." Beat Instrumental, Sep 1969

(unsigned), "New Thunderclap Single." Record Mirror, 4 Oct 1969

(unsigned), "Oh No! Not The Dreaded Thunderclap Newman!" ZigZag, Sep 1970

(unsigned), "Jimmy Has His Bent Frame Out Again."

Record Mirror, 9 Oct 1971

(unsigned), "Bent Frame In Provinces." New Musical Express, 13 Nov 1971

(unsigned), "Thunderclap & Others in Rock Panto!" New Musical Express, 27 Nov 1971

(unsigned), "Meaty Beaty." Record Mirror, 4 Dec 1971

(unsigned), "End Of The Crows?" New Musical Express, 2 Jun 1973

(unsigned), "McCulloch Joins Blue: Crows End." New Musical Express, 2 Jun 1973

(unsigned), "Jimmy Solo for RSO." Record & Radio Mirror, 22 Dec 1973

(unsigned), "McCartney: Crossroads yes Knebworth no." Record Mirror, 10 May 1975

(unsigned), "Wings Take Off On UK Tour." Record Mirror, 23 Aug 1975

(unsigned), "Wings tour preview." Record Mirror & Disc, 13 Sep 1975

(unsigned), "Jimmy's Broken Wing." Record Mirror & Disc, 10 Apr 1976

(unsigned), "Jimmy Breaks The Mould." Record Mirror & Disc, 1 May 1976

(unsigned), "Musical Chairs." Music Week, 19 Jun 1976

(unsigned), "Juicy Luicy." Record Mirror, 6 Nov 1976

(unsigned), "Wings' Jim Forms New Band." Record Mirror, 6 Nov 1976

(unsigned), "McCulloch Releases Single." Record Mirror, 29 Jan 1977

(unsigned), "Daltrey's One Of The Boys." Record Mirror, 16 Apr 1977

(unsigned), "Jimmy Quits Wings." Record Mirror, 10 Sep 1977

(unsigned), "Sixties Rock Package Cancelled." Music Week, 8 Oct 1977

(unsigned), "Album Reviews: L.A.M.F., The Heartbreakers."

Music Week, 15 Oct 1977

(unsigned), "Jimmy McCulloch, Was Guitarist In Paul McCartney's Wings Band (obit)." New York Times, 28 Sep 1979

(unsigned), "McCulloch's Death A Mystery." Melody Maker, 6 Oct 1979

(unsigned), "Jimmy McCulloch Dies." Record Mirror, 6 Oct 1979

(unsigned), "McCulloch Inquest." New Musical Express, 10 Nov 1979

(unsigned), "The 40 Greatest One-Album Wonders." Rolling Stone, 14 Jul 2016

Altham, Keith, "Speedy Keen: Speedy Words and Speedy Keen." New Musical Express, 5 May 1973

Altham, Keith, "The Jimi Hendrix Story." New Musical Express, 16 Nov 1968

Andrews, James, "Firebird In Jim's Wings." Sounds, 31 May 1975

Bienstock, Richard, "Radio Head." Guitar Player, Aug 2021

Black, Johnny, "Eyewitness: The 14 Hour Technicolor Dream, April 29, 1967, Alexandra Palace, North London." Q, Jun 1995

Boucher, Caroline, "Lucky Jim's just a thundering good guitarist!" Disc and Music Echo, 15 Jan 1972

Brocklebank, Jonathan, "Tragedy of the teenage genius Linda & Paul took under their Wings." Scottish Daily Mail, 27 Mar 2021

Brown, David, "Jimmy's New Branch Line." Record Mirror, 20 Nov 1976

Childs, Andy, "From Out Of The Shadows Comes Speedy Keen." ZigZag, Jul 1975

Clayson, Alan, "Speedy Keen Obituary." The Guardian, 6 Jul 2002

Cohn, Nik, "John Keen: How a Hooligan Romantic

Became a One Man Band." <u>Rolling Stone</u>, 5 Jul 1973

Evans, Jim, "Blowin' In The Wings." <u>Record Mirror</u>, 16 Apr 1977

Evans, Jim, "Faster Than Concorde." <u>Record Mirror</u>, 16 Apr 1977

Gambaccini, Paul, "Water Wings – McCartney Waives The Rules." <u>Sounds</u>, 20 Aug 1977

Gibbs, Vernon, "Thunderclap Newman: Hollywood Dream." <u>Columbia Daily Spectator</u>, 15 Oct 1970

Goldman, Vivien, "Keen's Mean." <u>Sounds</u>, 21 Feb 1976

Goldman, Vivien, "Speedy Keen: Y'Know Wot I Mean?" <u>Sounds</u>, 6 Mar 1976

Gormley, Mike, "Who's Peter Townshend? Producer for Thunderclap." <u>Detroit Free Press</u>, Aug 1969

Green, Richard, "Thunderclap's Posh Pad!" <u>New Musical Express</u>, 5 Jul 1969

Green, Richard, "Rock made Jim and Jack quit." <u>New Musical Express</u>, 16 Aug 1969

Green, Richard, "Pete's Thunder Claps!" <u>New Musical Express</u>, 21 Jun 1969

Green, Richard, "I'm Gonna Make You A Star Said Pete Townshend To Thunderclap Newman And He Meant It!" <u>New Musical Express</u>, 28 Jun 1969

Grossman, Lloyd, "Stone The Crows: Ontinuous Performance." <u>Rolling Stone</u>, 15 Feb 1973

Harvey, Peter, "Mischievous McCulloch." <u>Record Mirror & Disc</u>, 20 Sep 1975

Holman, Pamela, "The Who Drop Out... Of A Rally." <u>New Musical Express</u>, 27 Nov 1971

Holman, Pamela, "Sweat, Squirm and Scream." <u>New Musical Express</u>, 4 Dec 1971

Iles, Jan, "Jim's Flight Of Fancy." <u>Record Mirror</u>, 14 Aug 1976

Ingham, John, and Marks, Laurence, "Wings: The Band That's Alright Tonight." <u>Circus</u>, Sep 1975

Johnson, Derek, "Harper & Chips." <u>New Musical Express</u>, 18 Dec 1976

Johnson, James, "Strangely Missing That Barrow Boy Stagger: In Frankfurt With The Faces." <u>New Musical Express</u>, 4 Aug 1973

Kavanagh, Kevin, "Matching his big come back at Sam's Bar... Thunderclap Jones!" <u>Hornsey Journal</u>, 23 May 1986

Mabbs, Valerie, "Love Affair To Do A Led Zeppelin!?!" <u>Record Mirror</u>, 13 Sep 1969

Mabbs, Valerie, "Blue – Happy to earn your respect." <u>Record Mirror</u>, 28 Jul 1973

Mackie, Rob, "McCulloch: Happy with the Blues." <u>Sounds</u>, 9 Jun 1973

Mackie, Rob, "Keene: More Seedy Than Speedy?" <u>Sounds</u>, 1976

McKnight, Connor, "Andy Newman: Rainbow." <u>Time Out</u>, 18 Aug 1972

McLachlan, Patrick, "White Line: not to be sniffed at." <u>National Rockstar</u>, 20 Nov 1976

Mendelsohn, John, "Thunderclap Newman. Something In the Air." <u>Rolling Stone</u>, 18 Oct 1969

Mendelsohn, John, "Hollywood Dream." <u>Rolling Stone</u>, 15 Oct 1970

Middleton, Ian, " 'This hit has a sobering effect!' says 'PC' Newman." <u>Record Mirror</u>, 12 Jul 1969

Miles, "From the Marquee to the Met: Watching The Who." <u>Crawdaddy</u>! Sep 1970

Morthland, John, "Speedy Keen: Y'Know Wot I Mean?" <u>Creem</u>, May 1976

Moses, Ann, "Who's 'Tommy' Success." <u>New Musical Express</u>, 28 Jun 1969

Murray, Charles Shaar, "Paul McCartney: ...No Not Really In A Way Actually As It Happens." <u>New Musical Express</u>, 26 Jul 1975

Murray, Charles Shaar, "Speedy Keen – Interview." New Musical Express, 2 Aug 1975

Murray, Charles Shaar, "Speedy by name if not by nature." New Musical Express, 1976

Nightingale, Anne, "Water Wings." Record Mirror, 22 Oct 1976

Nolan, Hugh, "Who: Cattiest Group In The Business." Disc & Music Echo, 30 Nov 1968

Palmer, Tony, "The Hendrix Religion." Observer, 10 Nov 1968

Percival, Eamonn, "Listening To What The Man Said." Record Mirror, 31 May 1975

Petrie, Gavin, "Bright Blue." Disc, 14 Jul 1973

Pike, Jeffery, " 'The Best Is Still To Come': Jeffery Pike meets Jimmy McCulloch." Guitar, January 1975

Plummer, Mark, "Jimmy Crow." Melody Maker, 1 Jul 1972

Prophet, Sheila, "What A Wembley!" Record Mirror, 30 Oct 1976

Robinson, John, "We had to rely on our Motorheadness to get us through." Uncut, 11 Aug 2017

Scoppa, Bud, "Speedy Keen: Previous Convictions." Rolling Stone, 2 Aug 1973

Scoppa, Bud, "Blue: Blue." Rolling Stone, 8 Nov 1973

Scott-Irvine, Henry, "Heart of the Heartbreakers." Record Collector, 4 Oct 2014

Stewart, Tony, "Wings: A Complete Action Replay, New Musical Express, 18 Dec 1976

Sweeting, Adam, "Andy 'Thunderclap' Newman (obit)." Guardian, 3 Apr 2016

Swenson, John, "John Entwistle: Exile On Times Square, Beetle, 31 Dec 1972

Tan, Ronny & Reggy, "Townshend's Shadow Detaches Itself, Oor, Nov 1973

Thompson, Dave, "The Spencer Davis Group." Goldmine, 2 Apr 2004

Thorpe, Martin, "Wings… about to take flight again." Record & Popswop Mirror, 2 Nov 1974

Tobler, John, "Can You Believe It? Chatting with Pete Townshend." ZigZag, Jun 1974

Turner, Steve, "Pete Townshend: Genius of the Simple." Beat Instrumental, Dec 1971

Tyler, Kieron, "One Hit Wonder: Something In The Air." Mojo, 2011

Valentine, Penny, "The Unhappy Path of Thunderclap." Sounds, 21 Nov 1970

Walters, Charley, "Speedy Keen: Y'Know Wot I Mean?" Rolling Stone, 22 Apr 1976

Welch, Chris, "Singles: Thunderclap Newman – Something In The Air." Melody Maker, 24 May 1969

Welch, Chris, "Friday 13th – The Day Arthur Brown's World Blew Up." Melody Maker, 28 Jun 1969

Welch, Chris, "Galloping across the downs and a brief chat about Bix with Mister Thunderclap Newman." Melody Maker, 28 Jun 1969

Welch, Chris, "The Crazy World of Thunderclap Newman." Melody Maker, 19 Jul 1969

Welch, Chris, "McCulloch." Melody Maker, 23 Oct 1971

Welch, Chris, "The Return Of Thunderclap." Melody Maker, 27 Dec 1969

Wilson, Tony, "Now Pete's brainchild is set for the big screen." Melody Maker, 19 Jul 1969

Printed in the USA
CPSIA information can be obtained
at www.ICGtesting.com
JSHW022014040824
67521JS00001B/1